HAWKHURST

HAWKHURST

MURDER, CORRUPTION, AND BRITAIN'S MOST NOTORIOUS SMUGGLING GANG

JOSEPH DRAGOVICH

First published 2023

The History Press
97 St George's Place, Cheltenham,
Gloucestershire, GL50 3QB
www.thehistorypress.co.uk

British Library Cataloguing in Publication Data.
A catalogue record for this book is available from the British Library.

ISBN 978 0 7509 9889 5

Typesetting and origination by The History Press
Printed and bound in Great Britain by TJ Books Limited, Padstow, Cornwall.

MIX
Paper from
responsible sources
FSC® C013056
www.fsc.org

Trees for Life

CONTENTS

ACKNOWLEDGEMENTS

Thanks to my readers, Steve Schiavoni, Ryan Sardón Keller, Chris Holden, Neil Greenwood, Nick Dorrington, Will Morgan, my wife Jess, and my father Rick Dragovich, whose feedback has helped improve the many drafts of this book.

Thanks to all the people I have consulted over the course of writing this book: Lyndy Kessell at Parham House for her advice on Cecil Bishopp, Mike Huxley at the Cranbrook Museum for his advice on sources, and Professor James Walvin for his advice on race in the eighteenth century.

Special thanks to Paul Muskett for his advice and suggestions on sources.

Most of all thanks goes to my wife, Jess, without whose patient love and support this book would not have been possible, and to my 4-year-old daughter Annabel.

Map Data

INTRODUCTION

On 28 April 1847 the town of Goudhurst in Kent gathered for a celebration. Church bells rang, the townspeople hoisted flags and illuminated the belfry towers. They were celebrating the centenary of a battle. Not a battle against a foreign enemy, but against a gang of smugglers.[1]

The town was celebrating a momentous anniversary: the first time a local population had resisted violent intimidation by a vast network of organised criminals, the Hawkhurst Gang. For years, the gang had crisscrossed the countryside, operating with impunity and threatening anyone who dared to even look at them. The Hawkhurst Gang fought a guerrilla war with the government for years.[2] Goudhurst was the first community to challenge their dominance.

It is easy to look at the events that took place in Kent and Sussex in the 1740s through traditional romantic notions about smuggling: smugglers were part of the community, committing a victimless crime, prosecuted as much for their challenge to the social hierarchy as the laws they broke.[3] These ideas have been disproved by previous work on the subject. Smugglers throughout the eighteenth century were violent men, existing in a complex social and political web that saw people of all walks of life interact with the illicit trade. Successive governments would struggle throughout the century to keep the practice under control, launching spasms of enforcement that often coincided with other, external political crises. Yet the 1740s stand out in the history of smuggling as a period when the practice, and one gang in particular, rose to be a crisis in their own right that challenged the British state itself.

The period was an inflection point in the history of Britain, where immense political and social upheavals shaped the trajectory of the country for decades, and perhaps centuries to come. Foreign wars, economic downturn, and political revolution crackled throughout the decade. In this simmering potential, a band of criminals from a small Kentish village would sear itself into the historical record. The Hawkhurst Gang would not be the last gang of smugglers to terrorise the British countryside, but they were one of Britain's first mafias that would leave an impression on the region for centuries afterwards.

The Hawkhurst Gang is to Kent and Sussex what the Krays are to London, Al Capone is to Chicago, or John Gotti is to New York. They became a symbol of the bad old times of the mid-eighteenth century and a warning about the consequences of crime. Their memory is deeply rooted in the region. An obituary from the nineteenth century mentioned how the deceased personally remembered the depredations of the gang, and artefacts from Goudhurst's successful defence from the gang were being auctioned as relics 100 years after the battle.[4]

But the story of the gang is not limited to the south coast; at their height, stories of their activities were being published in newspapers all over the United Kingdom. A gang based in a village that, in the early twenty-first century, only has around 5,000 people, was the talk of London, the largest city in the world, and the entire United Kingdom.

Often, works on smuggling focus exclusively on the smugglers themselves: their methods and the violence they committed. But the story of the Hawkhurst Gang could not have happened without a confluence of events, crises, and social changes that radically transformed the country.

Today, tea is considered a fundamental part of British life and character. But this affection for the drink is a legacy of crime, empire and national competition. The tea we thoughtlessly put in our mugs warped every level of British society in the eighteenth century.

Tea, for all its banality, is a drug. It is a mind-altering substance (however mild) that is often consumed in a ritualised social setting. This is as true in the twenty-first century as it was in the eighteenth. From high tea, to colleagues gathering to gossip over a cuppa at the office, tea is valuable for its social function as much as its value as a drink. In the 1740s, tea consumption was skyrocketing in the UK, driven by elite tea services and those that sought to emulate them. This demand was satisfied by the ever-expanding colonial project, and eventually, a vast, trans-national criminal network.

As empire was flourishing and goods from around the world flowed into an increasingly wealthy Britain, the government sought to find ways to fund the country's participation in the interminable great power struggles of Europe. His Majesty's government needed ever-larger armies to fight on the Continent, and the navy that let Britannia rule the waves was hungry for cash. That money would come from taxing the production and trade of the realm. Tea, being initially associated with luxury, had a heavy duty placed on it, reaching 100 per cent of the price at one point.

Tea was not the only commodity commonly smuggled past the customs men. Everything from brandy to wool to lace was snuck past customs inspectors at one point or another. It was tea's relatively light weight and sky-high taxes that made it the engine that allowed the Hawkhurst Gang to grow into the force that it was. It is telling that when the gang broke open the customs house at Poole, they took all of the tea, but left the brandy.

There were times when south-east England looked like it was at war – because it was.[5] The Battle of Culloden in 1745 is officially the last pitched battle fought on British soil, but soon after Culloden, there were smaller battles between government troops and hundreds of smugglers. The government's legal and military battle with the Hawkhurst Gang resembles twentieth- and twenty-first-century conflicts with drug cartels in Latin America. It was a fight not just to limit illegal activities, but also one to bring areas of the country back under government control that had slowly slipped away. The Hawkhurst Gang and those like them were different to what had come before, violent paramilitaries that had shaken the foundations of law and order in two counties. It was these stakes that elevated the Hawkhurst Gang beyond the gangs of smugglers that preceded or followed them. Battling the gang wasn't just about the issue of taxation or law and order, it was a battle for the soul of the United Kingdom. They were more than just thugs running tea into London.

This running battle with smugglers is described in detail in newspapers across the country. Publications as far away as Scotland ran numerous articles about the guerrilla war in the south-east, feeding the nation with news not just of seizures and battles, but the exploits of individual smugglers and customs officers.

That fight would be led by people of all stripes, from grassroots local militias to people in the highest levels of government. They fought back against the Hawkhurst Gang to take back their communities and stop the violence that had taken over the region. Smuggling would still be a problem throughout the century, but it would never again cause the same sort of national crisis as the Hawkhurst Gang.

How Do We Know About the Hawkhurst Gang?

The gang's story plays out across a variety of sources, the most common being the records and correspondence of the people trying to stop them. John Collier, the Surveyor General of Riding Officers for Kent and Sussex, spoke extensively about smuggling in his surviving letters. His correspondence with customs officers in the field, as well as his political masters, provides an insight into the daily operations of the preventative services and the operational details of the Hawkhurst Gang. The upper levels of government were also concerned with dismantling the Hawkhurst Gang and smuggling as a whole. Parliamentary investigations, debates and letters among the Cabinet show how the wheels of the state sought to curb the abuses of the gang. Reports of seizures, captures and battles with smugglers were frequent fixtures of the national press.

Most scholarship on smuggling extensively uses the rich government records to glean information about smuggling gangs and how government forces attempted to combat them: sources like customs records and Treasury petitions (CUST and T series in the UK National Archives). There is comparatively little use of newspapers and other printed ephemera, partly due to how dispersed smuggling material is in daily newspapers throughout the period, and for past scholars, the difficulty of processing such a large corpus of material. This has coloured past smuggling research into looking at the smuggling conflict and the customs service in the way that it was supposed to work on paper. However, evidence described in newspapers suggests that the customs service, and its fight with the smugglers, did not function in the way described by government documents. On paper, John Bolton, who was captured and tortured by the Hawkhurst Gang, was a minor customs official. In reality, he was doing dangerous and complex police work that frequently put his life at risk.

Then there are the words of the smugglers themselves. Many of the Hawkhurst Gang were tried in the Old Bailey, the main court in London. During the eighteenth century, summaries of these trials were published and sold for public consumption as *The Proceedings of the Old Bailey*. Those sentenced to death were given a biography in *The Ordinary of Newgate's Account of the Behaviour, Confession and Dying Words of the Condemned Criminals Who Were Executed at Tyburn.** Both of these publications provide some of the only recorded words from the smugglers themselves. Through these sources we can glean some insights into the minds, motivations and structure of the Hawkhurst Gang. The *Ordinary's Accounts* had a moralising, cautionary intention to them, but they are the only voices we have from the Hawkhurst Gang itself. They should be used carefully, but it would be foolish to ignore them.

Some Ordinary accounts are constructed from newspaper stories when the subject was uncooperative, like Arthur Grey, one of the leaders of the gang. However, some contain details and events that are not found elsewhere, such as those of Sam Hill and John Cook. Comparative work has shown how Cook's and Hill's accounts often contradict newspaper accounts and other sources.[6] Rather than invalidate them as sources, this suggests that they are an authentic voice of the smugglers in question, instead of a government fabrication. The ones that are largely constructed, like Arthur Grey's, are almost identical to contemporary newspaper sources. It is unlikely the Ordinary was more creative with just Hill and Cook.

This book builds on the work of many local historians in south-east England over the last 160 years. The evidence around the Hawkhurst Gang is often fragmentary, but there is a lot of information available from combing over parish records, wills and other paper trails from the period. Mary Waugh provides the most complete account of smuggling in Kent and Sussex over the eighteenth and nineteenth centuries.[7] Henry Jones's articles in *Bygone Kent* are some of the most detailed studies of the Hawkhurst Gang available.[8] Paul Muskett writes about specific issues around smuggling, including military campaigns against the gangs and the lawyers that represented them in court.[9]

*   Often shortened to the *Ordinary's Accounts*.

These authors were writing in the 1980s and '90s, before the advent of a mature internet and mass digitisation of historical materials. Their studies were limited in scope to the materials that could be easily searched in physical archives. While this book also uses those sources, it uses digital research methods as well. The digital archives of Old Bailey Proceedings Online allows for a wider search of relevant material, not only for the Hawkhurst Gang, but also for the smuggling economy of London and its hinterland.

The Old Bailey trials provide a glimpse into how the smuggling economy functioned once it reached London. With the advent of digitisation and searchability, we can see a complex world of street dealers, crooked tea merchants, thieving dock workers and a whole host of other cogs in the illegal economy. The archive can also help answer some unanswered questions around smuggling that have plagued historians, such as how smuggling affected the markets for frequently trafficked goods. By studying theft trials where defendants stole tea, we can get a reasonable understanding about the 'street price' of tea during this period. This is information not available in higher-level government estimates on trade volumes.

Google's effort to digitise and distribute books has also been a boon to the study of the Hawkhurst Gang. Google Books is an invaluable database of more obscure sources that have enriched the story of the gang. Contemporary books and pamphlets contain a wealth of information about smuggling, the Hawkhurst Gang and the fraught politics of the early eighteenth century. Treatises on tea, magistrates' manuals, parliamentary debates and reports, and magazines all give rich details about the world in which the gang operated.

By incorporating new and more obscure material, this book tries to give a broader, fuller story of Britain's most notorious smuggling gang. Rather than take the previous approach of examining smuggling through a national or regional lens, it takes a deeper dive into the most well-known example of the period's smuggling gangs, looking more broadly than their crimes to encompass the political, social and military reaction to them.

A NOTE ON DATES

Dates in the early eighteenth century follow a different pattern to our modern standard. Until 1752, the UK had followed the Julian Calendar, and the legal year began on 25 March, so for official purposes, January in a calendar year would come after March. Dates in the book have been normalised to the year beginning in January.

A NOTE ON MONEY

During the period of this book, the primary currency in Britain was the pound sterling. Prior to decimalisation in the 1970s, one pound (£) was divided into 20 shillings (s) each of which was divided into 12 pence (d), making 240 pence to a pound.

Prices were generally denoted by numbers labelled with the denomination, so an amount of 2 pounds, 3 shillings and 8 pence would be written as £2 3s 8d. Though prices were not always 'simplified' into their highest-value currency. For example, the ancient property requirement for voting is listed as 40s not £2.

Prices appear as they were written in the source materials, unadjusted for inflation and in non-decimal notation.

This book deals with historical prices and money. The eighteenth-century economy was very different than the modern one, with different standards of living, material expectations and wealth inequality. Attempting to convert eighteenth-century prices to a modern equivalent would be misleading and lose historical context. On the facing page is a list of sample prices that gives a rough idea of the value of money during the period.

A NOTE ON MONEY

Property value requirement for voting	40s
7 Bushels wheat flour	£3[10]
1 Quarten Loaf, about 4lb of bread, 1740	8d[11]
3 Linen Shirts, 1740	18s[12]
Velvet Hood, 1740	2s[13]
Pair of Stockings, 1740	2s[14]
'Piece of Pork'(not further specified), 1740	6d[15]

GLOSSARY OF PEOPLE

Bishopp, Cecil
Sussex baronet and politician. Ran for a parliamentary seat in Sussex in 1734.

Bolton, John
A customs official in the Port of London and smuggler hunter.

Carey, Thomas 'Jockey Tom'
One of the leaders of the Hawkhurst Gang.

Carswell, Thomas
Customs riding officer. Killed by the Hawkhurst Gang in December 1740.

Curteis, Jeremiah
One of the leaders of the Hawkhurst Gang. Led the Hastings Outlaws prior to merging them with the Hawkhurst Gang.

Darby, John
Customs riding officer.

Dray, Freebody
Customs riding officer.

Duke of Newcastle
Thomas Pelham-Holles was a powerful landowner and important politician not only in Sussex, but also nationally. He served as Secretary of State for Robert Walpole and for his brother, Henry Pelham, after he succeeded Walpole as Prime Minister.

Duke of Richmond
Charles Lennox, 2nd Duke of Richmond. Friend and political ally of the Pelhams. Launched a wide-ranging campaign against smugglers in 1748.

Grey, Arthur
One of the leaders of the Hawkhurst Gang. Brother of William Grey.

Grey, William
One of the leaders of the Hawkhurst Gang. Brother of Arthur Grey.

Kingsmill, George
One of the leaders of the Hawkhurst Gang. Brother of Thomas Kingsmill.

Kingsmill, Thomas 'Staymaker'
One of the leaders of the Hawkhurst Gang. Brother of George Kingsmill.

Murray, William
Solicitor General of the United Kingdom.

Pelham, Henry
Brother of the Duke of Newcastle, MP for Sussex and Prime Minister from 1743.

Polhill, John
Customs riding officer.

Quaif, Thomas
A customs official in the Port of London and smuggler hunter. Friend of John Bolton.

Stanford, James 'Trip'
One of the leaders of the Hawkhurst Gang.

Ryder, Dudley
Attorney General of the United Kingdom.

Walpole, Robert
One of the first modern Prime Ministers of the UK until 1742.

PROLOGUE

On a spring day in China, a man picks a leaf from a bush. It is not a leaf idly picked. The man is a plantation worker and the bush in question is *camellia sinensis*, known more commonly as tea. He, along with many others working at the plantation, will pick several pounds of the fresh shoots during the day.

At the end of his day's picking, he takes the leaves to the roasting house, which is just beginning its work. The leaves need to be processed as soon as possible, lest they get too warm and spoil.[16] The roast house workers toil throughout the night, causing them to complain bitterly.[17] They blanch the leaves in hot water to wilt them.[18] Then the roaster takes over. He is the boss of the roasting house, and has the most skilled job in the whole operation.[19] Stirring the leaves in a shallow iron pan over a fire until his hands can't stand the heat, he is careful not to burn the leaves and ruin them. Once the leaves are roasted, he removes them with a fan-shaped shovel.[20]

While the leaves are still hot, rollers take each leaf and roll it into a little ball. The juice that seeps out of the rolled leaves is slightly caustic and burns the rollers' hands, yet they endure. As the rollers roll, another worker fans the finished leaves. The faster they cool, the more they hold their shape. If they aren't dry, the roaster roasts them again, then the rollers re-roll the leaves that uncurl. They repeat this cycle until the leaves are free of moisture.[21] Another worker then spreads the roasted leaves on a mat, sorting them for quality and carefully removing those that, despite the roaster's care, are burned.[22] They then store the tea to age it. When it is ready, they roast it again to drive out any moisture it might have accumulated during the aging process and pack it into tin chests protected by a fir-wood box.[23] The boxes contain about 100lb of tea, and any cracks in them are carefully sealed with paper in order to protect the contents on its long voyage.[24]

The tea makes its way from the plantation to the port of Amoy.* Waiting in the port is the trade mission to Batavia,** the capital of the Dutch East Indies.[25] The fleet of junks is packed with merchants, their goods, and immigrants bound for the colony. Its departure is a festive event. Sailors eat celebratory meals and make sacrifices to Ma-tsu, the goddess of the sea, to ensure a successful voyage.[26] After three weeks of hugging the coast, the fleet arrives at Batavia.

In Batavia, a ship, the last Dutch ship to return to Europe that year, waits patiently for the Chinese trade fleet. This last ship, colloquially called the Tea Ship, wants the Chinese fleet's cargo of tea.[27] It is loaded with hundreds of tons of tea, beginning its long journey.[28] Stopping in Ceylon*** for supplies and making its way around the Cape of Good Hope towards Europe, it arrives in Holland. The Tea Ship's long journey ends at the island of Texel,[29] a barrier island just north of Amsterdam, where smaller boats take the tea to the city's busy wholesale markets. Some of the tea is bound for Dutch coffee houses, but much of it is ultimately headed for Britain.

An Englishman living in Middelburg buys a large quantity of the tea, a few tons. He intends to send it to London, but he won't use the London Docks. His crew open the chests and pack the tea into loose cloth bags, which are themselves wrapped in a bag made from oilskin, a waterproof material. Each bag contains 25–50lb of tea.[30]

The crew load the bags into a small, fast cutter. Waiting for their moment, they quickly cross the English Channel to the coast of Kent, where they land at an isolated beach during the night. A gang of men are waiting.[31]

---

*   Present-day Xiamen, China.
**   Present-day Jakarta, Indonesia.
*** Present-day Sri Lanka

1

MURDER

25 December 1740

On Christmas night, as most people were sleeping off a day of celebration and festive revelry, the Hawkhurst Gang unloaded a cargo of tea near Hastings. Labouring under a near-full moon, the smugglers brought their cargo, almost a ton of tea, a few miles inland to a barn, where they stashed it and returned home for a well-earned drink and some rest.[32]

Not yet the most feared smugglers in Britain, the Hawkhurst Gang were one of many gangs making money by defying the tax laws, sneaking a wide variety of untaxed goods past the customs service. The gang was led by the Grey Brothers, Arthur and William. Sons of pub owners, they had fallen into smuggling at an early age.[33] There was also James 'Trip' Stanford, scion of a local wealthy family.[34]

However, they were not the only ones out on that cold winter's night. Thomas Carswell, customs riding officer, was on the hunt. Assisted by around a dozen dragoons[*] and customs agents, he followed the smugglers' tracks from the beach. Having found the stash, Carswell's men loaded a wagon and began making their way back to the secure customs house in Hastings.[35]

---

[*] A type of mounted infantry that carried short muskets and were often used for anti-smuggling duties.

But word of the seizure reached the gang, who quickly gathered in a local pub to discuss what to do. Their shipment was big, worth a small fortune, too much money to just let go. They would need to take it back, even though it was guarded by armed government agents. As they came up with a plan, Carswell and his men passed by the pub, unaware that they were taking their seizure right past its former owners. Spotting the revenue men, the gang would need to act fast if they were to save their goods.[36]

Trip Stanford and another smuggler rode back to Hawkhurst, their home and base of operations, as fast as they could, offering tremendous rewards for anyone who would come and help the gang recover the tea. They gathered weapons and met in a field just outside the nearby village of Hurst Green. What would happen next was going to be messy and violent. Preparing for a fight, the gang took off their heavy coats, stripping down to their shirts in the cold night. Drinking brandy, they swore damnation on anyone who fled before the tea was recovered.[37] It was theirs, and they rode off to take it.

Carswell's men were climbing the large hill into Hastings when the smugglers caught up with them: the thunder of hooves rose behind them as thirty smugglers charged up the road. Carswell had a choice: he could either abandon the wagon full of tea to the gang and flee, or stand and fight. He chose the latter, ordering his men to turn and fire. The crackle of gunfire and the smell of smoke pierced the still of the night, as the gang charged through the hail of shot with their pistols and blunderbusses.*[38] Horses whinnied, guns blazed, and a round bored deep into Carswell's skull.[39] He fell from his horse, dead. The remaining customs men could only surrender to the overwhelming onslaught of the smugglers.[40]

The Hawkhurst Gang had done it. They took the tea, the captive customs men and their new wagon back to the stash house in triumph. The gang made good on their promise, and rewarded those that came to help, giving them either 100lb of tea or 20 guineas, more than a year's wage for most people.[41] After killing Carswell, the gang would have taken the tea to a gathering just south of London. It is the sort of place where one could buy smuggled tea, wholesale. The London tea merchants bought half a ton of tea at a time.[42]

* An early type of shotgun.

Carswell's death launched a nearly decade-long manhunt for his killer, pursuing a gang that would become the terror of Kent and Sussex, the two counties between London and the English Channel. The Hawkhurst Gang were already known locally for their bloodthirstiness,[43] but the coming years would spread that bloody reputation nationally. In the 1740s smuggling would become a national crisis, bringing Britain to a fever pitch of anxiety.

In January 1741, the customs service published a wanted ad for Carswell's killers, offering £50 for anyone apprehending the suspects and £50 and a pardon for any of the suspects that informed on their fellows. As an aid to any would-be informants, the ad described the suspects that informers had already identified, providing some of the only physical descriptions of the gang. They were a group of men that would have been ordinary had they not also been gangsters. Ranging in age from their 20s to their mid-40s, they were multi-ethnic * and in a variety of trades; some scarred with smallpox, some with fair faces. They had a variety of nick-names and identities: Trip, Old Oatmeal, Beggerman.[44]

These men took on a lucrative but dangerous way of life. There were huge potential rewards for men that got into the smuggling trade in the mid-eighteenth century. Most smugglers were temporary workers, farmers and tradesmen that hauled cargo at night for some extra money. The ones that charged at Carswell, guns blazing, were more involved in the gang life.

Carswell's murder marks the start of the Hawkhurst Gang's rise as the most dangerous smugglers in Britain, followed by their bloody fall. They were largely a group of humble men, tradesmen from a small village roughly halfway between the English Channel and London. Men that saw a change in the criminal world of Britain and seized their moment. Some would become wealthy far beyond their station. Most would hang, die in prison, or find another violent fate. Some beat the odds and died in their beds.

---

* Richard Wenham is described as being of 'of a black complexion, with course hair', which indicates that he would potentially identify as Black today. Richard Wenham was almost certainly not a slave, but not what we would consider white today. He could have been from a variety of backgrounds; he could have been North African or Middle Eastern. It is an intriguing hint that London's rural hinterland was more ethnically diverse than we commonly assume. George Chapman's 'brown complexion' could also be an indication that he would not consider himself white today.

All were men who shaped their time in their own way, crossing paths with illiterate farmers, the most powerful men in the highest levels of government, and everyone in between. They made their mark with sword, shot and an enormous amount of tea.

2

TEA

The gang were willing to kill over tea, a commodity the British take for granted today as their national drink. However, the tea we casually fill our cups with each day warped every level of British society for nearly 100 years. It made criminal empires, bedevilled governments and turned eighteenth-century Kent and Sussex into a place that resembled the cartel-controlled areas of twenty-first-century Latin America.

The link between the British love of tea and the extensive organised crime that supported it was obvious even to people at the time. The tea that the Hawkhurst Gang were unloading in the moonlight had turned the United Kingdom into a quasi narco-state, an empire that projected itself into the world and was irrevocably changed by the new products, people, and plunder that came back. Tea was not the only stimulant that came in from far away, nor was it the only item that people smuggled in bulk past the revenue service. But the boom in demand, the nature of the product, and the political framework around it conspired to spin parts of mid-eighteenth-century Britain into a deepening cycle of crime and violence.

Tea, much like modern illegal drugs, was the perfect product to fuel a criminal empire. It was brought from abroad and could not be produced domestically, because long sea voyages spoiled the seeds.[45] It had a relatively high value to its weight and was legal to possess and use. But there was a good margin to be made if one could avoid paying the high taxes. Tea, being a stimulant, was also mildly addictive.

What made tea the driver of an entire criminal industry was its role as the lubricant of a vibrant, sometimes tumultuous public and private culture during the eighteenth century. Tea was a drink over which to socialise, conduct business, gossip, flirt, and debate the issues of the day. It was the drink of reasonable, civilised people – that was supplied by an uncivilised, violent, trans-national criminal network.

Tea fuelled the vibrant and raucous political culture that flourished in the hundreds of coffeehouses scattered throughout London, and the private, female-dominated social sphere in the home.[46] Having a cup of tea with a slice of toast for breakfast started in the first half of the eighteenth century. As early as 1712, a London tea dealer proclaimed: 'Drinking tea has grown so general, that it needs the less recommendation.'[47] By the 1730s, the stuff was everywhere. There was a tea for every taste and budget.[48]

As the wave of tea drinking crashed over Britain, people genuinely wondered whether this new drink was actually good for you. The early eighteenth century abounds with doctors debating over whether tea was better than tobacco or coffee or chocolate,[49] stories of housewives nearly driven insane by their tea addictions[50] and pundits pining for the good old days when British people drank beer for breakfast.[51]

The boom in tea consumption invited a tremendous amount of graft and dirty dealing. The rising demand for tea meant that many people were using it for the first time, and didn't know much about what they were drinking;[52] fertile ground for numerous fraudsters that would cut teas with any leaf that sort of looked like tea,[53] or use a variety of chemicals, like green vitriol, to dye cheap teas to look like expensive ones.[54] There was so much knock-off tea around that one anti-tea polemic declared the tea that 'the vulgar' drank 'neither in taste, smell or size of leaf, seemed to have any tea in it'.[55] Expensive tea wasn't much better. A treatise in 1750 noted that fine teas were a crapshoot; some tasted good and some would 'make any delicate person's stomach puke'.[56]

Smugglers were the most dangerous criminals attracted to Britain's tea craze. Smuggling was rife among most commodities during the period, but was especially prevalent around tea. Tea was *the* smuggled commodity in the mid-eighteenth century. It had no domestic competitor (if you don't count the various local leaves passed off as it) and was tremendously profitable to smuggle due to a quirk of how it was taxed.

Until 1745, tea was taxed by weight, rather than by its sale value.[57] That is, all tea had a flat 4s per lb tax in the 1730–40s. This tax got left behind as tea transformed from a rarefied luxury item to an everyday staple. It meant that all types of tea were taxed at the same weight, so that lower-quality, cheaper teas were in effect taxed more than their more expensive counterparts. Also, the level of taxation did not adjust for tea getting rapidly cheaper over the first half of the eighteenth century.

As late as 1707, a pound of tea would cost upwards of 60s, something only the very wealthy could afford with any regularity.[58] In that circumstance, a few shillings per pound was a reasonably small tax. However, in the 1710s, tea consumption rose dramatically outside the wealthy.[59] By the 1720s, the price had dropped to between 4–10s per pound. At those prices, a 4s tax becomes a significant part of the price, particularly at the bottom end of the market. The British government sleepwalked into making tea a lucrative item to smuggle.*

Much like modern drug cartels, eighteenth-century gangs could bring tons of untaxed tea into Britain. They benefited from a virtuous cycle in tea prices that increased the scale of smuggling operations throughout the early part of the century.

As the price of low-grade tea dropped, the tax became a higher proportion of the price. The more the tax was a proportion of the price, the more money could be made by avoiding the tax. The more money there was in smuggling, the greater the scale smuggling gangs could operate at. The greater the scale, the more tea could be brought in, which lowered the price.

This cycle fed the nation's crescendoing tea demand and helped create a crime problem that would reach a breaking point in the late 1740s. A parliamentary committee at the time estimated that out of the approximately 4 million lb of tea consumed in the UK, 3.2 million lb of

---

* Because smuggling was so widespread, it can be very difficult to determine what the actual price of tea was during the first half of the eighteenth century. Using trials from *The Proceedings of the Old Bailey*, we can get a rough sense of tea's 'street price'. Trials for theft listed the value of stolen items. By looking at trials where the defendants were accused of stealing tea up to 1760, we can see the rough retail price of tea. There were eleven trials between 1725 and 1750 where bohea and green tea, the two cheaper varieties, are listed as stolen. The price remains relatively stable, between 4–10s per pound. The most common price is 8s. While this sample size is small, it can at least show us the price within an order of magnitude (i.e. the price didn't shoot up to 40s a pound).

it was smuggled.[60] Tea, and the crime that it caused, insinuated itself into most areas of life in south-east England; from the farm hand working in the fields, to the dukes and duchesses in their parlours. The insatiable thirst for tea would drive political and social chaos, and cost many lives.

3

EMPIRE

At 12.45 on 14 March 1733, Robert Walpole rose to address the Commons.[61] He was about to make the most consequential speech of his political career. He stood in St Stephen's Chapel, the converted medieval church in central London where the House of Commons sat, the political parties facing each other across converted choir pews. What was once a house of God had become a house of politics. Galleries hung overhead for the men watching the debates.[62] Women had to watch through a ventilation hole in the ceiling.[63]

What Walpole was about to propose had been the subject of speculation for years, both in and outside parliament.[64] The road to the most violent tea smuggling gangs Britain had ever seen would not start with a tax on tea, but a tax on wine and tobacco. Walpole faced a chamber of hundreds of MPs, one of the fullest houses in living memory.[65] They listened to the speech in the lower part of the wood-panelled chamber. High above, the narrow public galleries contained members of the public that had come to watch the debate, peering down onto the chamber floor. The situation was tense. A crowd gathered outside the House of Commons in anticipation of the debate. They filled the passages surrounding the chamber, including the Court of Requests and Westminster Hall. Justices of the Peace and constables stood ready in the neighbourhood, in case the crowd of vintners and tobacconists descended into a riot.[66]

Parliament in St Stephens around 1709, Peter Tillemans.

Walpole began by acknowledging the need to better enforce existing taxes, noting how frauds had robbed the British Treasury of significant revenue. He then addressed the tremendous public outcry that had erupted in anticipation of his proposed taxes, and offered a conspiratorial explanation as to who was responsible:

'The smugglers, the fraudulent dealers, and those who have for many years been enriching themselves by cheating their country, foresaw, that if the scheme I am now to propose took effect, their profitable trade would be at an end; this gave them the alarm, and from them I am persuaded it is, that all those clamours have originally proceeded.'[67]

What followed was an eleven-hour, forty-five-minute debate about an excise tax on wine and tobacco, a proposed law that would throw British politics into turmoil for years. Walpole gave one of the best speeches of his political career,[68] proclaiming the disadvantage that honest merchants suffered from the smugglers, gangsters, fraudsters, and the corrupt customs officials that let it all happen. He described the numerous ways the dishonest skirted the laws and their sophisticated methods of fraud, at one point holding up the account book of a seemingly honest tobacco merchant that had been seized. The merchant had cheated on his taxes by carefully altering the book, pasting thin strips of paper over his previously recorded quantities. It was an alteration that allowed him to claim tax rebates on tobacco that he had never actually imported.[69]

Walpole was not proposing a new tax. His bill was trying to shift an existing tax from the customs to the excise. Customs duties were collected, and only collected, at the point goods enters the country. Excise duties, on the other hand, were collected in a number of places within the borders of the country. Excise duties could be avoided, but they weren't as easy to evade as slipping past or bribing a customs officer.[70]

★★★

Walpole was one of the United Kingdom's first modern Prime Ministers. By the eighteenth century, the fraught relationship between the monarchy and Parliament that had sent Britain into ructions of political violence since the 1640s had settled into a workable distribution of power between the two.

Walpole was one of the architects of this increasingly steady political settlement. In the 1720s and '30s, he had crafted a stable Whig party that enjoyed the support of the King through a mixture of guile, skulduggery and a healthy dose of political patronage. He was called the 'Great Man' by his contemporaries. Friend and foe alike acknowledged his political abilities. Walpole's tenure as Prime Minister lasted over twenty years, spanning two kings, a financial collapse and a war in Europe. To this day, he is Britain's longest-serving Prime Minister.[71]*

Nonetheless, on that day he was taking a political risk driven by necessity. The eighteenth-century British state was hungry for revenue, and always looking for new ways to fill the Treasury and pay off debts. War drove this hunger. Walpole's government needed money to buy weapons, ships, and pay the fighting men to use them.[72] By this time, Britain was a colonial power whose interest spanned the globe. From trading posts in India to the slave plantations in the Americas, Britain needed a navy to protect and tie the empire together.

The United Kingdom was not the only state spreading its tendrils abroad. Its rivals in Europe were doing the same, constantly tugging at the gossamer threads of early empire. They attacked each other's shipping, made moves against each other's colonies, and waged complex, brutal wars to reshape the political landscape in Europe. The eighteenth century was a period of almost ceaseless conflict, as colonial wars spilled over to Europe and vice versa.

However, parliament could not just raise taxes in whatever way it wanted, at least implicitly. Unlike modern governments, with their vast panoply of taxing tools, eighteenth-century governments had to settle with a much smaller collection of politically acceptable and feasibly collectible taxes. Land taxes had their limits from an economic and political perspective, and there would be no income taxes for several generations.

Hence, taxes on trade and industry were the bread and butter of the government's revenue. There had been an excise tax on various home-produced commodities for about fifty years, and though they were at times unpopular, they were an accepted part of government revenue. In 1723 Walpole had successfully added an excise duty on tea, coffee and sugar,[73] but these were relative luxuries at the time, unlike wine and

---

*   Like modern political parties, those in eighteenth-century Britain were complex and contained various personalities and political beliefs clustered around some sort of shared ideology. The Whigs were generally for the post Glorious Revolution settlement between King and parliament, where the monarch's power is limited and supported by parliament, particularly the issues around taxation and public money. Their main opposition party, the Tories, were for a stronger monarchy that deferred less to parliament. There was cross-pollination between the Tories and supporters of the exiled Stuart dynasty, known as Jacobites.

tobacco, which graced many tables or packed just about every pipe in the kingdom. Walpole's new tax would be felt by more, poorer people, on whom it would be more of a financial strain.

Walpole was making a tremendous political bet. Though they were unpopular, his success in adding excise taxes to similar items led him to believe that he could expand the excise further, reducing the government's reliance on customs duties, and the politically unpopular land taxes. There was also an election coming soon, one where the bill would hopefully provide a political boost by reducing land taxes, which affected every voter, and distributing the burden to the non-voting masses.[74] Walpole was a Prime Minister at the height of his political power, putting all of his clout on the line to reform the tax system in the face of vehement resistance and clamorous public opinion. He was betting that landowning voters would accept a reduction in their land taxes in exchange for more evenly distributed taxes on consumption.

That gamble was what brought the crowd to Westminster that day. The bill was the beginning of a fundamental redistribution of the tax burdens in the country that touched many more people than the oligarchs in parliament or the very small, landed electorate.

The result was disaster. From the very start, opponents of the bill equated the taxes on tobacco and wine with their most frightening political bogeyman, a general excise on goods. Grumblings about the existing excise taxes and land taxes aside, many saw a general excise on all goods as an unwarranted intrusion on domestic life. Even Walpole's allies were hesitant to support him in his big moment. The excise debate quickly took on a character that would sound as much at home in 1760s Boston as 1730s London: the bill was an assault on liberty itself. This was not just an argument over tax policy in parliament. The entire country got involved.

What followed was weeks of impassioned debates on the house floor and protests in the streets. Up and down the country, protesters burned government newspapers, and filed petitions against the scheme. Tobacconists and wine merchants sold their products in packaging that mocked the excise. The press went into overdrive. A flurry of pamphlets flew in either direction and newspapers sparred over the bill.[75]

Walpole himself got involved in this tumult personally. Newspapers reported that while he was attending a performance of the pantomime *Love Runs All Dangers*, one of the comedians ad-libbed some lines about the Prime Minister and his excise bill. After confirming that the political commentary was not part of the script, Walpole went backstage and 'with his own hands, corrected the comedian very severely'.[76]

The bill was doomed. In the weeks after its introduction, support for it dwindled to a precarious majority, until on 11 April Walpole put in a motion to postpone the bill, effectively killing it. A triumphant crowd heckled and harassed the MPs who had previously voted for the bill as they left the chambers for the day. Crowds celebrated the collapse of the excise bill by burning effigies.[77]

A week later, in the ashes of the failed excise scheme, the government regrouped. If customs duties could not be shifted to more enforceable excise duties, they would have to strengthen customs enforcement. Parliament quietly moved to establish a committee that would study the frauds and abuses in the customs service. New money would not come from the interior of the country, but from the border, directly tackling its growing gang problem. However, before parliament could attempt to pass an anti-smuggling bill, they would have to understand, and more importantly publicise, the scale of the problem.

June 1733
A few months later, the government began laying the groundwork for a major smuggling bill with an explosive committee report. Sir John Cope rose in his place and began to read the committee report that the government had commissioned in the immediate aftermath of the excise crisis. The report examined the 'various frauds and abuses of the customs' that had occurred in roughly the last ten years.[78]

He began with an expression of regret. Though the committee had been working diligently for over a month, it had discovered such widespread fraud in the customs operation that it had not been able to prepare as extensive a report as it would have liked, but the session was ending, and they felt that they should report what findings they had.[79] He proceeded to describe a complex and underhand world of avoiding customs duties that occurred in every part of the United Kingdom.

While illegal tobacco flowed into Britain through a series of cooked books and chummy customs officials, tea and brandy came into the country through well-organised and armed gangs. These gangs operated all over the country, from the rural coastline, to London itself. They simply bludgeoned their way through the customs barrier by force. The committee reported that smuggling gangs could reach forty or fifty members during a run, sufficient to overwhelm the customs officers, magistrates and troops sent to assist them.[80] It was shocking at the time, but a fraction of the scale smuggling gangs would reach in the next ten years.

The amount of tea and brandy smuggled was vast. In the roughly ten years before the committee's investigation, the customs service seized 251,320lb of tea and 652,924 gallons of brandy.[81] This is likely a small part of what was actually brought into the country. In the same period, the customs service alone* prosecuted over 2,000 people for tea smuggling. In return, at least 250 customs officers were beaten, wounded or otherwise abused in the line of duty. Six were murdered. At sea, the customs seized 229 vessels for smuggling, burning 185, and pressing the rest into service.[82]

Cope then revealed their star witness, Gabriel Tomkins, a smuggler currently sitting in jail for returning from transportation.** [83] Tomkins was no ordinary smuggler, he was the long-time leader of the Mayfield gang, one of the most successful gangs in south-east England. Tall and solidly built, he had a face pitted with smallpox, bordered at the top with a thick, black unibrow. His left arm was scarred where a pistol ball had passed clean through.[84] In his early 40s, he was the very definition of a hardened career criminal.

Tomkins was a new breed of gang leader. The easy money from tea transformed the old, traditional smuggling gangs, called owlers, into heavily armed mafias that would shoot, slice and beat their way through any resistance. First arrested for smuggling in 1716, in his early 20s, he had spent the last decade and a half in and out of jails, evading the law, returning from transportation, and spending years at large despite a £100 bounty on his head.[85] Just the year before, he was parading his gang, swords drawn, past a major Kentish town, fresh from a battle with the customs service.[86] Tomkins made a plea deal with parliament, promising to give information in exchange for clemency, sitting before the committee to explain the system that shipped tons of the tea into London.

---

*   The committee report excluded the excise service, which likely prosecuted more individuals.

**   Transportation was the practice of sending convicted criminals to the colonies for a pre-defined period. Returning before your sentence was complete was a crime and was often punished with death.

He started by naming several grocers and shopkeepers in central London and Southwark, just across the Thames. Shipping between 15,000–20,000lb of tea and coffee per year, he would bulk buy goods in the Netherlands and land them along the coast of Kent and Sussex. The gang would then move towards London (the destination was always London) in an armed convoy of ten to twelve smugglers. Travelling at night, they would stash the bulk shipment in a series of dedicated safe houses, 5 or 6 miles outside of the city. They would then bring the tea into London 100–200lb at a time to their buyers, careful to time the watch changes to make the exchange. The gang would get 5–6s per pound for tea, which meant at the average street price of 8s per pound, the grocers were making a very handsome profit to reward their illegality.[87]

The gangs in the countryside were violent and organised, and were not any more restrained when they ventured into London. At 2 a.m. one day in May 1733 the watch stopped two women in the street who had baskets on their head containing 177lb of tea. Knowing they had been caught, the women offered to show the watchmen the location of a stash house where there was more tea. They followed the women to the house, but when they reached it, the women shouted, 'Robbers, Robbers!' Hearing their cries, smugglers appeared in the street and savagely beat one of the watchmen to death.[88]

The parliamentary session wound down, but everyone's eyes were on the election that would take place in the first half of next year. Walpole and his Whig party had been unassailable for a decade. This was the election to topple them, and Walpole's political opponents knew it. The bitter fight in parliament and the surrounding public outcry ensured the election would be about taxes, the excise and smuggling. The terrible genie of popular uproar was out of the bottle, and the coming electoral storm would whip the gangland along Britain's watery border into overdrive.

4

CORRUPTION

In the twenty-first century, the English Channel is one of the busiest water-ways in the world; it was no different in the eighteenth. For centuries, the Channel was a place of conflict and exchange between numerous communities on either side. Clinging to the edge of its stormy waters, these communities traded, fought and intermingled. In hindsight, the Channel seems like a clean dividing line between two eighteenth-century superpowers, the United Kingdom and France. It was anything but in the eighteenth century. In many ways, the communities along the Channel had more in common with one another than they did with their respective national capitals in London, Paris and Amsterdam. The Channel was more a watery frontier, a place where ethnic identities and national control ebbed and flowed in a tangled web of blurred identities, international competition and organised crime that would see the most contentious election in a generation.*

The towns, ports and islands along the Channel had an independent character that often translated into various forms of legal autonomy. The Channel Islands were under the control of Britain, but had special tax regimes and could legally trade with France during times of war until the late seventeenth century.[89] Dunkirk was a free port where trade was loose and people did not ask many questions.[90] On the British side, the Cinque

---

* Morieux very cogently makes this argument in *The Channel: England, France and the Construction of a Maritime Border in the Eighteenth Century.*

Ports of Kent and Sussex – Hastings, New Romney, Hythe, Dover and Sandwich – were the frontier towns of the Channel.

The Cinque Ports were coastal towns that had made a deal with the English crown in the Middle Ages: they would provide the fighting ships needed to protect the realm, and in return they would receive some special legal and political rights that lingered long after their naval significance had faded away. They had some legal and jurisdictional autonomy from their surrounding counties, such as with arrest warrants. But their major privilege was political. Each of the Cinque Ports elected two members of parliament, called barons, to Westminster, making them prime targets for political bosses.

Their political importance stood in contrast to the fact that the ports had been in decline for years. Daniel Defoe, the English author and politician on a tour of Britain, described crumbling, dirty places perched on the edge of the sea. He wrote of 'old, decayed, miserable' towns[91] presiding over 'ill repaired, dangerous, and good for little' harbours.[92] The idea that each of these dirty little towns had as much parliamentary representation as the counties that surrounded them was ridiculous to Defoe. This iniquity was not just a moral issue; the ports had very small electorates that were easily captured by small groups of powerful politicians that were plugged into the intense electoral web.

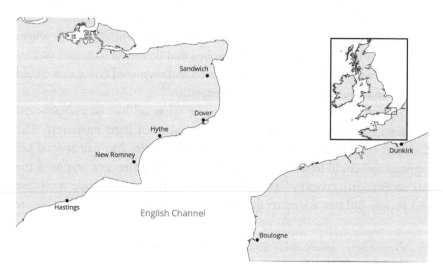

Cinque Ports and important French ports.

Elections during the eighteenth century were elections of oligarchy. Property requirements meant that a very small portion of the population was eligible to vote. In Kent that year, fewer than 8,000 men voted.[93] Constituencies were based on ancient boundaries and rights, not population, creating a strange patchwork of deeply unequal voting districts. Voting was not secret, which made it straightforward to enforce any private deals. Powerful families or individuals often controlled very small constituencies like the Cinque Ports. Using their influence over the extremely limited electorate, they could hand-pick the candidates they sent to Westminster. Even in constituencies with meaningful numbers of voters, networks of patronage determined political outcomes.

In Sussex, those networks were controlled by the Pelham family, headed by Thomas Pelham-Holles, the 1st Duke of Newcastle.* Staunch allies of Walpole and his Whig party, Newcastle and his brother Henry Pelham served in Walpole's Cabinet as Secretary of State and Paymaster of the Forces.** Through a series of inheritances, Newcastle was one of the largest landholders in the country.[94] The Pelhams exerted political control over the county through a series of agents and allies, but their political fortunes and influence were tied to Walpole and the Whig political establishment. Newcastle was willing to do everything in his power to make sure that the constituencies under his influence elected Whig candidates, most of all his brother Henry, who was standing for the county of Sussex.

The Pelhams' political enemies in Sussex saw their opportunity in the 1734 election and pounced. Most of the candidates with their political knives out were from the opposition Tory party, but some were rebel Whigs who opposed the excise tax, or the government in general. Unlike modern British politics, parties were not centrally controlled by a formal leader. There was no one regulating who was and was not included in a party. One could be a Whig in their politics, but be in opposition to the government.[95]

---

* The Duke of Newcastle was Pelham-Holles's title. Though he did not spend a great deal of time in the north of England during this period, he had homes and estates in the south-east that he used while politicking in London.

** A Cabinet position responsible for financing the army.

Portrait of the Thomas Peham–Holles, Duke of Newcastle by James MacArdell (mid 1700s).

One of those opposition Whigs hoping to ride the wave of discontent following the excise debacle was Sir Cecil Bishopp, a local baronet who was already installed as an MP for a tiny constituency in Cornwall with fewer than 200 voters.[96] However, Bishopp's family had deep roots in Sussex. Based in Parham House, an Elizabethan-era estate that his family had owned for hundreds of years, Bishopp had grander ambitions than being a seat-filler for a powerful Cornish family. Though he was a Whig, his opposition to the excise bill gave him a shot at unseating at least one of the Pelham political machine's candidates.

Bishopp opened the campaign trying to establish his credentials as a Whig (albeit one trying to unseat a government MP), a Protestant, and an enemy of excise taxes. He and his running mate glad-handed landowners in the countryside rankled by the excise bill, which the press referred to as the 'country interest'. The nuance of how the excise might reduce their total tax bill was lost among the fear of excessive taxation. His anti-excise message went over well, with Bishopp and his running mate coming to rallies where people cheered, rang bells and waved anti-excise banners.[97]

Newcastle responded to Bishop's campaigning in the countryside with largesse in the towns. He spoiled the Cinque Ports on behalf of his candidates,[98] at one point leading 1,000 would-be voters on a hunt for a single, terrified stag. The mob chased the poor animal to the beach, where it threw itself into the frigid English Channel in a vain bid for freedom. Celebrating on the beach,* the hunters drank three barrels of beer and ten gallons of brandy as boats dragged the stag back, alive.[99] The Duke of Richmond later wrote to Newcastle thanking him for the 'polite entertainment'.[100]

Despite the duke turning on the tap for the election, the outcome was far from certain. The press reported Bishopp and his running mate's support was increasing in the county to the point where the election could go either way.[101] Privately, the Pelham brothers' confidence in an election victory was also starting to waver. Henry wrote to Newcastle that he thought they would win, but that voters in the country were staunchly against the government. The only thing that would ensure their victory, by Henry's estimation, would be their ability get votes through personal influence.[102] They would need to get creative.

---

*   The newspaper article does not indicate raucousness, but given the liquor involved, it is near impossible that they were waiting quietly.

Newcastle had a lot of tools at his disposal to persuade people to vote his way. Elections at the time were generally free and fair, though not without their share of arm-twisting and manipulation. Since votes were not secret, powerful people could use a variety of rewards or punishments to get those in their orbit to vote a certain way. This was like an early eighteenth-century pyramid scheme. If one could secure a powerful man's (or woman's*) support, they could secure the votes of everyone under them in the pecking order. The levers that different politicos had varied by their place in society. Those lower down could offer a favourable business deal, or threaten to break one – or if they had some sort of political clout, they could pass out favours or offices in exchange for support. Managing this complex web of relationships could swing an election. The people were riled up about the excise, but they could be persuaded to vote for the government if it suited their personal interests. Newcastle had a huge advantage in this regard: vast resources, and a direct line to the government. He could offer lucrative and powerful government jobs to make sure he got the votes he needed, shaping the very workings of state administration to serve his political objectives.

The vote in Hastings was in trouble. One of the Cinque Ports, it sent two MPs to parliament, two seats that the Pelhams could not lose. A canvas of the town's electorate showed a worrying number of undecided voters. In the game of political patronage, an undecided voter was a voter that could be persuaded.[104] Newcastle knew that if he could secure the right person, the right link in the patronage chain, he could keep Hastings in the Whig camp.

John Collier was that crucial link. A lawyer and politician, he was a power player in local Hastings politics. Collier had already done some election work for the Pelhams, but he was not firmly on the side of Newcastle.[105] He was the key to Hastings, but he wasn't going to come cheap. Newcastle would have to go big.

In November 1733, the Treasury appointed Collier as Surveyor General of Riding Officers for Kent.[106] He was now in charge of the riding officers patrolling the coast, netting a plush salary of £250 and an office in

---

*   Women could not vote until the twentieth century, but landowning women could still influence the voting men under their control. Bishopp seems to have sought the support of Lady Darby during the 1734 election.[103]

Hastings for his trouble.[107] Collier was effectively the top anti-smuggling agent in one of the most gang-infested counties in Britain.*

But securing Hastings was only one of many elections that Newcastle was trying to win. The most important race was Sussex county, where his brother, Henry, was on the ballot, fighting a close contest against Bishopp and his anti-excise campaign. Sussex had a much larger electorate than an individual town like Hastings. With almost 4,000 voters,[108] securing the support of one influential person was not going to be effective among such a large voting population. Newcastle turned to an unorthodox tool of persuasion.

Organised crime was embedded through all levels of society in Kent and Sussex, which was a hotbed of smuggling from the moment there were customs laws to defy.[109] Since the Middle Ages, the English government had attempted to limit the export of wool, seen as a strategic commodity, and across the Channel, France had a thriving cloth industry that was hungry for English wool. Attempting to prop up domestic cloth producers and starve their economic rivals, the English government put a tax on exporting wool out of the country. A thriving smuggling industry sprang up ferrying illegal wool past the early customs service to the more lucrative French markets.[110] By the 1730s, the illegal trade was sometimes putting pressure on the legal economy in Kent. Farmers reported having to increase their wages to compete with the smuggling gangs.[111]

Wool production was an important agricultural activity and source of wealth in the area, especially in the Romney Marsh, an area of coastal wetland. Fertile, criss-crossed with waterways and dotted with rich feeding grounds, the marsh is perfect for raising what Defoe described as 'an

---

*   There seems to be some disagreement between the Treasury warrant books and Saville's collection of Collier letters. The Calendar of Treasury Papers says that Collier was appointed for both Kent and Sussex, while Saville (and indeed Collier himself) say that it was just for Kent. But the Treasury papers frequently list William Battine as the Surveyor General for Sussex. It is also possible that Collier was Surveyor General for part of Sussex, and the western half was covered by Battine, who would later play a large role in the Galley and Chater murder investigations. Winslow states that Collier was Surveyor General for Kent and East Sussex. The line between Collier's and Battine's jurisdiction is unclear. Collier's surveys only included Kent, but he seems to be in charge of the investigations around Thomas Peene's death, which occurred firmly in Sussex. It is possible that the Treasury record is a mistake and that Collier is exercising his influence near Hastings.

infinite number of large sheep'.[112] Farmers could get 33 per cent more for their fleeces in France than in British markets, if they could avoid the high export taxes.[113]

That was where the smugglers came in. By the end of the seventeenth century, the wool smugglers of Kent and Sussex took on the name owlers, a reference either to the hoot-like signals that they used to communicate, or to the fact that much of their activity took place at night.[114] Coastal farmers would strike a deal with the local owlers to take their wool across the Channel, past the customs patrols.[115] To protect their investment, the farmer would also lend horses and men to the gang. When the goods were successfully shipped off to France, the whole group would throw a raucous party, with plenty of punch and singing.[116] Owling wasn't just business, it was social; a community ritual of coastal life. The owlers were an integral part of the larger agricultural system in Kent and Sussex, and socially integrated into the wider community, to the point where their neighbours were willing to support them, even when they were in trouble with the law.

The very landscape of the Kent and Sussex coasts assisted anyone wanting to clandestinely sail goods across the Channel. Soaring white cliffs stand tall over the sea, giving way to protected coves and flat stretches of tidal beaches.[117] The sheer cliffs are very dangerous and almost impossible to navigate without deep local knowledge, and a horse willing to risk its own life.[118] Farther inland, the cliffs and beaches give way to a patchwork of wetlands, forest and abysmal roads.[119] The whole area was perfect for smuggling, from its economy, to its culture, to the land itself.

While the hardened, violent gangsters like Gabriel Tomkins were getting all the ink, there were numerous other lower-key smugglers that had more political connections than Gabriel Tomkins, the bricklayer from Tunbridge. Newcastle had something to trade when one of these smugglers landed in jail. He didn't just have the power to influence government appointments, he could also influence the justice system.

In theory, Newcastle did not have the power to issue or approve pardons for criminals. As Secretary of State, his job was to receive petitions for pardons, gather the relevant legal opinions from the original judge, and pass them on to the King for a final decision.[120] But that does not seem to be how it actually worked with Newcastle. He was very high up in the government and had a great deal of formal and informal power in Whitehall. In reality, Newcastle could decide whether a request for a pardon was granted, or a prisoner should go free.*[121]

Through his agents like Collier, Newcastle could make deals that traded votes for clemency. His ability, and willingness, to deal in judicial influence seems to have been well known among voters connected to smuggling, who actively reached out to Newcastle, offering large tranches of votes in exchange for helping a smuggler that was currently caught up in the justice system.[122] These petitions from blocks of forty to sixty men could be aggressive, promising to vote for Newcastle's opponents if he didn't help their man out.[123] The voters demanding Newcastle's assistance may have been active smugglers, people who depended somehow on smuggling, or simply people who had a social connection to the imprisoned smuggler. The reality was likely a mixture of all three.

These weren't trivial proposals: fifty voters was more than 1 per cent of the electorate in Sussex. Moreover, the promise to support the other side if their request was refused meant that the actual effect on the election outcome was double. Intervening in even a few smuggling cases would have a significant impact on the election, especially one as tight as 1734. How this game of 'Better Call Newcastle' started is difficult to determine. Did the smugglers take a punt and succeed, or did Newcastle have a reputation as man who could make things happen, and was open for business?

Collier had helped Newcastle negotiate one of these clemency deals a few months before he was appointed Surveyor General.[124] Now he was on the other side of Newcastle's nascent judicial-electoral complex. As part of his job, Collier conducted an annual inspection of all the customs riding officers under his command. Using that inspection to monitor popular feelings towards smuggling, he could determine where smuggling would have a political impact.[125] By installing Collier as Surveyor General, Newcastle had shaped a law enforcement organisation into a political tool. The customs service in Kent and Sussex enforced the customs laws, and in doing so gave Newcastle a steady stream of potential vote-securing favours. Newcastle's unique mix of political power and proximity to

---

*   Goodwood MS 155 contains a 1743 account from an excise officer where a
     well-connected smuggler is released from prison before his trial partly on the word
     that Newcastle thought he should go free. Winslow also mentions that Collier saw
     Newcastle as the key to John Grayling's freedom in 1744. It is clear that Newcastle
     putting his finger on the scales of justice was a common occurrence.

organised crime turned normal eighteenth-century electioneering into a potent and dangerous cocktail.

***

Polling took place in the spring of 1734 amid considerable election violence throughout the country. In Kent, the political temperature and anti-excise fury was the hottest. Maidstone, the main polling place for Kent, saw a mob drag a voter from his horse and beat him to death.[126] Newcastle was told that if something wasn't done about the riots in Sussex, they might erupt into full-scale insurrection.[127] In Bristol, 'one of the greatest mobs that ever was seen' poured their fury at John Scrope, Walpole's Treasury Secretary and one of the most vehement advocates of the excise bill.[128]

William Hogarth and Francois Morellon de La Cave, *The Polling*, 1758.

As the election and polling raged on, Scrope sent a letter to the Treasury stating that former gang leader Gabriel Tomkins would be employed 'to detect smugglers'.[129] In giving evidence to the parliamentary committee, he had not just escaped justice, he had secured a plum government job as a riding officer, working for the newly appointed Surveyor General, John Collier.

The Whig campaign in Kent ended in disaster, the Tories sweeping away the government candidates. In Sussex, Newcastle's intense campaigning and dealmaking delivered the election for the government.[130] Walpole would hang on, but he had been severely wounded; his power as a Prime Minister never recovered.[131] To help secure victory in Sussex, Newcastle had shaped the law enforcement and judicial system for political gain.

Eighteenth-century elections were filled with shady deals, mutual back-scratching, and electioneering that would be considered naked corruption in twenty-first-century Britain. However, Newcastle's smuggling-driven political machine was corrupt even by eighteenth-century standards. His contemporaries, even his ostensible political allies, considered what he did in Sussex an unscrupulous bargain.

Years later, in 1752, Horace Walpole, Robert Walpole's son, MP, and perennial frenemy of the Pelhams, visited the Hastings area. The Hawkhurst Gang was long gone. Walpole stopped on Silver Hill, near the spot where Carswell had died twelve years before. Looking north, the hill overlooks a long stretch of the Kent and Sussex border, including Hawkhurst,[132] the village at the centre of so much death and mayhem over the preceding decades. Writing of the experience to a friend, he levelled the blame squarely at Newcastle:

> On our way, we had an opportunity of surveying that formidable mountain, Silver Hill, which we had floundered down in the dark: it commands a whole horizon of the richest blue prospect you ever saw. I take it to be the individual spot to which the Duke of Newcastle carries the smugglers, and, showing them Sussex and Kent, says, 'All this will I give you, if you will fall down and worship me.'[133]

The words that he attributes to Newcastle were not his, they were the words that Satan used to tempt Christ in the garden (Matthew 4:9). The gang may have been the instrument of chaos, but Newcastle was the devil on their shoulders. The man who would be Prime Minister for seven years, who led the family that would hold the office for nearly twenty, had in part built his political power on organised crime.

5

SMUGGLING

1735

Despite having no background in law enforcement, and retaining his role as an agent for the Pelhams, John Collier began the serious work of a customs leader in earnest. He may have been appointed as part of Newcastle's political machine, but he still had a job to do. Most of that early year involved trying to clean house among the customs services and control the biggest smugglers along the Romney Marsh. Over the summer, he investigated some allegations against two customs officers, the brothers John and Thomas Jordan, who were reportedly running a racket. Dragoons would make seizures on their own, without a customs officer present, sell any seized horses back to the smugglers for an exorbitant fee, then sell any cargo they took to the Jordans, who would fence the goods themselves.[134] However, the investigation frustratingly came to nothing. John Jordan remained in his job, and was even later promoted to a supervisor of riding officers.[135]

Later that year Collier would need to defend his officers legally after they confronted the Hawkhurst Gang. At the end of October 1735, Thomas Carswell was on patrol with several other customs officers and a handful of soldiers. Carswell was a friend of Collier's, an important and well-connected man in Hastings politics. He had been promoted within the customs service a year before Collier became his boss as Surveyor General.[136] Carswell's killing in 1740 was possibly a revenge killing, one born out of mutual hatred with the Hawkhurst Gang, who he had been battling for years in the cat-and-mouse smuggling game. In 1735, that game turned deadly, the first record we have of the gang.

October 1735

One moonlit night in October, Carswell had reason to suspect that a smuggling run was going to take place, and led a small detachment of customs officers and soldiers to intercept it. As a riding officer, Carswell could command other agents of the customs service or request assistance from the military, bringing handfuls of soldiers as additional firepower while he was out on duty. At Hollington, a few miles outside Hastings, they waited for the smugglers. A road that went from the beach into the countryside ran through the area and was the most likely route for the gang. It was high and flanked by trees and hedges, an ideal spot to observe the run, or spring an ambush. The customs men split up into two groups. Carswell, a sergeant and three other soldiers formed one group, while the two other officers took two soldiers to form another. The groups separated roughly 200 yards down the road, hid themselves in the hedges, and waited.[137]

The night was clear and the nearly full moon* illuminated the road. At about midnight, a lone man on horseback rode up from the beach; a scout for the gang, sent ahead to see if the route and the landing sight were clear. He apparently did not notice the officers hiding in the hedges, because fifteen minutes later a noisy gang with their pack horses rode up behind.[138]

Thomas Pettett, a bystander who had been watching the smugglers closer to the beach, heard the crackle of gunfire. Pettett had got wind of the run at the pub, and decided to see it for himself. There were, after all, rewards for turning in smugglers. He had seen the scout and the smugglers pass, but after they left his sight, he heard the gunfire. Two or three shots rang out and the gang came back towards him in a rout, whipping their horses in utter chaos. The smugglers broke through fences into the surrounding fields. Some dumped their goods and fled, while others broke through more fences and tried to salvage the run. Pettett overheard the fleeing smugglers say they could stash their tea in Turner's Hole, a prearranged stash area in a nearby barn.[139]

---

*   Ninety-two per cent full according to www.moonpage.com (Accessed 21 July 2021).

Later, at an alehouse close to the scene, Thomas Peene lay dead. The customs men had found him lying in the road after the gang fled; taking him to the alehouse and calling the coroner to examine the body.[140] They had fired at the smugglers in the confrontation, and the coroner confirmed the worst. Peene had been shot twice in the back of the head, and died instantly. The coroner concluded that someone had shot Peene, though there was no indication who.[141]

Peene was a carpenter who lived in Hawkhurst, a village about 12 miles* from Hollington. He had roots in neighbouring Sussex and must have been relatively young. He had married his wife, Elizabeth, a few months before,[142] and was almost certainly one of the smugglers that night rather than an innocent bystander in the wrong place at the wrong time. There was no reason for a carpenter to be that distance from home in the middle of the night.[143] The gang themselves were also from Hawkhurst, and must have been relatively new on the smuggling scene, joining the area's established but growing gang culture. The confrontation at Hollington is the first record of a mafia that would come to terrorise Kent and Sussex, and the British state. Even at this early stage, they had already earned a fearsome reputation as a violent gang. Thomas Pettett, in his letter consenting to be a witness of the incident, warned how bloodthirsty the Hawkhurst Gang were. Coming forward as a witness might cost him his life.[144] Peene's role in the gang is unknown, but official reports reckon that he was a temporary worker,[145] the sort of person that took up smuggling to supplement their income. Peene was not by reputation a gang leader.

After Peene's death, the legal investigation carried on into the following year. The coroner's inquest gathered the customs officers present at the shooting to give evidence. By their own admission, the customs men fired at the smugglers. The soldiers who discharged their weapons were arrested for manslaughter.[146] Courts were quick to prosecute customs officers and soldiers that killed smugglers, partly because the local area was sympathetic to the smugglers, but also because there was a persistent fear of using military force to enforce the law. There were no professional police forces at the time, and smuggling gangs were violent and heavily armed criminals. Even so, there was a long-standing fear of a professional

* According to Google Maps. Collier states it is 16 miles in SAY/287. I've gone with Google in this case.

military being used to erode civil liberties. Large standing armies that enforced the law were the domain of imperial despots in Europe. The rights of free Englishmen were not going to be denied by the King's soldiers. Hauling every soldier that killed a smuggler into court was as much a check on government overreach as it was supportive of smuggling gangs.

Once the shooters were arrested, the customs officers gave their own, often self-exonerating, accounts of what happened that night. According to the officers, they left the bushes and presented themselves to the smugglers, attempting to seize the goods and their horses. The sheer sight of the officers convinced the smugglers to flee from the first group led by Carswell. Carswell called out to the other group to stop the fleeing gang. As they attempted to stop their retreat, the gang attacked them with the thick ends of whips and clubs. Under assault, Mr Hide, the officer in charge of the second group, ordered the soldiers to fire on their attackers to intimidate them. The smugglers ran past the officers, who followed in hot pursuit. Some distance down the road, they discovered Peene, lying dead in the road. Not one of the customs officers saw or knew who killed Peene. Carswell reckoned that Peene had been trampled by horses in the retreat.[147]

It was unlikely to convince the coroner, who wrote in his report that Peene had sustained two wounds from musket fire to the back of his head.[148] Pettett testified that he only heard two or three gunshots.[149] Two shooters hitting the back of a man's head with smoothbore muskets, at night, while they were in the process of being attacked at close range, would be nothing short of a miracle. Even if they were firing at the backs of the fleeing smugglers, it would have been a difficult shot, especially if they were shooting to scare the gang off. Peene, even if he was riding a horse, would not have made it any distance down the road with the sort of injuries he sustained.

Peene's wounds and Pettett's testimony likely indicate that the customs officers fired first, ambushing the smugglers. Customs officers appearing while gunshots erupted from the hedges, instantly killing one of their gang, seems a more likely cause of the outright panic that Pettett described in his testimony. Whatever happened at Hollington, it seems as if the customs officers were covering something up. Early in 1736, one of the soldiers' case was put before a grand jury. Carswell, several other customs men, and Peene's new wife Elizabeth gave testimony. The jury found the evidence lacking[150] and the charges were eventually dropped. While the authorities were keen to make sure that soldiers and customs officers showed up in court, that does not mean that they would be convicted.

May 1736

In May, the government introduced a red-blooded law and order bill, pithily described as 'for indemnifying persons, who have been guilty of unlawfully importing goods and merchandise into the kingdom, upon the terms therein mentioned and for enforcing the laws against such importation for the future'.[151] The bill was dripping with frustrated, legislative rage. It offered a small carrot: a general pardon for any smuggling offences before 17 April 1736. Except murderers; they were still on the hook. Those that committed smuggling offences after that date could expect the legal hammer to come down. There were generous bounties for captured smugglers, with informants not only receiving a pardon but payment for their services.[152] Convicted smugglers would hang rather than be transported.[153] You don't come back from the end of a rope.

Anything that looked like smuggling was made a crime. Assembling by the coast while armed was criminalised.[154] Simply loitering by the coast without a good reason earned you a month of hard labour.[155]

In addition to cracking down on smugglers, the law afforded some protections for customs officers. Any person accused of assaulting customs officers could be tried in any court in England rather than where the offence took place.[156] Fair trials were hard to come by in areas where large swathes of the community were involved in smuggling. Soldiers were generally unpopular, and the government found it difficult to make smuggling charges stick in local courts.[157] When judges were presiding over seizures, they were to concentrate on the actual case against the accused, rather than examining how the seizure was made by officers.[158] Customs officers could also legally respond with force when they were attacked.[159]

Objections to the bill in the Commons were tepid. Walpole had just won an election, and though his majority was greatly decreased, he still had control of his caucus. The smuggling bill was as offensive to civil liberties as the excise bill, yet there was no revolt in parliament or public outcry. The simple, calculated fact was that this bill didn't affect nearly as many people or constituencies as the excise bill. During the excise crisis, opponents could imagine a world where everyday items like soap, mutton, bread and butter were taxed in some eighteenth-century version of the Beatles' song 'Tax Man'. It was a different matter entirely when the government was cracking down on the crime-ridden coastal fringes of the kingdom to enforce taxes that were already on the books. Politically, opposition was a non-starter.[160]

In the Lords, however, resistance came from an unexpected source. Lord Hardwicke, the Lord Chief Justice and a Walpole ally, panned the bill. Crimes of implication were new and dangerous. It was impossible to prove that a person had the intent to smuggle.[161] In an argument that would be familiar to modern Americans, he said that the bill infringed on an Englishman's right to bear arms, which were a check against tyrannical and arbitrary government, using troops to suppress legitimate dissent.[162] It was no less than a ploy to take everyone's guns away.[163]

An important part of the bill that explicitly allowed customs officers to use force when met with force was Hardwicke's next target. If customs officers were not going to be hauled into court every time they shot a smuggler, they would shoot first and ask questions later. The government was already effectively taking citizens' weapons away, now they were going to legalise military violence on civilians – heavily armed and violent civilians, but civilians nevertheless. This was the road to tyranny. Trigger-happy customs officers and troops might 'imagine that clubs, or even fists, are offensive weapons and such might be opposed by powder and ball'.[164] If Carswell had been in the room, he could have attested to the accuracy of the statement. That is exactly what his men had done the previous year at Hollington.

Lord Hardwicke ended with a dire prophesy:

> I am afraid, that instead of preventing smuggling, it will render desperate all those who shall hereafter embark in that pernicious trade, which will make them more bold and enterprising than they ever were heretofore; and their common danger will unite them closer together, which will make them more powerful and formidable.[165]

In 1740, political moves in Vienna, more than 800 miles away from Hawkhurst, would plunge Europe into another struggle between the great European monarchies, and turn the Channel into a wartime border between Britain and France. The war was an opportunity for the

Hawkhurst Gang. The French would welcome them as the enemy of their enemy, supporting their business and cultivating their favour. But the gang, and the government's perception of them, would change dramatically. They weren't just criminals, they were possible enemy agents.

6

THE GANG

Gabriel Tomkins needed to get out of town. The star customs officer, the media darling, was not what he seemed. In reality, he had turned his office into a hustle that allowed him to prey on both sides of the smuggling conflict.[166]

The former gang leader, who had earned himself a customs officer job by testifying to parliament, spent the remainder of the 1730s quickly climbing the ranks of the customs service, earning a promotion and becoming a sheriff's bailiff in Sussex.[167] He was good at seizing tea from smugglers and the papers loved him for it. They followed his exploits and the impressive size of his seizures – 600lb of tea here, 800lb there.[168] He seemed to have a magic touch.

His career was nearly cut short in 1736, when he almost got himself killed at the hands of his former colleagues. Tomkins went to Rye, a port town in east Sussex, to arrest smuggler Thomas Moore.[169] Arresting Moore was no trouble, but Moore's friends hastily intervened, offering to pay a £300 bail bond for his freedom, which Tomkins took. Everything seemingly resolved, the group even shared a drink together.[170] However, as the drinks flowed and the princely sum he had paid for bail sunk in, Moore became less happy with the situation.

That evening, Moore and his posse burst through the door of Tomkins's room at the Mermaid Inn. He was going to get the bail bond back from Tomkins, and presumably also go free.[171] ⁹Tomkins, facing down the angry mob of smugglers in his room, refused. They grabbed him, dragged him out through the streets, beat him, and threatened to drown him in a salt marsh. However, murdering him, or at least murdering him here, was a step too far. They instead would put him on a boat to France, to face an uncertain fate.[172]

News of the commotion reached Nathaniel Pigram, captain of a local customs sloop.* Pigram started a search for Tomkins in all the ships in Rye harbour. Luckily, the customs crews found him before the smugglers could set sail.[173] Visiting Tomkins shortly after his rescue, John Collier saw the 'violent and barbarous' treatment that had befallen his employee.[174] Tomkins almost lost his life for nothing. Rye was one of the Cinque Ports, with its own jurisdiction.[175] The Sussex warrant Tomkins had was not worth the paper it was written on and would likely not hold up in court. But maybe that was the point, to leverage a useless warrant to shake a smuggler down for £300.

After Tomkins's brush with death, he was working with his old friend and mentor, Jacob Walter. A tall, thin man in his early 60s, he and Tomkins had been working together for decades, were transported together and both appeared in the same wanted ads. The bullet wound through Tomkins's left arm came from the time that he had broken Walter out of London's Fleet prison.[176] Tomkins had been receiving goods for Walter, providing a safe avenue of selling them and no doubt taking his cut.[177]

Tomkins had also started shaking down other smugglers and pocketing the proceeds. Taking illegal tea from smugglers was technically a seizure, which turns into straight robbery when the customs officer simply keeps what he seizes. But who are the smugglers going to complain to? The pickings were apparently so rich they were too much for one corrupt customs officer to cover. So he did what any good manager does: delegate, unofficially deputising a man named Thomas Black, who pretended to be a customs officer, seizing goods at gunpoint. Black was eventually picked up by real customs officers, but escaped. He went on the run with Tomkins's protection.[178]

Tomkins even tried to steal the seizures that were reported. In 1739, he conspired with a customs bookkeeper to get John Collier's report of a seizure thrown out, making it bureaucratically disappear. Once it was off the books, he could pocket it without anyone being the wiser. The plan fell

---

*   A small, fast sailing ship often used by the customs service.

apart when one of Tomkins's employees tipped off Collier.[179] All of this evidence convinced Collier that Tomkins was too crooked to continue in his various posts.[180] The jig was up.

Tomkins was 50 years old when he resigned his commission and fled into the night.[181] No doubt grey was creeping into his dark brown hair and large, black unibrow. He had taken his knocks: from the smallpox that scarred his face, to the bullet that passed clean through his left arm. He had faced gunfights, transportation, and the hangman's noose. He had always made it through.[182] It was, once again, time to start over. He made his way to London in the still night.[183]

★★★

Smuggling tea had become big business, and the business was booming. Illegal tea was flowing like water through south-east England. The red meat anti-smuggling bill of 1736 did not make a dent in the trade. The Hawkhurst gang were one in a whole constellation of gangs that were operating in Kent and Sussex, interfacing with a fleet of cutters ferrying tea and other goods between nearby countries and the coast. One newspaper estimated in May 1740 that smuggling gangs had been so efficient that they had 'since the last frost drained those countries, at a moderate calculation, of near 200,000lb weight of that commodity'.[184] But the up-and-comers in the business were the Hawkhurst Gang. They were importing a lot of product, making a lot of money, and operating in an area where the justice system was weakened by fear and political meddling. Life for them was good.

With business booming and tea flowing, the Hawkhurst Gang went on the offensive, waging an aggressive war against the customs service. Runs had just become too large and frequent to hide them effectively. The previous decades saw runs performed by gangs of thirty to forty. By the middle of the 1740s, runs could involve hundreds of smugglers and as many horses. It was crime on an industrial scale. No amount of intimidation, community spirit or bribery could keep hundreds of men and horses working on the beach a secret. Secrecy was not an option to protect a run, the only other option was to keep law enforcement away with force.

Smugglers were always armed, but they had turned into paramilitary organisations, riding through their territory with pistols, blunderbusses and short cavalry swords called hangers. By the mid-1740s, their bludgeoning and intimidation had managed to eliminate nearly all government resistance to their business. In 1744, one of Collier's subordinates had to apologise for submitting an empty report, explaining that it was 'morally impossible to be otherwise; so long as the coast is infested with such numbers of smugglers'.[185] Outgunned and outmanned, customs officers had to content themselves with observing the gang as they went about their business and attempt, sometimes unsuccessfully, to stay out of their way. Collier sat as the reports from front-line officers poured in, describing an unchallenged smuggling trade.

The Hawkhurst Gang was most active along a stretch of coast between Hastings in the west and Folkestone in the east. It included Romney Marsh, where the owling trade flourished twenty years earlier, and Dungeness, a small, triangular peninsula, like an arrow pointing almost directly at Boulogne. Dungeness was, in essence, a giant pile of small stones called shingle, flanked by wide, flat, sandy beaches. A former island that became connected to the mainland after apocalyptic storms in the thirteenth century,[186] grasses and small shrubs clung to the low, windswept pile. It was essentially a large, natural jetty, an ideal place to land cargo, and organise the men needed to do it. At the base of this triangle is Lydd, a village on the edge of the sandy headland, dominated by an ancient church. Smugglers could stay in Lydd while they waited for the cutters to come in.

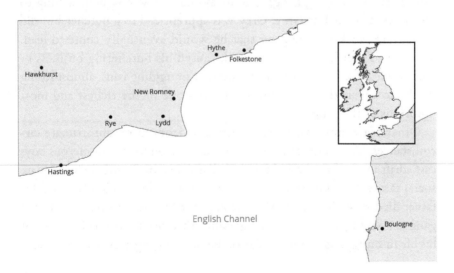

Dungeness and principal operating area of the Hawkhurst Gang.

Customs officers dutifully recorded the Hawkhurst Gang's frequent comings and goings. In the Lydd area alone, they made at least forty-eight smuggling runs in the year between September 1743 and September 1744.[187] Officers stationed at Lydd observed the gang in the area almost every day.[188] The gang came and went as it pleased, bringing in tons of tea. The quantity of tea coming over the beaches almost certainly dwarfed the legitimate trade.

The smugglers that would make headlines a few years later are often present in the officers' reports. The Grey brothers, Trip Stanford and the Fuller Brothers were among those the officers recorded as leading the gang, running their operation with an efficiency that would turn modern managers green with envy. Getting dozens or hundreds of men and horses to show up for work is not trivial in the twenty-first century. Doing it illegally in an age where the best communication technology was word of mouth implies a superior management nous. The cutters came on an almost daily basis and there was always a gang of smugglers waiting to unload them.

Hawkhurst sits at the confluence of several main routes from the coast to London. It was a natural place for smugglers to gather and became the town for anyone wanting to get into the business. The men themselves presumably came for the lure of smuggling, like Trip Stanford,[189] or were local boys that fled humdrum professions, pulled by the persistent siren calls of the smuggling gangs that always needed young men willing to take risks, like Arthur Grey. Grey was apprenticed to a butcher but did smuggling work for the gang that he would eventually come to lead, so much so that his smuggling work caused his butchering business to wither. He risked his legitimate savings on smuggling runs, almost losing it all. However, the risks paid off: he was one of the richest and most notorious of the gang.[190]

Other Hawkhurst Gang members came from more unfortunate circumstances. The gang provided a home and haven for the numerous boys cast adrift by misfortune and family collapse in a time with an inadequate social safety net. Richard Mapsden was from a decent family, until his father died when he was 9. Abandoning his education, he fell in with the gang at a young age, an illiterate gangster that would spend almost all of his life in smuggling.[191] Samuel Austin joined the gang at such a young age, he could hardly ride a horse. His father had fallen into unemployment, casting the family into poverty.[192]

The Hawkhurst Gang was really a conglomeration of numerous micro-gangs, operating in a decentralised system. Each gang leader had his own crew of twenty to thirty smugglers. Crews could operate independently, or as part of the larger group to handle larger shipments. The smugglers would arrange a time to meet a shipment, where they would arrive heavily armed. Once the boat arrived, they would load the goods onto horses and stash them in their network of safehouses, ready for market. If the revenue services tried to interfere, they were usually armed well enough to scare them off.

But the Hawkhurst Gang stopped at the sea. They controlled many of the routes from the coast to London, and had ties with merchants in Holland and France, but they needed to get goods across the Channel. They needed an ally with the connections, one who could make a dedicated partner.

Enter Jeremiah Curteis, alias Pollard. Rumoured to be the son of the mayor of Rye, he ran the Hastings Outlaws, also known as the Transports, with John Grayling, notorious captain of a smuggling cutter.[193] The Outlaws worked closely with the Hawkhurst Gang, providing the ships that brought their goods across the Channel. Curteis was a tall, thin man, with a light complexion set against a reddish beard.[194] *

---

*   There seems to be some confusion about the Outlaws and the Transports. Waugh (p.94) asserts that they were the same gang. Both gangs seems to be operating at the same time and seem to have similar behaviour. CUST 148/12/629 and CUST 148/12/613 describe very similar behaviour as well as the oath to the French King. I think that these two gangs were one and the same, led by Jeremiah Curteis and John Grayling. In addition to their similarity in the sources, there is some linguistic reasoning to support this idea. The Transports were likely called that because they were comprised of men that had returned from a sentence of transportation early, which was a crime. Anyone returning from transportation was committing a felony punishable by death. This meant that these men were, by the legal definition, outlaws. It is not rock-solid evidence, but it is strong enough where the argument is valid, in the absence of better evidence.

In May 1744 they appear to have provided the service, shore to shore, for the Hawkhurst Gang.[*] The Outlaws brought their cargo from a stash house near the coast to Hythe, in broad daylight.

The Hawkhurst Gang then arrived, armed to the teeth, and took it from there. The gangs were using their own specialities to form a brutally efficient system for getting tea into London. The Outlaws used their skill in sea transport, and the Hawkhurst Gang used their arms and network of inland safehouses to get the tea to market.[**] [195]

Smugglers got their goods in French and Dutch towns across the Channel, the most prominent of which was Boulogne, a port town around 20 miles south-west of Calais. Boulogne was the capital of the smuggling world in the eastern English Channel, a vast hub of illegal commerce, where goods from Europe and the world could be bought and snuck into Britain.[196] The town was a huge market for English smugglers, and everyone knew it.

Even in peacetime, the French could stick it to their perennial rival by fostering the smuggling trade. French authorities and merchants knew they were supplying criminal enterprises and either didn't care, or wanted to encourage it. Boulogne traders send out advertisements in French and English, and the French government removed port taxes for commonly smuggled goods and provided some military protection to smugglers.[197] The gang could also use the town as a refuge if the heat from the authorities got too much or they needed medical care after a shootout with the customs service.[198]

Boulogne was also a very convenient place to dispose of people. Deaths were frequent in the running gun battles between smuggling gangs and the customs service. Homicide rates in Kent had been in decline since the Middle Ages, with the exception of the 1740s.[199] Among all this murder, there was a conspicuous lack of outright assassinations from smuggling

---

[*]   It is difficult to ascribe precise gang affiliation to a particular individual at a particular time. Like a lot of organised crime, gang identities can be fluid and individuals could work for different bodies of smugglers that had some sort of identity, particularly when those organisations aren't competing. In terms of Curteis being the leader of the Hastings Outlaws in 1743, I am basing that judgement on Waugh arguing that Curteis was the leader of the Outlaws with Grayling, and that the customs reports indicate that the Hastings Outlaws were still active in 1743–44. The Outlaws seem to fall off the face of the Earth after Grayling gets transported, so my assumption is that Curteis took what was left of the gang and merged it with the Hawkhurst Gang after Grayling was caught. Waugh also assumes Curteis merged his gang with the Hawkhurst Gang, but does not specify a time or reason.

[**]   The source suggests a sea–land split between the two gangs.

gangs. The type of killings that we would later associated with modern organised crime didn't seem to happen. For all their willingness to shoot at and beat anyone that opposed them, they never seemed to deliberately 'whack' people.*

Kidnapping to Boulogne and other cross-Channel towns was an alternative to murder, which brought legal problems, but also possible social problems in their community as well. Murdering someone's relative risked creating a whole family of informants. The gang was relatively careful to avoid the worst excesses of violence, but kidnapping inconvenient people was another matter. This was an era when interpersonal bondage was common. The empire enslaved hundreds of thousands of Africans, violent press gangs would abduct men for forced labour on ships, and transportation was a common punishment. Abductions by smugglers were shocking and worth reporting in the press, but were likely not as abhorrent, or legally prohibited, as they would be today.

Gangs, and in particular the Hawkhurst Gang, resorted to kidnapping when they captured customs officials or soldiers, using the swarm of cutters illegally criss-crossing the Channel to dispose of their unfortunate captives. Anything they had witnessed would remain unreported.

What happened to captives once they reached France isn't clear. Gangs could have waited to kill their captives once they were away from Britain, though there is no mention of this at the time. Kidnapping could also have been an intimidation tactic. In 1742 Curteis kidnapped two customs officers, John Darby and Freebody Dray, as they attempted to seize a shipment of goods, eventually returning the officers home, unharmed.[200] Though the message was clear: co-operate or they might not come back next time, an eighteenth-century version of Pablo Escobar's *plata o plomo*.**

---

*   Part of this is the difficulty with the extant sources. There are coroners' records, and newspapers were quick to report violence from smuggling gangs. However, these records are not necessarily complete. Murders by smugglers might also be recorded as other types of murder. There don't seem to be any unexplained murders in the primary materials, or in the secondary scholarship. Whatever the reason, it is a peculiar aspect of a particularly violent period.

**   Translates as 'silver or lead', the idea that authorities should either accept a bribe or expect a bullet at the hands of the cartels.

One of the most horrifying, but likely, scenarios is that they were sent to be forced labour in the French galley corps. In the first half of the eighteenth century, the French had a massive fleet of galleys, large ships propelled mainly by oars, rather than sails. The galleys were a military force in the Mediterranean, but also served as floating prisons for the nation's criminals. Thousands of the prisoners, convicted of crimes from theft to manslaughter, toiled on the galleys, chained together in brutal conditions.[201]

Smugglers were the second largest group of convicts on the galleys after thieves.[202] Gangs could turn their captives over to legitimate authorities as smugglers, or more likely had some sort of deal with the French authorities to take their prisoners and not ask questions. Any protests by the prisoner would have been for nothing. Those running the galleys probably heard it all. By the late 1740s, the British press believed and reported that smuggling gangs doomed their captives to a wretched life below decks on a French galley.

The Outlaws' connection to the French ran deeper than just business. The gang had allegedly sworn allegiance to the King of France, had free rein of French ports, and were providing transport services between the two countries, notwithstanding that some of those transported to France were brought there against their will.[203] The gang also reportedly drank toasts to the Stuart pretender to the British throne, living in exile in France;[204] a common act of political protest that got the attention of the British authorities, who were on the lookout for any signs of dissent. Support of the Stuart royal line, known as Jacobitism, had boiled over into violence several times in the decades after they were deposed in 1688. It is unknown whether the Outlaws' connections to the French were formed out of shrewd business sense, or genuine political feelings. Whatever the Outlaws' motivation, customs officials were afraid that the Hastings Outlaws were not just a group of smugglers, but anti-government insurgents, at a time when the cold war in the Channel was about to turn hot.

7

WAR

March 1744

The Duke of Newcastle was in his London home, Newcastle House, with a member of the Hawkhurst Gang, Abraham Walter. Originally from Hawkhurst,[205] Walter had just returned, or more accurately escaped, from France, bringing the Secretary of State information that was a matter of national security.[206]

Newcastle's political fortunes had only increased since the 1734 election. Walpole's government, which he had served loyally for years, had collapsed in 1742. Newcastle's brother, Henry Pelham, whom he had fought so hard to keep in parliament, rose to Prime Minister in 1743 when Walpole's successor died in office. Newcastle's electioneering and willingness to deal with the smugglers had paid off. Pelham kept Newcastle on as Secretary of State, forming a powerful alliance that would control British politics for the next decade. But there was a war on, and Newcastle could use his connections with smugglers in other ways.

For four years, the machinations of European monarchs had once again plunged the Continent into senseless butchery. Move and counter-move around the Austrian throne had mobilised tens of thousands of men in a brutal game of chess across dozens of countries and pulled in nearly every major player in Europe. The King, George II, was drawn into the conflict around his ancestral lands in Hanover, in northern Germany.[207] He personally travelled to Germany to lead the war effort. With him was the Duke of Richmond, Newcastle's friend and political ally. Sending Newcastle frequent accounts of the fighting, Richmond kept him abreast of the horrors of war against the French: cannonades, cavalry charges, men killed and maimed, whole companies of troops annihilated for little gain.[208]

British and French troops had been fighting each other in support of their allies on the Continent, but their mutual border along the Channel had remained largely free of direct military confrontation. The French supported the smugglers in the Channel with access and tax-free tea as a way of stirring up trouble for their neighbour.[209] However, in late 1743, the French made a deal with the Spanish to fight Britain directly.[210]

Abraham Walter was one of those smugglers that the French so happily supported. Travelling to Boulogne for reasons he never made clear,* Walter had witnessed something troubling, even for someone who was used to the turbulent and violent smuggling life. Two English cutter captains,** men used to taking abductees to France, were themselves swiftly arrested by the French authorities, taken to Dunkirk, and banned from seeing anyone including their own families. Walter and the captains' worried families pleaded with the mayor of Boulogne, who did nothing other than tell them that the captains would come to no harm. It wasn't the mayor's call, the order to arrest them came all the way from the French King. However, the mayor let slip to Walter that the captains were to be taken back to England on the transports, though Walter should keep that piece of information to himself (he didn't).[211]

Walter had to find out what was going on for himself, and went to Dunkirk. When he arrived, he saw that the port wasn't just busy with its normal hum of traders and smugglers, but was full of ships and fishing boats, packed to their gunwales with soldiers, artillery and defensive barriers.[212] France was preparing to invade.

Most troubling of all, they were loading around 20,000 extra muskets, along with additional equipment, weapons intended for the thousands of English dissidents and criminals they expected to join the invasion.*** The political turmoil and gang-fuelled chaos in England must have been clear

---

* Though this was likely smuggling.

** These captains were likely smugglers.

*** Whether they expected criminal gangs like the Hastings Outlaws, who had sworn allegiance to the French crown, or expected those anti-government elements of society to take up arms, the French clearly thought that there would be significant native support for their invasion.

enough to see across the Channel. If the British government was losing control of Kent and Sussex to the smuggling gangs, they stood no chance against a co-ordinated force of French regular troops.[213]

The invasion force was packed full of rebellious British: Irish rebels, and English Jacobites, who supported the overthrow of the current king in favour of the Stuart dynasty, which was deposed over half a century ago. The pretender's eldest son, Charles Edward, lurked a few miles away and his personal secretary was in Dunkirk.[214] The French weren't coming just to fight, their aim was regime change.

The plan was relatively simple. Four French warships were to come up to the south-west of Britain, drawing the British fleet into an engagement. While the defence fleet was distracted, the Dunkirk invasion would sail all the way up the Thames estuary directly into London. If the fleet could not be drawn away, they would land at Dungeness or Pevensey Bay, Hawkhurst Gang territory,* making their way through Kent towards the capital.[215]

The French officers were practically jovial about their impending invasion of Britain. While visiting an English merchant in Dunkirk, Walter witnessed French officers changing their money, figuring that no one would accept their French livres in the freshly invaded country. They kindly offered to take any letters the merchant had for England, sure they would be there in the next few days.[216]

The only thing that spared the UK from invasion was the Channel itself. Days of violent winds and heavy weather decimated the fleet, driving ships aground and sinking more. Commanders tried to order the ships back into the harbour, but returning to port was too risky. Even ships anchored in sheltered areas near the harbour suffered badly. The French admitted that 600 soldiers had drowned, but Walter knew that the number was far greater. The invasion fleet in disarray, Walter made his escape from Dunkirk, travelling back to England via Ostend.[217]

It was shocking and detailed intelligence, but there was a problem. It was clear why Walter was in Boulogne when he originally embarked on his adventure.[218] He was a smuggler, and a member of one of the most notorious gangs in south-east England: the same gang that was shooting,

---

* The source does not explicitly say the landing site was chosen because it was gang territory, but it seems like an odd choice, given that it is not the closest landing place to Dunkirk.

beating, kidnapping and robbing the area into oblivion. The word of a smuggler was unlikely to be credible, and Newcastle, the Secretary of State, sitting down with criminals, at least openly, would cast doubt on the intelligence.

Someone in the room had a solution. Walter's testimony had already been written down, signed by him and Newcastle. The heading of the document read 'The information upon oath of Abraham Walter, of the Parish of St Bride, London'. In a stroke of euphemistic inspiration, they inserted with a caret after Walter's name, the word 'currier [courier]'. It was technically true.[219] Despite the criminal source of the information, Newcastle took the intelligence seriously.* [220] The French would wait another year before trying again, but the testimony must have given Newcastle an inkling of just how vulnerable Kent and Sussex were to French attack, and how the smuggling gangs he had implicitly supported made that vulnerability worse.

---

*   Newcastle would mention intelligence about preparations at Dunkirk around the time of the Jacobite Rebellion. The previous February, Newcastle wrote to Richmond thinking that the French would invade from Dunkirk up the Thames. Walter's testimony seems to be the first that suggests they might land in Kent.

8

ESCALATION

Money and the new anti-smuggling law saw the traditional boundaries around the smuggling trade dissolve in the first half of the 1740s. The relatively limited conflict between smuggler and revenue office escalated into something that began to more closely resemble a terrorist insurgency. The constraints and unspoken rules began to loosen, unleashing ever-escalating violence on the customs service and eventually the community. The Hawkhurst Gang started out as one of many smuggling gangs in Kent and Sussex, but in the 1740s it would grow in scale and violence to the point where it gained de facto control of the area, seizing a unique place in the history of British smuggling.

The 1736 law had criminalised so many aspects of smuggling and incentivised informing to such an extent that most smugglers could be put at the end of a rope at any time. Rather than give up smuggling, the gang closed more tightly. The only thing keeping them safe was each other, everyone else was a potential snitch or an officer that stood to make a tidy sum by sending them swinging in the breeze. It had become life and death.

Just as the gang got more closely bound together, the shadowy political support they enjoyed kept the important smugglers out of jail and off the gallows. Carswell's 1740 murder was a compelling argument to the Hawkhurst Gang that they could operate with an impunity that previous gangs did not enjoy. Carswell had been dead and buried for years, and not a single member of the gang had been convicted of the murder, despite an intensive manhunt. Most of the gang was indicted by a grand jury shortly after the event, but no charges were brought. Two were charged with being involved in the smuggling run where Carswell was killed, but they were acquitted. Arthur Grey was picked up in 1742 but was admitted to bail, and the charges against him simply vanished.[221] John Mackdonnell was arrested as well, but was acquitted.[222] The gang was literally getting away with murder; what was the government going to do about beatings, kidnapping or threats?

Smugglers concentrated on causing physical pain or embarrassment to the customs officers they captured, never reaching the point of simply murdering them outside of a confrontation. Someone would come to take their place, and there was likely a social price to pay for simply executing respected members of the community. Besides, the beatings and humiliation generally worked. By 1743, the customs officers from Dover to Lydd were giving little interference to smuggling gangs. Those that did often had cause to regret it.

On one occasion, the gang pulled an officer off his horse while he was on patrol, 'broke his head', and locked his horse up until the early hours of the morning. They then landed their goods at their leisure.[223] In another incident, a customs officer named Parker seized a load of tea from the Hawkhurst Gang. As Parker brought the tea back to the customs house in London, three of the gang, including Club James, rescued the tea and dragged him back to a pub. Pointing cocked pistols at him, they threatened to shoot him if he ever touched their goods again. Undeterred and perhaps made of stronger stuff, Parker stayed on the beat, enduring numerous threats, and a few shots directed his way.[224]

Another officer was captured by the gang after an attempted seizure around Lydd.* They forced him to lead one of their pack horses on foot to their stash house in Sandhurst, 20 miles away from Lydd.[225]

Riding officer John Darby received the most concentrated ire from the Hawkhurst Gang. Victim of the property maxim that location is king, he lived in Lydd, epicentre of the gang's coastal operation.[226] His house was near the centre of town, where he could see who was coming and going from the gang's almost-daily landings around Dungeness.** Darby

---

*   Though never explicitly stated, the gang was likely to be the Hawkhurst Gang. Sandhurst is about 3 miles away from Hawkhurst.

** Based on Darby's letter to Caro, he must have been fairly near All Saints Church, in the centre of town.

was more willing to name names in his reports to Collier than his contemporaries.* Frequently mentioning the Greys, Trip Stanford and Curteis, he was nearby, had an eagle eye, and knew the gang's leadership.

In return, the Hawkhurst Gang made Darby their whipping boy. While trying to make a seizure in 1741 with another officer at Lydd, the customs men were beaten by a gang of smugglers with clubs.[227] The next year, Jeremiah Curteis kidnapped Darby and his colleague Freebody Dray, taking them to Boulogne, and apparently treating them well before returning them:[228] a trip they might not come back from next time.

Despite this crescendoing mistreatment by the gang, customs officers still occasionally tried to do their jobs. Whether this was out of a sense of duty or bloody-mindedness, officers did take their chances when they could. They seemed to be relying on the unspoken rules in the traditional game of smuggler and officer. Violence was generally restricted to confrontations while smuggling was taking place, the gangs did not just outright murder officers or beat them in their homes. It seems like a strange line today, but the shootouts that rang out all over Sussex and Kent were just business, and when officers went home to their families, they were generally left alone. John Darby and other officers might have kept trying out of a belief that the smugglers would not actually kill them. The long-standing rules of the game and social consequences would keep them relatively safe.

However, as smuggling got more intense, and gangs like the Hastings Outlaws and the Hawkhurst Gang gained de facto control of more territory, the legal and social constraints that protected officers when they were off duty began to unravel. Violence begets other violence, and the more the gang got away with, the more violent they became. It was not enough to shoot at officers as they tried to seize goods or to violently rescue their cargo – the smugglers started to proactively attack officers while they were off duty. Attacking an officer in the street, showing up armed to their house, or threatening their loved ones and property became part of the smugglers' toolkit.

'Sir, my life is in great danger and if you could be my friend [in] any way no one would so gratefully acknowledge it than [me]', John Darby wrote to his superiors in spring 1744. The Hawkhurst Gang had paid a visit to his house, armed. He was thankfully not home. A few days later,

---

* Based on my observations of TNA CUST/148/12.

the gang again came to his door, but had been dissuaded from acting by the presence of soldiers encamped in the nearby churchyard. A group of armed gangsters showing up at your door is frightening; twice in one week shows a terrifying persistence. The gang might be third time lucky, because the soldiers in the churchyard were supposed to march away on another assignment soon.[229]

A few months later, Trip Stanford and William Grey showed up at Darby's farm in Sussex. After finding he, once again, was not home, they threatened to burn the farm to the ground.[230] The final straw came when Darby was staying in an inn and received a night-time visit from gang leaders Jeremiah Curteis and Richard Smith, who forced their way into the room and threatened to carry him away again on a less pleasant trip to France. Fleeing out of the room, Darby hid from the smugglers. Searching for him, they cut the bridle off his horse, saying they would kill him if they could find him. This was too much for Darby. He fled to nearby Hythe with his family, lying low from the gang.[231] The game had changed. Officers were not safe off duty anymore, and they knew it.

9

LONDON

The gang had effectively neutered the riding officers on the coast and in the countryside. The sheer mass of armed men during runs meant that arresting smugglers, or more accurately important smugglers, when they were actually smuggling was nigh impossible. But the coast was not the only place the customs service attacked the smuggling system. Once tea was landed, the gangs stored it in a series of stash houses in the countryside, and crucially in the capital. Gangs could muster a substantial force to defend rural stash houses or could move the tea away if they got wind of a raid, but London was a more difficult place to operate in. In the urban hustle and bustle it was harder to gather the same number of armed men as in the counties, and harder to see a raid coming. The customs service began raiding urban stash houses.

In October 1743 customs officials got a tip-off of a stash house on Kennington Lane in south London that was actively guarded by armed smugglers. Threatening 'the loss of their heads' if the officers approached the house, the smugglers were ready for a fight. The customs assembled twenty officers with musketeers as backup, locked and loaded. Squaring up to the house, they demanded to enter. The smugglers dared the officers to lay siege, and they obliged in a shootout that lasted three hours, damaging the house and undoubtedly sending the neighbourhood into chaos. Eventually the smugglers relented and offered a deal. They would allow the customs officers to search the house, but only if they would pay for the damage from the firefight. The officers agreed and entered

Musketeers on the Streets of London. Detail from William Hogarth, *Industry and Idleness*, 1747.

the house to find the tea. However, the preceding three hours had given the smugglers time to move their goods. They found nothing, returning home empty handed, 10s poorer.[232]

The customs service were also keen to capture wanted smugglers when they could, as well as raiding stash houses. To do that they would need a certain breed of men in their employment, men that were willing to hunt down and arrest some of the most dangerous criminals in Britain, with violent friends, and powerful political allies: men like John Bolton.

Bolton had been working in the customs service since 1735, moving to London from Chester in the north of England.[233] On the books, he was a petty bureaucrat, supervising loading and unloading at the port of London for a modest £35 a year.[234] But Bolton wasn't just a pencil pusher, he was also hunting smugglers in the city and the surrounding countryside at the behest of his bosses in the customs, an eighteenth-century Eliot Ness.* His dangerous confrontations with smugglers seemed to be a common occurrence. Bolton's boss once said that he 'sent him [Bolton] upon different occasions, where his life has been in great danger, and he always behav'd as a faithful servant ought to do'.[235] Bolton was a successful hunter too, at one point splitting with his crew a handsome £50 for collaring a smuggler.[236]

Bolton often worked with his friend, Thomas Quaif, another minor official[237] cum anti-smuggling agent. Quaif could have had a lucrative smuggling career if he hadn't found himself on the other side of the law. He was born in Hawkhurst in 1706, likely growing up with the same men that had turned his home town into the smuggling capital of England.[238] Together, they formed an eighteenth-century buddy-cop duo fighting organised crime in London's urban jungle.

Bolton was even tried for murder after a stash house stake-out in London went wrong. The smugglers managed to outwit Bolton and Quaif by leading them away from the stash house with a grocer's servant carrying a bag of tea as a decoy.

However, the drop didn't go entirely to plan and the smuggling gang killed a constable on their way out of town. Bolton looked enough like the killer to be accused of the murder by one of the survivors. But it seems to have been a case of mistaken identity, Quaif and Bolton's boss vouched for his whereabouts, ensuring Bolton was acquitted, free to hunt smugglers once again.[239]

Customs service jobs were political appointments, beholden to whatever social circles could control the placement. Jobs like riding officers were relatively prestigious and were handed out as favours in the wheeling and dealing of political and electoral life, which means officers weren't necessarily selected for their knowledge of smuggling. But the lower ranks of the service seem to have been less juicy prizes in the patronage system. It appears that customs bosses could appoint the dull, workaday jobs at the port more freely and they seemed to use these positions to hire people who had more skills than connections, and use them to combat smuggling in the city. Giving them a customs appointment, no matter how minor, gave such men the ability to make seizures and arrests as well as legitimise their anti-smuggling work. It is possible that Bolton and Quaif were

---

*   A famous US prohibition officer in the early twentieth century.

Depiction of London port, Boitard, 1757.

former smugglers brought in to hunt smugglers, or they simply had the knack and the chutzpah to track down dangerous criminals for a living.

Arresting smugglers away from the coast and raiding stash houses wasn't always successful, but it afforded a much-needed response to the smugglers' aggression against customs officers. In theory, the 1736 law gave officers broad powers to arrest people that were reported as smugglers, or that attacked officers in the course of their duties. In practice, it was not only difficult to arrest smugglers successfully, it was also difficult to make the charges stick in the local courts. Potential witnesses received as many threats as customs officials and smuggling gangs were tight-knit enough to make informing reasonably rare. There was also the issue of actually arresting a smuggler. Gangs were good at protecting their members from the law. They usually outgunned and outnumbered officers, despite those officers having military assistance. Even if they did successfully take a suspect into custody, their friends were often willing to rescue them.

Capturing gang members was made harder by the fact that they had a man on the inside of the customs service: a prominent lawyer who had been in the pocket of the smuggling gangs for over a decade. Serving as a clerk to the solicitor of the customs service, he had access to privileged information and gleefully sold it to the gangs, tipping off his gangster clients of any arrest warrants, and burying any potentially damning information.[240]

Though the odds were generally stacked in favour of the smugglers, the customs service did have some success in making high-profile arrests, which would only serve to strengthen the Hawkhurst Gang.

10

MAFIA

John Grayling made a mistake, one that cost him his freedom. Grayling was a sailor, one of the many smugglers that specialised in avoiding the law at sea. Calling the gang he led with Jeremiah Curteis the Hastings Outlaws was not just for effect, it was a legal truth. In 1736, Grayling and his gang beat and wounded a sailor on a customs cutter, earning them seven years' transportation to the colonies in 1737.[241] Grayling could not be kept away for very long and returned in 1738, forming the Outlaws and carrying on his smuggling business, this time living out of Boulogne.[242] Curteis and Grayling continued smuggling for years, safely out of the reach of the law in France.

However, the exile life in Boulogne wouldn't last forever. The war with France* complicated things for smugglers. The sudden arrest and detention of smuggling captains before France's failed Dunkirk expedition must have rattled Grayling, regardless of whether he himself had been arrested or not. To the French, the smugglers were disposable. For decades, politicians in Britain had been decrying the tyrannical, arbitrary rule of absolute European monarchies like France. It seems that Grayling had seen this tyranny at first hand with the sudden arrests of the cutter captains in Boulogne, and it was not to his liking.

---

* The War of Austrian Succession.

In May 1744 the government had issued a proclamation to ease a manpower shortage in the navy: anybody guilty of smuggling who was willing to join the service would be pardoned.[243] When a copy of the proclamation arrived at Boulogne, Grayling saw his chance to come home. In June, Grayling and six other Outlaw gang members sailed back to Hastings, requesting the Duke of Newcastle to confirm that the amnesty applied to them.

Newcastle dithered, kicking the question to the Attorney General. Newcastle was Secretary of State, and his brother was the Prime Minister. He likely could have made sure the amnesty applied to Grayling and the other Outlaws. Newcastle had partly built his power base on his willingness to trade judicial favours for votes, and Grayling and the Outlaws almost certainly had votes to trade. One of the agents working on the case referred to Grayling as 'Sir Grayling' in correspondence.[244]

But times had changed. The chaos of the 1734 election had given way to the Pelhams having a solid hold on Sussex. Newcastle's candidates had run unopposed since. The closest Sussex had to a competitive election was in 1740, when Newcastle's rival, the Duke of Somerset, threatened to run a challenger if Newcastle didn't replace one of his candidates with Cecil Bishopp. Newcastle coolly replied that they would just have to let the voters decide. Somerset blinked, the challenge never materialised.[245] The simple fact was that Newcastle did not need the Outlaws or whatever votes they might have to offer, not like he did a decade before. Why bail out a gang that had reportedly sworn allegiance to the French? However, Grayling and the Outlaws took the fact that Newcastle had deferred to the Attorney General as a good sign.[246] They were so confident that their pardon was secure that they shipped all their clothes and furniture to Hastings.[247]

However, clemency was not a done deal. After they arrived in Hastings, it became clear that their inclusion in the amnesty was complicated. And there was the issue of returning from transportation.[248] The mood in Hastings began to sour when one of the lawyers started to lose confidence that the decisions would be in their favour. Thinking it was safer to return to Boulogne and wait out the Attorney General's decision, they ran. Grayling never made it back to Boulogne. A privateer attacked his cutter as he fled, landing him in prison.[249] In a final blow while he languished in Newgate, Collier informed him that the amnesty did not apply to him. He would need to be tried.[250]

Grayling was to be transferred by thirty armed soldiers from Newgate Prison to Horsham in Sussex, 40 miles away through gang territory. A rescue attempt was a near certainty. Arriving in Croydon, a town south of London, they got word that the Outlaws* were waiting for them in a village down the road. The soldiers were in a difficult situation. Grayling had to arrive in Sussex where he could be tried, but doing so would mean walking into a trap.[251]

The officer in charge of the mission had a flash of brutal ingenuity. They would stay in Croydon another day. He came to Grayling that evening and told him that at the first sign of any rescue attempt, he would personally shoot him through the head. He must have seemed sincere, and Grayling was successfully taken to Horsham without incident.[252]

The law eventually provided Grayling and the other Hastings Outlaws the salvation that bullets could not provide. Grayling was a Hastings man, and the Hastings establishment was pulling what strings it could to secure his release. This included Collier, who was caught in a conflict of interest between his roles as Newcastle's agent, Surveyor General of riding officers and as part of the Hastings political establishment. Collier was not coy with his lobbying, writing that if Newcastle didn't intervene, Grayling would hang.[253]

Grayling was generally a more sympathetic case than most smugglers; not only was he connected with the well-heeled of the town, he had also more or less turned himself in, throwing himself on the mercy of the King. His case was also legally ambiguous, which Collier and the other Hastings elite could use to lobby for his release. It took nearly a year, but the persistent lobbying of Collier and others managed to save the captured Outlaws from the hangman's noose. In 1745, the navy managed to slice open the legal Gordian Knot and recruited them into the service.[254]

---

* The newspaper article did not name the gang waiting in ambush, but it is safe to assume that it was the Outlaws, or even the Hawkhurst Gang.

Grayling's arrest and newfound navy career effectively ended the Hastings Outlaws as a gang. Curteis was not caught up in the incident, becoming the sole leader of the gang when Grayling went to prison. Once it was clear that Grayling was out for good, Curteis merged what was left of the Outlaws into the Hawkhurst Gang.[*]

By the end of 1744, the pressure of being in the Hawkhurst Gang must have caused some members to crack. The war had distanced the cosy relationship between the smugglers and the French,[255] and Grayling's arrest must have spooked a few higher-level smugglers.

The tight-knit Hawkhurst Gang had a traitor that landed one of its major players in jail. In November 1744, Thomas Quaif arrested Thomas 'Jockey Tom' Carey in a pub near London, based on information provided by Club James, one of his fellow gang members, who had earlier been enthusiastically threatening to blow a custom's officers brains out.[256][**] Arresting Jockey Tom would have been a major coup for Quaif. He was one of Carswell's suspected killers and had been high up in the gang for years. A few weeks later, another one of Carswell's killers, John Mackdonnell, was also taken into custody.[257] The gang was not so safe anymore, their high-level members suddenly finding themselves sitting in prison. It was time to strike back.

★★★

In late November 1744 the Hawkhurst Gang, 100 strong, marched into Bexhill, near Hastings, in the middle of the day, flags flying like a private army. They were marching to a smuggling run, but they had a point to prove first. Bexhill had a detachment of troops stationed to assist the customs service. The 100-strong gang descended on their quarters,

---

[*]   I'm basing this on the fact that after Grayling was arrested, there is no mention of the Transports or the Hastings Outlaws in the records as far as I can determine. Curteis was already working closely with the Hawkhurst Gang, and going forward the gangs seem to be effectively one.

[**]   The newspaper article names the informant as Club George, but this is very likely a reporting error on behalf of the paper. I've found no evidence of a smuggler by that name. Club James was a known Hawkhurst Gang member, and he is known to have betrayed the gang around this time (and been punished for it). It seems too coincidental to have two smugglers with the nickname 'Club' betray the gang at the same time. An error is the simpler explanation.

confiscating weapons and beating up some of the twenty terrified soldiers. Outnumbered five to one, the troops offered up little fight.[258] With any possibility of organised resistance out of the way, the gang went to settle a score.

Philip Bailley, a riding officer, got it worse than many other customs officers because he wasn't just an obstacle to their business, he was a part of it. They came to kill him because he had ended the collaboration, having recently 'broke his trust'. You can start working with the Hawkhurst Gang, but you don't stop without endangering your life, *plata o plomo*.[259] Club James, the snitch, would learn this lesson soon enough. The gloves had finally come off, and murder, the deliberate, premeditated, targeted kind, was now an option.

The Hawkhurst Gang marched, hooting and shouting, to Bailley's house, coming for blood. The smugglers searched the house, swearing they would kill him if they found him. But Bailley had managed to get enough of a head start to evade the horde of revenge-filled smugglers and slipped out of the house. Frustrated and angry that they couldn't get their hands on Bailley, the gang proceeded to destroy his house and all his possessions. They broke every stick of furniture, smashed every window, sliced every curtain to ribbons, and destroyed his shop in a fit of collective rage.[260] The family fled to neighbours, their home completely uninhabitable.[261]

Whipped into a murderous frenzy, the gang then descended on another customs officer named Walsh, torturing him with blows and cuts from their hangers. Showing a modicum of compassion, the gang let him escape with his life, a few of the gang keeping the rest from murdering him.[262]

Having torn a path of violence and destruction to the coast, the gang proceeded with their actual job for the day, unloading a run of tea. The vessel they were unloading was a custom-built smuggling cutter, recently launched from Folkestone, estimated to be the largest of its kind to date.[263] Obliterating any resistance wasn't just a statement, it was a way of clearing space for the massive run. The Hawkhurst Gang had begun to look more like paramilitaries, heavily armed and able to achieve complex, violent operations, picking military targets ahead of time and taking out potential leadership.

But the run wasn't entirely problem free. A group of armed soldiers, perhaps led by Bailley himself,[*] moved to confront the gang.[264] As they completed their unloading, the smugglers split up to store their cargo in several stash houses. Stopping to refresh their horses at a nearby village, the officers encountered a small group of smugglers riding rapidly towards them, perhaps an advanced guard, or as a warning to the town that the main body of the gang was coming through. Firing, in a likely mix of abject fear and vengeful rage, the soldiers killed one of the smugglers on the spot.[265]

The destruction of Bailley's house made national news.[266] Something was different now. Both sides upped the ante in November 1744 and would fundamentally change the conflict over smuggling in south-east England into a guerrilla war. After Bailley's house was destroyed, the customs service ordered more military assistance into the area: two troops of cavalry to Kent and two to Sussex.[267] The customs also seemed to have more fire in their bellies when apprehending the gang. At the end of November, they apprehended two smugglers at Brighthelmstone in Sussex. Not going without a fight, the smugglers put up a fierce resistance, which was met with the soldiers running one of smugglers through the chest with a bayonet, seriously wounding him.[268]

The stakes in the game were higher, and whatever restraint both sides had shown each other before had slipped away. It would make conflict all the more dangerous and deadly.

[*] There is some disagreements between the sources. The customs report of the incident indicates that the encounter between this second group of soldiers and the smugglers happened on the same day as the smuggling run. Sam Hill's account, which asserts that Bailley personally led this group as revenge, happened three days later at Sandwich Castle. They both agree that a smuggler was killed in the confrontation. I've decided to go with the official reports at this point. Sam Hill's account is around eight years after this event, while the customs report is at most a few weeks. Hill's memory of the details is likely wrong, and attributes the killing of the smuggler as Bailley taking revenge for his house.

II

BOLTON

18 December 1744

John Bolton sat in the King's Head Inn in Shoreham in Kent.[269] With him were his colleagues John Jones,* a tidesman, his old friend Thomas Quaif and Club James,** who had taken a new name since his information landed Jockey Tom in jail. He was going by Peter Floyd now, and was helping Bolton and Quaif on their latest assignment.

They had been to the far east of Kent, unsuccessfully trying to arrest John Jenner, another smuggler.[270] Quaif and Bolton were working far from their usual area in London, though the fraught climate in Kent and Sussex meant they were better suited to arrest smugglers than the riding officers stationed along the coast. Darby had been driven into hiding, Bailley's house lay in ruins and Walsh was nearly killed by a

---

*   John Jones was likely a customs agent; there is a John Jones that is a tidesman in Bristol. However, John Jones is such a common name it is difficult to be sure.

**   The sources seem to disagree about whether Peter Floyd or Club James was with Bolton at Shoreham that day. I've not found any record of Peter Floyd other than in reference to this incident. Henry Jones in *Bygone Kent 20*, p.717, argues that Peter Floyd might be an alias that Club James began using after he started working with the customs agents. This is the most likely scenario. Club James helped Thomas Quaif capture Jockey Tom the month before and Club James's surname is listed as Floyd in the report where he threatens a customs agent (TNA CUST 148-12-605). Different sources would have referred to Club James by what name they knew him. Bolton must have known him by his alias, hence his later testimony that uses Peter Floyd. In this account, I will treat them as the same man.

mob. Bolton and Quaif lived in the capital, further from the reach of the gang. It was one thing to gather 100 smugglers to terrorise a riding officer in a lone house, it was another to march that same army of smugglers into London. Quaif had an advantage against the Hawkhurst Gang as well. He was a local man, born in the village, and must have grown up with most of the men he faced on the other side of the law. It might be why Club James trusted him enough to help arrest Jockey Tom the month before.[*]

They were stuck in Shoreham, a village in northern Kent on the outskirts of London, because of a lame horse that needed to be reshod, an eighteenth-century flat tyre.[271] Waiting for the farrier to finish his work, their peaceful boredom was shattered by terror. Gunshots, lots of them, were coming from outside. The Hawkhurst Gang were in town, Arthur Grey and Jeremiah Curteis at the head of a posse.[272] Bolton and his crew knew why they were there, and that they were in grave danger.[273]

They hid as best they could, but it was the horses tied up outside that betrayed them. The gang knew they were hiding, and announcing their arrival with gunfire had the village running for cover. No one was around to help them.

---

[*] The following account is derived from a variety of sources. The customs men's capture caused a stir in the press and within the government itself. It is also central to several trials of the Hawkhurst Gang members years later, some of which involved Bolton's own testimony. Lastly, some of the gang recorded their own versions of the story in the *Ordinary's Accounts of Newgate* before their executions. These sources often contradict each other, and I have tried to maintain a hierarchy of reliability among the sources in constructing the story, but will note when I've made an interpretive call. I generally take Bolton's testimony under oath as the most factual, though it is almost certainly carefully curated in the trial to make a particular legal point at the trial and abridged for publications in the *Old Bailey Proceedings*. Smugglers' accounts and government reports are next and are used to cross-check the numerous press accounts of the incident or fill in the details of Bolton's testimony. For example, Bolton testifies in Peter Tickner's trial that he was just with Jones and Floyd. However TNA T 29/30/107, an entry in the Treasury record book, mentions that they took evidence from Thomas Quaif, while several press reports indicate that Quaif was there when the smugglers took them, but managed to escape. That is sufficient for me to conclude that he was there, but he was not included in Bolton's testimony because he himself was not actually captured by the gang.

There were eight, heavily armed smugglers outside the inn, but simply rushing inside to take the customs men was a dangerous proposition. Barging their way into the building was asking for a well-timed blunderbuss to kill half of them before they could even lay a hand on Bolton and his companions.

However, there was a safer, though arguably more brutal method. Calling into the building, they gave the customs men an ultimatum: come out, or they would raze the building to the ground. Facing the choice between a certain death by fire and the infinitesimally greater chance of surviving whatever the smugglers had planned, the customs men came out and surrendered to the Hawkhurst Gang.[274] As they exited, Quaif saw his moment and somehow escaped the smugglers,* leaving his friend John Bolton and the others to face whatever Curteis and Grey had in store for them.[275]

The gang did not kill them immediately. In one sense that was too good for a snitch like Club James; in another, murdering a lawman in cold blood is something they had not actually done before. When they had captured customs men before, they had taken to beating and humiliating them, but then let them go home. A customs officer that remembers the beatings and torment of a meeting with the gang must have been preferable to dealing with their replacement, who would likely shoot first and ask questions later knowing that his predecessor had been so cruelly murdered. But Bolton and Jones were different. They were strangers, agents from the city sent to hunt them down. There was no local social network protecting them. However, they certainly knew Club James, the traitor who was now in the company of lawmen. They would need to make an example out of him. Taking their weapons and money, the gang tied the prisoners' hands behind their backs, put them on horses, tied their feet to the stirrups and started for home.[276] They would figure out what to do with them later.

---

* The press reports at the time say that Quaif had the good fortune to escape and that the smugglers let Jones go before going to Hawkhurst. Bolton's testimony says that Jones was taken to Hawkhurst with them. Subsequent press reporting also indicates that Jones made it back to London about the same time as Bolton did. It is possible that the press reports confused Jones with Quaif and it was just Quaif that got away, perhaps because the gang knew him from their childhoods, or he was involved with them somehow. However, Quaif had just put one of their friends and associates into Maidstone Jail, so it seems strange they would just let him go, unless all of their rage was directed at Club James.

Whipping the customs men as they left town, they embarked on the 30-mile ride to Hawkhurst.[277] It would have been a long trek by horseback, especially if one is whipped while tied to a horse. Setting out at noon, they made it back to Hawkhurst in the early hours of the morning, trudging through the dark winter night. Despite the ungodly hour, capturing Club James was too good to wait until morning. They took Club to see the boss, William Grey,* at his house.[278]

William leapt out of bed, almost naked, bounding down the stairs to find the beaten, bedraggled Club standing in the middle of his house. Grey was followed by his similarly delighted mistress, a local woman who had left her husband to live with the tea kingpin of the south-east. Club had done the unforgivable, he had informed. Jockey Tom, their partner in crime, who had been there with them when they killed Carswell four years ago, was in jail because Club had run to the law. William was angry, to the point of murder. He took a blunderbuss in his hand, about to decorate his home with a spray of shot and pieces of Club James.[279]

At that terrifying point, John Cook, William's servant and fellow smuggler, stepped in to talk some sense into him. Whatever Cook said to Grey, it was effective in saving Club's life, for now. Grey satisfied his rage by smashing the butt of the blunderbuss in Club's face with all his might. His mistress followed up with a lit candle pressed to Club's newly battered face.[280]

Bolton and the others were held chained in Hawkhurst for four days. The gang stripped the customs men above the waist, and began to carve at them with their hanger swords, a torture that had been meted out to Walsh the month before. The smugglers were toying with them, making them suffer.[281] Club naturally got the worst of it. One newspaper following the story reported that Club was 'almost cut to pieces with their hangers'.[282] As the customs men suffered, the mood in Hawkhurst was almost bacchanalian. Years later one of the gang would recall how they had 'entertained' the customs men while they were in town.[283]

---

* John Cook describes the capture of Club James in his Ordinary of Newgate account. His master is never named, only referred to as the mysterious G. Henry Jones estimates that it must have been William Grey. The Grey brothers were the leaders of the gang at the time and Cook's account names Arthur Grey as one of the party that captured the customs officers. I agree with this argument and use it here.

While Bolton, Jones and Club James were being tortured, the gang convened to figure out what to do with them.[284] They wouldn't kill them outright, but they couldn't just let them go. They had already done enough to catch charges, and this wasn't just the normal beating they had meted out to the customs men. This was serious, shocking stuff of the kind that gets attention. Taking a group of government agents home and torturing them for days meant the press was closely following the story. Where they were and what was happening was not a secret. They needed to get rid of them before someone tried to rescue them. The gang would stick to their tried and tested method of making people disappear, sending them to the galleys in France.[285]

On 20 December, it was time for the gang to start preparing for their next run. They would dispose of the prisoners on the same boat that brought the goods. Bolton, Jones and Club, their bodies beaten and sliced, were once again tied to horses and taken 25 miles over road to New Romney, at the base of Dungeness. They waited for the cutter for two days, guarded at night by a smuggler that went by the name Poison, who beat Bolton's already battered body.[286]

Once the word came that the boat was near, they were on the move again, this time to Lidlight, a lighthouse at the end of Dungeness.* The gang had gathered around 200 horses and the 100 men for the run, a small army of workers and horses mustered for industrial-scale crime. Their feet crunching in the shingle,** they picked their way through the scrub on the windswept peninsula to the beach. The army of smugglers began to unload the cutter's cargo, 5 tons of tea along with some wine and brandy.[287] There was a fortune of tea on the beach, with an approximate street value of £4,000, enough to buy an opulent house, or fund the operation of the most dangerous criminal gang Britain had ever seen.

One of the smugglers gave the prisoners a swig of the brandy that they were transporting. A small act of humanity towards the men who had gone through days of hell. Bolton and the other prisoners watched as the gang unloaded the cutter with a small boat, making several trips back and forth to fully unload the cargo.[288]

---

*   There is no place called Lidlight in the area today. The best estimate I can make for Lidlight would be the lighthouse at the end of Dungeness.

** The beach near the point in Dungeness goes from flat sand beaches to shingle.

Once the boat was empty, it was time for the prisoners to board, bound for their new life as a galley rower in the French prison fleet.[289] But something was wrong. The captain of the cutter would not take the prisoners on board.[290] What the gang had done to the customs men was so brutal and so public, he wanted nothing to do with it.[291] Smuggling was one thing, even making people disappear into a French prison ship was OK, but this was a whole other level. The argument soon got heated, and then the shooting started. As the firefight between the cutter crew and the gang raged, Bolton and Jones took their opportunity to escape, perhaps assisted by the quick-thinking John Cook.[292]

Club James was not so lucky, and was never heard from again. Some reports claimed that the gang managed to convince the crew (at gunpoint) to take Club to France after all; however, one indicated a more gruesome fate. Many beaches in Britain are flat and shallow, and tidemarks can be hundreds of yards apart. When the tide was out, the smugglers took Club to the low-tide mark, staking him down to the beach. The incoming water did the rest, slowly rising, almost imperceptibly, until it covered the terrified Club.[293]

Bolton and Jones took days to make it back to London, arriving in town on 3 January.[294] They were battered, beaten, lacerated, and no doubt exhausted, but they were alive.

The national press picked up the story and papers as far as Scotland were reporting on the gang's savagery, putting the Hawkhurst Gang in newspaper readers' imagination. Smuggling was rife all over Britain, but only the Hawkhurst Gang were capturing revenue officers, torturing informants to death, and selling people as slaves to Britain's perennial enemy. The rumour mill spun at a dizzying pace over the fate of the captured customs men. Names were changed and the accounts of the torture became ever more lurid. Papers reported that the smugglers intended to 'cut them into Stakes [sic] make a bonfire and broil them',[295] that the gang tied the men to trees and whipped them until they begged for death, at which point the smugglers told them that they had much more in store for them.[296]

The evolving saga of Bolton, Jones and Club James was an early form of breaking news, with papers posting regular updates on the story. The Hawkhurst Gang had arrived, both as a potent force in the south-east and the most famous group of smugglers in Britain. They had broken free of the normal pattern governing smuggling for generations and had become a law unto themselves. The local customs officials were largely powerless, and customs agents sent from London were met with the sort of violence rarely seen outside of armed conflict. The Hawkhurst Gang were a growing national emergency, one that would be temporarily eclipsed by another political crisis to the north.

12

REBELLION

On 16 April 1746, the Duke of Cumberland's army faced the rebel army across a boggy field outside Inverness, the Battle of Culloden. The rebels, composed mostly of Scottish highlanders, stood ready for battle at the behest of Charles Edward Stuart, known as Bonnie Prince Charlie, the heir to the exiled Stuart dynasty and the great enemy to the Whig–Hanoverian establishment. It was the most significant challenge to the ruling British government in a generation. The fate of their movement and the fortunes of their bonnie prince were to be settled on this windswept moor.

The rebel highlanders, dressed in tartans and berets, charged towards the government lines, swords in hand. Broadsword met bayonet in a swirling melee. Heavily outnumbered by government forces, the rebel army,[297] the hope of a Stuart restoration, and the last serious attempt at Scottish independence until the twenty-first century, was crushed.

Culloden was the end of a twelve-month period that took the British state to the brink, where war, civil strife and the smuggling crisis in the south-east reached a crescendo that threatened to topple the British government as it had existed for the previous half century. It was the year of rebellion, one where the Hawkhurst Gang seized de facto control of Kent and Sussex, brushing away any setbacks the government had previously inflicted, and turning the green and pleasant land into something that looked more like a twenty-first-century narco state.

The Hawkhurst Gang stopped looking like a bunch of smugglers and started to look a lot like paramilitaries. Politicians like Newcastle had let the smuggling genie out of the bottle for political gain, but it had grown into something that no one could control.

As John Bolton dragged his beaten and wounded body back to London, the Hawkhurst Gang had already made another massive run through Romney.* Three hundred of them rode through the town, brandishing their pistols and cutlasses. The people who witnessed such a spectacle dared not leave their homes out of sheer terror.[298] It was better to leave them be, lest they fall afoul of the gang that had recently tortured a man to death.

Smuggling runs had been steadily increasing in size over the last decade. Where thirty to fifty smugglers working a run were commonplace in the mid-1730s, the number had risen to 100 smugglers for a large run in the early 1740s. Despite the pressure the customs service had been able to apply in London and through some big arrests, the gang had swept away most meaningful resistance from officers in the countryside by the end of 1744. Runs began to grow to hundreds of smugglers, and hundreds of horses at a time, bringing in tons of tea per run.

The larger the run, the more profitable it was, enjoying the same economies of scale as legitimate businesses. The customs service must have known when a run was happening if 300 men were expected to show up. Those men could not just materialise out of the countryside, and getting 300 people to do anything requires a lot of planning and organisation. Bolton witnessed what was a typical operation by the gang. Runs took days to plan, and co-ordinating with the incoming boat meant that the gang often had to wait nearby until it arrived. The towns they chose as staging areas were small; small enough that hundreds of armed men waiting around for several days could not be kept quiet.

As with other mafias that would come later over the centuries, there were likely plenty of witnesses that could have testified, if they were willing to come forward. Successfully prosecuting people in a more-or-less liberal democracy requires that the government is able to arrest suspects and gather enough evidence to secure a conviction. Finding witnesses that

---

*   This is almost certainly the Hawkhurst Gang because they were the only gang in the area that could pull together a run of this size.

were willing to risk their lives, especially after the likely murder of Club James, was going to be almost impossible.

The 1736 law was predicated on the government having the local strength to meaningfully arrest suspected smugglers, and that they stay in jail until their trial. The year 1744 proved that the government did not have that ability in the face of the Hawkhurst Gang. Knowing that a run is taking place is useless if customs officials cannot muster the force required to stop it, or pursue the smugglers as they dispersed their cargo to their network of safehouses in the county.

Even if the military strength existed to confront the gang, the collateral damage that such a confrontation would have caused must have been a consideration. Hundreds of smugglers holed up in a town would have been hard to root out without significant civilian casualties and property damage. When the customs service killed someone who was clearly a smuggler, it was cause for an investigation and the trying of government agents.[299] A shootout with hundreds of smugglers could engulf a whole town and endanger the lives of the people in it. Trying to use major military force to fight large groups of smugglers is not law enforcement, it is counter-insurgency. Limiting civilian casualties must have been a motivation against mass troop deployments. The army was also busy fighting the war in Europe, and deploying significant force risked setting off long-simmering political anxieties about domestic military presence as a slide into authoritarianism.

But there was little local customs officials could do other than ask for more troops. The Hawkhurst Gang's assault on the authorities had got the attention of the Treasury. After the gang ransacked Bailley's house and nearly killed Walsh, Major Battine, the Surveyor General for West Sussex, requested a stronger military force 'to hinder the smugglers committing any more riots' in Sussex.[300]

However, the troops that were stationed in gang territory began to see the futility in risking their lives fighting an overwhelming horde of smugglers. In early 1745, riding officers in Folkestone in Kent requested more military support due to the 'great increase in the smugglers in those parts'. The closest troops were stationed in Deal, only 17 miles up the road, yet they refused to march more than 5 miles from home.[301] Why risk what happened to those troops in Bexhill?

Morale among the troops stationed in the counties seems to have collapsed by early 1745. The soldiers were content to let smugglers run rampant, even when they were in small numbers. In February 1745, six smugglers rode into Lewes in Sussex, weapons drawn, pistols cocked and blunderbusses pointed out at anyone who would oppose them. They were daring anyone to start trouble. No one did, even the soldiers stationed in town.

The gang walked up to an inn and ordered the innkeeper to bring a bottle of wine outside to them. When the wine didn't materialise fast enough, one of the smugglers decided to go in and get it, on the back of his horse. Adding insult to injury, the gangster snatched the sergeant's halberd* from the no-doubt stunned troops drinking in the inn. Wine and halberd in hand, the smugglers rode out of town, shooting into houses as they went, nearly killing a bystander with their fire. The soldiers never tried to stop them.[302]

Whatever strategic reason the Hawkhurst Gang had for sweeping away any law enforcement had given way to the giddy, violent revelry of men unrestrained. They were the law and they knew it. People had better fall into line, or they would be met with violence and destruction. In February 1745 a group of smugglers wrecked an inn, assaulting the owner and breaking every window in the place.[303]

Anything that seemed like resistance to the gang's rule was met with creative, statement-making violence. In June, the gang attacked an army recruitment drive at a country fair near Hawkhurst. Locking the recruiters in cages, they commandeered the recruiters' drum and beat for volunteers to join the gang, offering a five guinea sign-on bonus.[304] **

Despite the violent mood in the counties, the customs service still made what seizures and arrests they could. Thomas Quaif made a small 500lb seizure in early 1745.[305] In April, the customs service hit back at the gang with a daring dragoon raid into Hawkhurst itself, arresting sixteen smugglers.[306]

---

*   A bladed weapon at the end of a long shaft that was the symbol of a sergeant's rank in the army.

**   It is possible that the stories in contemporary newspapers were exaggerated or sensationalised in order to sell papers to a smuggler-hungry readership. Whether the papers got all the facts right of these individual incidents is beside the point. People believed these stories, and the outrage against smuggling played some part in driving political action. The rise in smuggler outrageousness also seems to track with internal government documents.

In a separate raid that month, customs arrested Old Jolly, another Hawkhurst Gang member.[307]

But the arrests never seemed to result in any of the gang actually going to trial, much less being sentenced. That same month, the *Westminster Journal* ran an editorial asking why smugglers 'seldom come to any punishment'. In particular Jockey Tom, who had been arrested six months before on the evidence of Club James, was not on the list of upcoming trials. Like the tide that snuffed out Club James, the charges against Jockey Tom receded as quickly as they appeared.[308]

The press began to call for parliament to do something about the downward spiral in the south-east. The *Newcastle Courant* wrote that the smugglers' daily outrages 'calls loudly on the legislature for punishment',[309] and the *Derby Mercury* prophesied, 'If some stop is not made to this sort of rebellion, the consequences will evidentially be fatal.'[310]

Rebellion was a strong word, and was not taken lightly by anyone at the time. The Hawkhurst Gang and other smugglers in the area were challenging the state, breaking down the very fundamental proposition of any government: they will protect you if you follow the law. The Hawkhurst Gang were not following the law, and no one in their territory was being protected from their predations. However, the gang's rebellion would be overshadowed by another, much larger, rebellion in the north.

★★★

In August 1745 the long-feared Jacobite rebellion began. Charles Edward Stuart, the man who haunted the dreams of the ruling Hanoverian dynasty, launched his attempt at the British throne from the highland town of Glenfinnan. Quickly taking Edinburgh, the rebellion gained momentum and began hurtling south.

Stuart was heir to the Stuart dynasty that had ruled England, Wales and Scotland from the death of Elizabeth I to when they were deposed by William and Mary in a largely bloodless coup that is today remembered as the Glorious Revolution. The Stuarts had ruled as absolute monarchs, invoking the idea that kings ruled by the will of God and not the consent of parliament. Their conflicts with an increasingly assertive parliament led to civil war in the 1640s, the end of which saw Charles's great grandfather, Charles I, become the first English monarch to face execution. After a short, dreary period of commonwealth under parliament's victorious civil war commander, Oliver Cromwell, the monarchy and the Stuarts were restored to the throne in 1660, only to be deposed again in 1688 when they threatened to take the firmly Protestant country back into Catholicism.[311]

What followed were Protestant monarchs constrained by a parliament that we would largely recognise today. Dominated by the Whig party, the British government during the early eighteenth century was dedicated to Protestantism, and the supremacy of parliament over the Crown.[312] These were the ideals that parliament had fought for in the civil wars a century before, and they defended those ideals vigorously. Hailing English freedom, they decried the tyrannical, absolute monarchs on the Continent holding their subjects in 'slavery'. However, a part of the population was not happy with the direction of the country, and longed for the return of the Stuarts, and their absolutist kingship, to the British throne. These supporters of a Stuart restoration were called Jacobites* and their continuous agitation was the defining culture war during the first half of the eighteenth century.

Jacobitism had numerous adherents during the period, drawn to the cause for a variety of reasons. The specific goal of restoring the Stuarts was often a catch-all for a number of grievances against the Whig–Hanoverian establishment.[313] It was not that Charles Edward was their man, he was just not the current man in power. Various groups dissatisfied with the status quo had some support for the Jacobite cause: Catholics excluded from political life, Scots angry at their political union with England, and indeed anyone unhappy with the numerous political, economic and social changes that were transforming Britain.[314] Their association was often loose and contradictory, such as Protestants supporting the restoration of a Catholic king.**

Jacobitism had bubbled over into the rebellions of 1715 and 1718 that rocked the country and exiled some of the political class. The Stuarts lurked in European exile, harboured by rival countries like France, which hoped to weaken the UK on the international stage with internal division.[315] With the Stuart pretender to the throne hovering on the margins

---

*   After the latinisation of James, the regnal name of the last Stuart king.

**   This is an oversimplification of a complex subject that has had a lot of good scholarship over the years. However, it is a reasonable explanation of Jacobitism for the purpose of this book.

of British political life, Jacobitism was a real threat; a persistent, gnawing danger that engendered a certain paranoia in the Whig establishment. As a result, Jacobitism became a good way for anyone to make the powers that be deeply uncomfortable. Drinking to the pretender's health, or making some other nod to the Jacobite cause, was countercultural, a way to bond with other dissatisfied people into a common cause, even if they didn't really believe much in that common cause, or that cause ran counter to their own interests.

The countercultural aspect of Jacobitism made the ideology attractive to criminals. Crime, and particularly the organised kind like smuggling, requires a certain disdain for authority.

Expressing Jacobite sympathies was a good way for smugglers to thumb their nose at the authorities they had been trading shots with the night before. Smugglers' politics were likely as varied as the general population's, but that does not mean they did not recognise how much Jacobitism bothered those in power.

John Collier, during his customs inspections in Kent, was always on the lookout for Jacobite sympathisers in his jurisdiction. He investigated whether some smugglers were Jacobites, such as Jockey Tom and the Whenam family.[316] However, Collier did not implicate every smuggler in the county as being a secret agent for the Stuarts. During the Jacobite Rebellion, the smugglers of Kent and Sussex would find themselves on both sides of the conflict, some expressing support for the rebels, and some acting in the interest of the government. Despite this mixed reaction to the events up north, the rebellion would accelerate anti-smuggling feelings that were already developing in the counties.

The rebel army marched south through the autumn of 1745, reaching as far as Derby by early December. They had expected more support coming from English Jacobites, but the recruits were very thin on the ground.[317] Drinking to the pretender's health to get a rise out of people is one thing; picking up a musket and fighting the government is another.

However, the rebels reaching that far south into England sent Kent and Sussex into an electric panic. Newcastle had received intelligence, similar to that which Abraham Walter had provided a few years earlier, of another French plan to invade from Dunkirk.[318] The whole Sussex establishment set about making preparations to defend London, with a paltry force of 6,000 troops. Reinforcements were coming, but if the

French invaded before they arrived, they would not be able to put up much resistance.[319] Trying to cut the French off before they landed, the fleet was patrolling more intensely, searching for signs of the enemy force. What was inconvenient for the French was also bad news for the smugglers, though this did not seem to stop them in the short term.

The fear of a French invasion was exacerbated by the fact that the Hawkhurst Gang carried on business as usual. On 11 December, the gang made a run in Pevensey Bay* so large that it made just about everyone think that the French invasion had begun.[320] A few days later, news of the mistaken invasion had to be retracted in the newspapers.[321] Nevertheless, it was a clear sign that the borders were not secure and that the extra patrols were fallible.

Under this heightened, fearful atmosphere, Newcastle ordered Collier to deputise the whole customs service to patrol for the French and gather what intelligence they could of their intentions, reporting the findings directly to both Newcastle and the commander of the Channel fleet. Collier had already doubled patrols around Hastings.[322]

Collier even employed some smugglers to gather intelligence on the French coast. After their boat had been seized by customs, two Hastings smugglers offered to spy for the British off Boulogne and Dunkirk. Collier vouched for their character and requested that they be given a boat and allowed to carry out their spying, under the supervision of a navy lieutenant.[323] It wasn't full-throated patriotic duty that the smugglers were performing, but Collier was unlikely to stick his neck out for someone he suspected of harbouring rebel sympathies.

While waiting for reinforcements, Newcastle mobilised as much of the county's defences as he could, and received a number of volunteers. The mayor and gentlemen of Chichester, a town that a customs officer had declared several months prior contained 20,000–30,000 Jacobites, formed a militia to defend the government.[324] Cecil Bishopp, the perennial thorn in Newcastle's political side, whose father and brother were Catholic, gathered together other like-minded landowners and proposed to Newcastle that they seize the arms and horses of

---

*   Pevensey Bay was identified by Abraham Walter as the original target of the French landing in 1743. A beach suitable for landing tea with an army of smugglers is also a good place to land an actual army.

all the Catholics in coastal Sussex,* to prevent them from assisting any French invasion. Newcastle and the King agreed with the proposal.[325] There seemed to be a mutual coming together, at least in Sussex. Old political opponents worked together; the customs service employed smugglers. Even as the rebel army retreated back to Scotland to regroup and the acute threat of invasion receded, Kent and Sussex remained on high alert.

However, not everyone was consumed by communal spirit in the face of the Scottish and French threat. On 29 January, John Collier received word that two men had tried to buy passage to France at Hooe, a nearby village and the base of one of the area's smaller smuggling gangs. The men were Jacobites, trying to get to France for unknown reasons. However, they were not smugglers, but landowning gentry from good local families.[326]

James Bishopp, younger brother to Cecil Bishopp, and his assistant had originally commissioned a small boat to sail across the Channel. But the weather turned stormy, nearly drowning them. They landed back on the Sussex coast and made their way to Pevensey, searching for another way to get to Boulogne. Connecting with the local smugglers, they made their way to Hooe, hoping to finally hire a boat out of the country.

However, the smugglers at Hooe were suspicious of Bishopp's eagerness to get to France and the princely sums that he would pay them to get there. They decided to lie to Bishopp, saying there were no boats to France. Everyone was afraid to go.

Sensing something amiss, Bishopp ran, the Hooe smugglers in pursuit. They captured Bishopp and, in a strange inversion of the natural order, the smugglers, specifically Jockey Tom, sent for a constable.[327] As though fetching a constable was not enough, they reported Bishopp directly to Collier, who immediately informed Newcastle.[328]

Collier was at a loss at the sudden patriotism of the gangsters that he had been fighting for the last decade. 'I cannot take upon me to determine to say wheather [sic] the motives of stopping and confining those persons came from a true regard to the service of their country or a diffidence of one another, but I have applauded their zeal and indeed they were hearty and honest in their assistance.'[329]

*   Chichester and Arundel.

Bishopp knew the jig was up and that his dreams of turncoating to the French were over, though he was still determined to stick it to the government, even in confinement. He lived it up while he was confined in an inn, awaiting transport to London, implying that he would pay the bill when it was time to leave. But when it was time to pay, Bishopp petulantly said that 'he was a state prisoner and therefor could contract no debt', stiffing the innkeeper and going off in 'a surly, abrupt manner'.[330]

His brother's arrest by smugglers in a pub was a disaster for Cecil Bishopp, who had been part of the defence preparations, likely in part to head off any suspicions that his family ties made him a Jacobite. He wrote to Newcastle, apologising for his brother's behaviour and distancing himself from James, who he had not seen in twelve years: 'I am as incapable of guessing at his intentions, as of any other stranger.'[331] Nevertheless, Newcastle and Collier started to investigate Bishopp's other family members.[332]

James Bishopp never explained why he wanted to go to France, but he had a great admiration for the French and their military prowess.[333] However, his intentions were clear to everyone. Richmond wrote to Newcastle: 'I fancy his [Bishopp's] designs must have been treasonable because My Lord Gage [an opposition politician] assures me they are not.'[334]

13

RETURNING HOME

The months after James Bishopp's arrest would see life return to normal in the south-east. Charles's retreat back to Scotland meant that the threat of an immediate French invasion ebbed away, and in April Culloden would finally end Jacobitism as a significant political threat.

Despite examples of smugglers assisting in the effort against the French, it did not inure the government to them. Whether they were Jacobites or not was beside the point. The smugglers in Kent and Sussex acted in a violent, defiant and lawless way that looked a lot less like the other smuggling gangs across the country and more like the rebel army that the Duke of Cumberland had chased down in Scotland.

Richmond was among the military commanders fighting Charles's army in northern England.[335] He returned home to a Sussex where the Hawkhurst Gang and other smugglers were shooting up towns in drunken rampages, threatening customs officers out of their jobs, and ransacking the property of anyone who got in the way. Richmond wrote to Newcastle in late January: 'The smugglers hereabouts lately and wherever they go they declare themselves rebels. I think it a much more serious thing than people seem to apprehend in London.'[336] The Hawkhurst Gang may or may not have explicitly been Jacobites, but they acted like rebels in almost every sense of the word.[337] Indeed, they were more successful than the Jacobites hurtling to their doom in the Highlands; smuggling gangs were often better organised, richer and more successful in fighting government troops. The gang was a rebel group that needed to be crushed by a state that had just deflected a serious blow to its legitimacy.

Even before the Jacobite Rebellion started, the papers were publicly calling the smugglerss a rebellion, and customs officers were comparing the Hawkhurst Gang to a standing army. After the Jacobites were defeated, the press started to rope smugglers into the same group as the rebels. The *Newcastle Courant* printed a letter from Hastings saying that the London smugglers operating near Hastings, 'Have the assurance to wear a uniform … and call themselves Prince Charles's volunteers.'[338] During the rebellion, a newspaper published a story where an Irish officer in French service had snuck into Sussex and was drilling smugglers into a regiment.[339] It is difficult to know how much of stories like this were true, or just wartime paranoia – but even before the rebellion, the Hawkhurst Gang looked like a small army. It would be very easy to see the gang as waiting allies for a French invasion.

An article running in several newspapers called on parliament to do something about the new rebel threat. 'It is hoped that the insolence of the smugglers on the Sussex coast, at this critical juncture, when we are threatened with an invasion from France, will contribute more than all the schemes ever yet proposed towards procuring of more effectual laws against the practice of smuggling.'[340] It would.

★★★

In March 1746, parliament presented a committee report on the 'Causes of the most infamous practice of smuggling, and consider the most effectual methods to prevent the said practice'.[341] The 1736 Act had failed to do anything about the smuggling problem nationally, but in particular in Kent and Sussex.

Parliament had already acted the year before to try to curb the problem. In mid-1744, they had reduced the duty on tea in the hope that it would reduce smuggling in general. It was successful; tax revenues went up after the reduction went into effect, meaning more tea was going through legitimate channels.[342] Smuggling that went on in the ports and the small-scale operations were likely the first victims of the tax cut. The report indicated that, despite government efforts, Britain was an even bigger smuggling nation in 1745 than it was in 1733. Smaller gangs dotted every conceivable coastline: ninety smugglers per run at Yarmouth, fifty smugglers in Suffolk.

Goods flowed from Ireland, the Isle of Man, as well as the Welsh and Scottish coasts.[343] For all its ubiquity, smuggling elsewhere did not reach the scale of the Hawkhurst Gang, serving the massive London market.

The report was especially damning in the estimates of the sheer amount of tea that was smuggled into the country. The United Kingdom imported about 4 million pounds of tea a year, and it was estimated that any sort of tax was paid on only about 800,000lb of it, which means that 80 per cent of tea was smuggled.[344] Legitimate traders were unable to keep up with the economics of tea smuggling. Even after reduction, taxes on tea were still higher than the cost of smuggling, fuelling the huge network of smugglers all around the country.[345] Only about 5 per cent of smuggled cargoes were seized, which was an acceptable loss for the gangs, who just passed the costs on to their consumers, about 4d per pound. It was a small, implicit tax the customs service imposed on the gang.[346]

Over the past decade, English merchants had totally taken control of the international supply chain. Dealers living and working in places like Boulogne, Calais, Dunkirk, Flushing and Middleburgh bought foreign tea to supply a fleet of British cutters with product, sixty of which served Flushing alone.[347] Smuggling was a uniquely British problem. Other countries supplied the raw materials and made it easier for smugglers to operate, but the people operating the supply chain were British from beginning to end.

However, the rebellion, and the wider European war, had recently made life much harder for the Hawkhurst Gang. The increased patrols and additional troops meant to defend against the French had a chilling effect on smuggling in Sussex and Kent. Runs were harder to get to shore and some cutters had shifted eastward, towards the extreme end of Kent, to avoid the patrols.[348]

A freak fortune of war thousands of miles away had also been a major blow to the gang. In the Far East, a British man-of-war had seized two French tea ships as prizes. Combined, the ships contained about 1.3 million lb of tea, 13 per cent of the tea annually imported into Europe. Instead of dragging the two prizes back to a British port, the captain that captured the ships sold them and their cargo to the Dutch for cash. Hoisting their flag over the two laden tea ships, the Dutch sailed back to Holland, bringing a glut of tea to Dutch markets, and starving the French market that the Hawkhurst Gang depended on. The beneficiaries of this Dutch tea bonanza were the gangs in Suffolk, who were closer to Holland

and were not swamped with jumpy patrols. The East India Company tried to absorb the surplus of Dutch tea, but at that point they were competing with the smugglers, and the smugglers often won out.[349]

The reduction of duties was also hard on the gang, squeezing their margin at a time when the market had shifted elsewhere. However, the double blow of a shifted market and lower margins on their cargoes meant that they had to cut costs somehow, and rather than going out of business, the Hawkhurst Gang doubled down on their core competencies: violence and economies of scale. The total amount of tea going into Kent and Sussex versus Suffolk may have shifted, but the size of the runs increased, and cowing any law enforcement with terror tactics made those large runs possible.

The committee report included testimony of smugglers willing to testify to escape punishment, as Gabriel Tomkins had done over a decade before. One of those smugglers was Abraham Walter, the 'currier' who had given Newcastle intelligence about the French invasion plans in 1743. Walter was not just a member of the gang, he had connections across the Channel. His brother had been a tea merchant in Dunkirk, but since the war with France, had moved to Middleburg in the Netherlands. Walter was sitting in Newgate on a smuggling charge, and was willing to talk to parliament about the Hawkhurst Gang's operations in more detail.[350]

Smugglers could gather large numbers of men to go on a run, but it was the Hawkhurst Gang that was best at mobilising the numbers needed to make the truly big runs. Walter testified that the Hawkhurst Gang could muster 500 men in an hour.[351] The gang that assembled at Hurst Green and killed Carswell in 1740 numbered only about twenty to thirty men. The gang's operational capacity rose twentyfold in five years.

But Walter's assessment of the customs and fleet activity's short-term effect on the gang was dire: it had all but stopped smuggling in the area.[352] During the Jacobite Rebellion, more than 2,000 troops had been sent in to suppress smuggling.[353] By the end of January, the *Kentish Weekly Post* prematurely declared smuggling dead in Sussex.[354] The war and rebellion had silenced any objection to massed troops used for law enforcement, and more crucially brought intense naval patrols. The government could use military force to bring down the gang, but it would be politically unsustainable outside of wartime.

For all the customs service's failings in the countryside, they seemed to have succeeded in driving the smuggling gangs out of London through their use of stash house raids and anti-smuggling agents like Bolton.

Where once the gangs could bring a ton of tea into London at a time in the dark of night, they now needed a swarm of couriers carrying small amounts of tea, called duffers, to get their product into the city, 25lb at a time.[355] Though it was easier and cheaper to get tea into the country, it was harder to get it into London at scale.

However, the setback was temporary. Walter testified that 90 per cent of the population would be willing to help the smugglers and could rely on smugglers to rent horses from them, and pay in advance.[356] The rebellion had put the gang down, but not out.

The 1736 smuggling law and 1744 amnesty were dismal failures that did not account for how interdependent smuggling was with the violent, armed culture of the gangs. While there were amnesties around smuggling itself, there were no amnesties around carrying firearms or violence. The report tells a story where a man gave up smuggling, but was arrested for carrying firearms along the coast. When news of his arrest came out, anybody who had left the smuggling life went right back in. Why stop making money when you're likely to get arrested anyway? Several people arrested for carrying firearms after leaving smuggling died in Newgate, the tragic result of the last decade's broken, reactionary policy.[357] The issue was not getting arrested for smuggling, it was getting arrested for all the things you did while you were smuggling. The gangs provided a real protection from prosecution. If a smuggler left the gang, there was no one to rescue them if they were arrested, and no one to stop them getting arrested in the first place. Carrying firearms along the coast was an integral part of the smuggling trade. If there was no amnesty for carrying firearms, there might as well have been no amnesty at all. The gangs stayed together.[358]

A customs officer testifying before the committee went even further. If parliament were to pass another amnesty, it would need to include a pardon for murder, as most smugglers had been involved in one.[359] The gangs had become something more than business associations. They were communities that were durable beyond the simple economic calculations of tea duties and profit margins. They were bands of the men that existed outside the social order, held together and defined by the laws they broke and the people they hurt. Because most had shared in the lawbreaking equally, they could not leave, even if they wanted to get out: Club James failed to learn that lesson and lost his life. Leaving to try and return to a normal life risked being arrested for something else, and getting a pardon by informing risked a brutal end at the hands of your former fellows. Smuggling was a prison from which you could not escape.

Parliament was also trapped in a cycle of high taxes and punitive laws. The report sensibly concluded that smuggling was caused by high taxes,[360] but its other conclusions were more troubling. The carrots and sticks parliament could employ would not necessarily break up the gangs that were now more lifestyle than businesses. A general pardon, even one that included murder, would be political suicide. The press were already calling for harsher punishments and letting smugglers literally get away with murder would cause a political storm that would doom the effort to failure. The Hawkhurst Gang that had taken over Kent and Sussex, only to be temporarily laid low by the total focus of the British government, was not going to be so easy to eradicate. But it needed to be done. The Jacobite rebellion had turned the chaos taking place in Kent and Sussex into a national problem. The state needed to be asserted, especially along their very thin, watery border with the enemy, or it could fail.

★★★

Horace Walpole wrote in June 1745, 'the Parliament sits on, doing nothing, few days having enough to make a House'.[361] The rebellion had sucked all the political oxygen out of Britain and sent parliament into a legislative torpor. A smuggling bill languished in the legislature for months, going through amendments over the course of many weeks, often being delayed and put off for other, more pressing business; like debating bills to encourage coffee growing in the colonies and bills to better prevent swearing.[362] In the immediate aftermath of the rebellion, the smuggling fever in the press had subsided. As the French threat ebbed away, so did the urgency to pass a tough anti-smuggling law. Business slowed as interest in running the country hit a low. The political establishment of Britain turned inward to the parade of Jacobite rebels and traitors flowing into London.[363] *

---

* A search of the British Newspaper Archive on 20 January 2022 for the word 'smuggler' is indicative of how public attention had shifted in the months after Culloden. January, February and March have thirteen, eleven and thirteen hits for the search term (which includes the plural) respectively, while the rest of the year range between two and nine hits of the term.
The peak after Culloden was May and June (nine and seven hits) with most months having under five. It is a small sample size, but can give a rough estimation of the public mood. Spot checks of the results include far fewer references to Kent and Sussex smugglers.

The leftover military presence and the heightened coastal patrols that continued after the rebellion also kept the smuggling trade down for the first half of the year, with few runs reported in the press.[*] The gang, losing its primary source of income, began to diversify into other types of crime. A well-organised and armed group of men, when starved of their primary occupation, can more simply be used for theft.[364] They began doing home invasions, stealing items that they could fence in London. The robberies were concentrated in neighbouring villages and seemed to be systematic, a tributary system in an ironic simulacrum of taxation.[365]

While the coastal smuggling trade had been disrupted by increased troop presence, the gang viciously defended their existing revenue streams. In January 1746, the excise tried to fine a Goudhurst man for selling liquor without a licence, normally a petty crime. However, the excise men were threatened with murder by Hawkhurst Gang leader George Kingsmill.[366] Goudhurst was gang territory and no one interfered without losing their lives. The gang were either running protection rackets in the surrounding villages, or running other lines of tax-avoiding business directly, in either case keeping tight control over neighbouring communities. In this they were unique among smuggling gangs: they didn't work with the community, they controlled it, taking what they wanted. As the revenue from smuggling dried up, they put the screws down harder in places like Goudhurst.

The rebellion, and the gang's increasing oppression, also soured the smugglers with the general public. Reports of confrontations with the public ranged from the petty, such as smugglers trading insults with bystanders, to the dangerous, where a mob of townspeople in Lewes, assisted by two customs officers, chased a small band of smugglers out of town by force, the beginning of a militia movement.[367] Having turned to robbery and preying directly on the community more intensely than they had before, the smugglers seemed even less like loveable rogues than they had during the Jacobite rebellion. The strong community support that Abraham Walter had boasted about to parliament was beginning to slip away.

Smugglers, either in rage or desperation, escalated the violence even further. In April 1746, a group of smugglers was suspected of robbing a warehouse containing port wine recovered from a wreck. They slit the warehouse guard's throat and hung the body nearby. The week before,

---

[*]   See previous footnote about newspaper searches.

they had kidnapped two customs officers and wounded several militia. The *Kentish Post* reported that the smugglers 'daily exercise themselves in a regular military manner'.[368]

In the lean times of 1746, the Hawkhurst Gang turned on each other as well. Arthur Grey and several of the gang robbed Samuel Hill of £150, attacking and nearly killing him, before briefly fleeing the country.[369] The fissures within the gang were starting to show now that the pressure was on. The leaders had their own crews that they used during smuggling runs, and there was little love lost when the opportunity to work together stopped. Hill was Jeremiah Curteis's man. Arthur Grey likely thought that he would be gone before Curteis could take revenge. Arthur's brother, William, smoothed things over by promising to pay for the money that Arthur stole.[370]

In late June, parliament passed the smuggling bill that had been held up for months. Gone were the amnesties, carrots and sticks. The law was a bloody-minded piece of legislation that empowered the customs service and military to break up the gangs, by force.

The most radical part of the legislation was the gazetting system. Smugglers that had credible evidence against them were to have their names published in the *London Gazette*, the official government newspaper. They would be ordered to appear for arrest to a magistrate within forty days, with the notice to be published twice in successive issues of the *Gazette*. The order would also be sent to the sheriff of the county where the alleged offence took place, to be posted in public places like market towns, and would be publicly proclaimed (shouted out loud by a town crier) in two market towns on two successive market days between 10 a.m. and 2 p.m. near where the alleged offence took place. Failure to comply with this order was a felony punishable by death.[371]

The gazetting system turned the judicial battle between government and smuggler on its head. Instead of the burden being on the government to arrest a potential smuggler, hold them in jail and try them with witnesses and evidence, it was on the alleged smuggler to turn themselves in and face the court system. The facts of the initial charge were not important initially, simply failing to show up was punishable by death. From the government's perspective, it turned a very difficult case to prove, that of someone participating in a smuggling run, to a very simple one, that they failed to appear when gazetted. The system was similar to a draconian anti-poaching law.[372]

For the smuggler, it presented an impossible choice: turn yourself in to be tried for a crime you know you did (or at least you thought you would be convicted of regardless) which was punishable by death, or go on the run, thus committing a crime that was punishable by death. It was a brutal part of the law passed by a legislature that had run out of options and wanted to break up the big smuggling gangs at all costs. Such a law was unlikely to have passed in the fractious, liberty-proclaiming days after the excise crisis. But the times had changed, the aftermath of the rebellion tipped the balance between safety and liberty in safety's favour and parliament's legislative malaise had denuded the chamber of anyone willing to make an argument for civil liberties. The smugglers were rebels, and would be put down like so many highlanders shot dead at Culloden.

Simply harbouring a person known to be gazetted was grounds for transportation.[373] Anyone who failed to appear after forty days of being gazetted automatically had a £500 bounty on their heads, a huge incentive to inform, or to hunt down offenders. Informers were also acquitted and given their share of the reward.[374]

The law made a token effort at amnesty. Anyone smuggling before 24 June 1746 could pay the appropriate taxes, and sign up as a sailor in the navy.[375] It was a deal few would take, given the failure of previous amnesties.

The law stood to be a game changer, and one that was in untested legal waters. Punishing failure to turn oneself in with death was exceptionally harsh, even in capital-punishment-crazy Britain. Parliament likely knew that it was a law that would get challenged in court. Rich smugglers had good lawyers. The potential for tyranny this law posed was clear. Parliament put a sunset clause in the law: it would only be in force for seven years after it was passed.[376] The law was there to solve a very specific problem, and would do so with brutal efficiency.

★★★

In September 1746 the authorities at Rye found out that they had a wanted criminal in their midst. Gabriel Tomkins, who with accomplice Nathaniel Miller had robbed the mail coach between Chester and London, was in town.[377] Having been a smuggler, an informant, and a corrupt customs officer, Tomkins had been lying low for years. That all changed when he returned to crime, dabbling in postal robbery.[378] He was back in his old haunts, hanging around in Rye. But someone had spotted him in town, and the hunt was on. The postal service in Rye called the constables, who gathered a posse and began to search the town for Tomkins and Miller. Seeing the law coming for them, they decided to get out of town, fast. One step ahead of the posse, Tomkins and Miller jumped on one horse and beat it out of town, two desperados running for their lives. The constables jumped on their horses and ran after them in a high-speed pursuit. The constables shouted to them to stop and, when they inevitably didn't, fired at the fleeing robbers. Miller was hit, sitting behind Tomkins. He fell, gravely wounded from the speeding horse. Tomkins left his accomplice bleeding in the road, fleeing as fast as he could, his mount now carrying half the weight. He got away from the law men, who were shouting to any passers-by to help apprehend him.[379]

★★★

Legislatures only pass laws, it is the job of the executive to put those laws into effect. That job fell on the Attorney General of the United Kingdom, Dudley Ryder. Ryder was a career lawyer and politician. Representing the constituency of Tiverton most of his life, he began his government career as Solicitor General* under Robert Walpole.[380] Promoted to Attorney General in 1737, he continued in the office after Henry Pelham, Newcastle's younger brother, became Prime Minister in 1743.

Ryder was known by his peers as a scrupulous man in the execution of his duties as Attorney General. He applied the law neutrally, even in the face of political and family interest. In the aftermath of the white-hot election of 1734, he refused to support Walpole's attempt at settling an election dispute in favour of defeated government candidates, one of whom was his brother-in-law. They had lost fair and square. To Walpole's credit, Ryder kept his job. Walpole would later describe Ryder as 'a man of singular goodness and integrity; of the highest reputation in his profession'.[381]

Ryder oversaw the applications of the smuggling law personally, assisted by his Solicitor General, William Murray. Murray was a Scotsman, a member of a dedicated Jacobite family. His brother had been Secretary of State for Charles Edward Stuart, and another brother had fled into exile

---

*   Deputy to the Attorney General.

as a Jacobite. The fact that Murray rose so high in the government was a testament to his ability as a politician and as a lawyer. Walpole regarded his talents highly, once saying that he spoke 'divinely'.[382] His talents were enough to overcome anti-Scot bigotry in the high levels of government. Richmond once remarked about Murray: 'The only objection that can be made to him is what he can't help, which is that he is a Scotchman, which (as I have a great regard for him) I am extremely sorry for.'[383]

This legal dream team set about executing the new law to try and crush the smuggling gangs around London. But they first needed a target and witnesses in order to bring the smugglers in. The Hawkhurst Gang would soon oblige them.

14

DOWNFALL

Goudhurst, 21 April 1747

At five o'clock in the afternoon, fourteen men[384] of the town were expecting visitors. However, the visit they were expecting was not a social call. The men were armed and waiting for a gang that had promised to burn their town to the ground: the Hawkhurst Gang.

The militia had taken up defensive positions and were ready for the gang's attack. The smugglers came in broad daylight, two hours before sunset. Fifteen of the gang approached the town, armed and ready to exact revenge – revenge for having the audacity to resist them.[385] * Patiently, the militia waited for the smugglers to make the first move.[386] They were disciplined, led by William Sturt, who the legends say was a veteran returned from the war in Europe.[387] They also likely knew the law; shooting first meant that they were liable to be charged with assault or murder.

The smugglers rode up to the waiting militia and unleashed a volley at the standing townspeople.[388] None of the militia were hurt, but it was all the provocation they needed, the battle was on. A firefight ensued, and when the smoke had cleared, two of the gang lay dead, and the others fled

---

* There are a lot of myths around the battle of Goudhurst, such as accounts after the fact and nineteenth-century commemorations of the battle. I have tried to stay close to contemporary sources, either ones that I have found, or ones outlined in Henry Jones's articles in *Bygone Kent*.

the field. George Kingsmill, one of Carswell's murderers, and another of the gang were killed, their bodies abandoned by their fleeing comrades.[389] The militia quickly buried the two dead smugglers.[390] They had stood up to the most feared smuggling gang in Britain, and Sturt was a hero.[391]

The battle of Goudhurst, as it would come to be called, marks the beginning of the end for the Hawkhurst Gang. They tested their control of the local communities they had previously subjugated and had found that their threats and force of arms were no longer sufficient to overawe even the communities close to Hawkhurst. The gang's power, and the gang itself, were beginning to unravel.

The Goudhurst militia were the most visible manifestation of a phenomenon that had been growing since early 1746: the local population in Kent and Sussex were turning against the gang that they had supported or condoned for a decade. A heady mix of patriotism, the gang's own predations, and the persistent sense that government was doing nothing prompted the creation of several local militias designed to hunt down and stop the Hawkhurst Gang.

The rebellion had changed the mood in Kent and particularly Sussex. During the rebellion, the whole area was trying desperately to gather its defences while nervously peering across the Channel for any sign of the French invaders. Under this oppressive cloud of threat, most smugglers were business as usual, or at least trying to operate business as usual, scuttling back and forth to the enemy that was coming to destroy them. Even after the threat of invasion subsided, Britain was still at war with France and the smugglers' perceived refusal to stop made them tantamount to rebels. Smugglers were not just defrauding the government out of much-needed money, they were probably giving information to their most hated enemy, the French.[392] They didn't seem like good Englishmen anymore in the insecure, fragile-feeling aftermath of the rebellion.

The military preparations for the invasion cut off smugglers' normal line of business. While that would not necessarily bother the part-time smuggler contracted for night labour on a run, it did affect the leaders of the gang and their cadre of lieutenants, where smuggling was their full-time occupation. Fewer runs, or runs that turned little profit, were taking away their livelihood. The gangs were well armed, and with a ready network to funnel goods into London, the next best option was simple robbery. Smugglers began robbing houses, or shaking people down on the road. While smuggling seems like a victimless crime, robbery certainly does not.

They also muscled their way through other, pettier robberies. In late March 1747, the gang went on a bender through several pubs. Drinking what they liked, they threatened to shoot anyone that dared ask them to pay.[393] The victims were the local population, which must have reinforced the notion that the smugglers weren't really part of the community anymore. With the tea trade shifted to Suffolk, Kent smugglers started to go back to the old owling trade, smuggling wool out of the UK to France. This time, however, they were not allies helping farmers get the best price for their wool. If a farmer did not want to sell his wool, they would just take it.[394]

The Grey brothers seem to have got a taste for robbery in late 1746 and early 1747. After robbing and beating their fellow smuggler Sam Hill in 1746, they robbed a coach owned by a well-appointed woman around the beginning of 1747, stealing a gold pocket watch with diamonds, two other watches and three guineas.[395] They were both arrested in January: their robbery trials were delayed throughout the spring.[396] They seem to have either been acquitted or had escaped by April.

Because there was less profit in smuggling, every run counted, which meant that smugglers had to take more risks retrieving goods that the customs service seized. The gang began breaking open customs houses and rescuing goods, exposing them to more legal jeopardy and demonstrating a violent streak that was likely not lost on the locals. Soldiers simply passing through Hawkhurst were now in danger. A member of a highlander regiment passing through Hawkhurst was beaten nearly to death.[397] In the same way that poverty prompts some to commit crimes and violence they would otherwise not commit, the lean times during and after the rebellion drove the smugglers to do the same. When it came to the Hawkhurst Gang, smugglers that stopped smuggling started acting like regular criminals.

At the end of March 1747 the gang tried for another big run, one too large for the Hawkhurst Gang to do alone. They joined forces with two other gangs, one based in Folkestone and another in Sussex. The run was a veritable who's who of the smuggling world. Even Gabriel Tomkins, fresh off his spectacular escape from Rye, took part in the run.[398] Eleven tons* of tea were coming in the cutter, a huge cargo that would need co-ordination,

---

*   This is the high estimate from the various sources. Given that three gangs showed up, it is likely an accurate estimate.

and a lot of time.[399] The gangs met on the beach at 9 a.m. in Reculver, north Kent, working to unload the massive cargo. Suddenly, a group of customs men, at the head of a militia, attacked the assembled smugglers.[400] It was every gang for itself. The Folkestone gang managed to get away with their part of the goods, but the Hawkhurst men were not so lucky, and had to abandon the huge haul:[401] upwards of 3,000lb of tea, along with spirits, coffee and handkerchiefs.[402] The tea market was still disrupted by the captured French ships. They were smuggling what they could, getting as much as they could out of this one run.

The Hawkhurst Gang were furious about what happened on the beach. The Folkestone gang had abandoned them when it counted, leaving them with nothing. Jeremiah Curteis and the other gang leaders demanded that the Folkestone gang share their part of the haul. The Folkestoners refused, but the Hawkhurst Gang weren't going to let that be the end of it.[403] In an act of pure bravado, the gang marched deep into the Folkestoners' territory and surprised them at Wingham, a village outside Canterbury. The Folkestone men couldn't have expected to see the Hawkhurst Gang show up, and must have been terrified as they themselves were unarmed. The Hawkhurst men fell upon the unarmed Folkestone gang, beating and cutting them in the middle of the street. If they wouldn't share their haul, the Hawkhurst Gang were at least going to give them some scars to remember them by. Curteis and the gang took three horses from the Folkestone men, in addition to their pound of flesh.[404]

Normally, customs officers would find it difficult to disrupt a run in progress by a large smuggling gang, even in broad daylight. The time of the run meant that the participating gangs were either desperate, or felt they had sufficient numbers to ward off any customs attack. Mustering three smuggling gangs, especially one as heavily armed as the Hawkhurst Gang, must have been a reasonably potent force.

The customs service recruited a local militia to help break up the run, similar to the citizen mob that drove the smugglers out of Lewes the year before.[405] * It was likely the first time that the gang had encountered

---

*   Uriah Creeds's Ordinary account says that, 'But on a sudden they heard a Noise of Persons above coming towards them, which proved to be some Custom House Officers, and others, whom Creed call'd the Militia of the adjacent Country.' Who this militia was is unknown, though it could have been the Goudhurst militia. However, their numbers seemed to be too small to dislodge what the *Kentish Weekly Post* called 'a large gang of smugglers'.

significant citizen resistance allied with customs officials. Big runs had rarely been disrupted by a dedicated customs attack before, so their experience during this one must have made them realise how serious a problem these militias had become. They had had a militia right on their doorstep, which might be why they decided to attack Goudhurst a few weeks later.[*]

The run at Reculver, and the Hawkhurst Gang's savage beating of the Folkestone men, was a windfall for Ryder and Murray. The Folkestone men were wounded and angry about what had been done to them on their own turf. They were no match for the Hawkhurst Gang in terms of weapons, bravado and bloody-mindedness, but they could take advantage of the new smuggling law. They were witnesses to the whole run, after all, and knew names. Instead of getting even with guns, they got even in the courts.[406]

Two weeks later, on 14 April 1747, John Cook and four other Hawkhurst Gang members were ordered to surrender themselves in the *London Gazette*, by the 'information of the acrediable person upon oath'. The charge was not the run that led to the Hawkhurst Gang beating the Folkestone men senseless in the streets, but a smaller run with the Folkestone gang in early February.[407] Cook and the other gang members had forty days to turn themselves in, otherwise the government would be coming for them. Cook predictably didn't turn himself in, and was arrested by a group of dragoons on 30 June.[408]

---

[*] No one is entirely sure why the Hawkhurst Gang decided to attack Goudhurst. Jones argues in *Bygone Kent 22* that someone in Goudhurst may have been responsible for the gang having a wave of arrests right after the run, though he admits that it is speculation. Goudhurst is puzzling because it occurred several months before the government announced that violence against smugglers was allowed (SAY/296). The earliness is likely a clue as to why the attack took place. Grassroots resistance to smugglers (whether it was driven by local customs officers or not) was growing throughout 1745, 1746 and early 1747, and Winslow argues that the gang were running protection rackets in the neighbouring villages (p.155). The militias had finally grown enough to cause a problem to the gang, and it was time to stamp it out. Throughout this period, the Hawkhurst Gang seems to be the most violent smuggling gang in the country. Even before 1745, they seemed to resort to violence much more than other gangs, even those in other parts of the country. Attacking Goudhurst seems within their normal behaviour. They could cow the local villages by scaring them away from organising. Even if it didn't stop other militias forming, they could clear the closest one out.

It was unlikely to have been the first time that Cook or any of the gazetted smugglers were arrested, but this time was different, because of how the 1746 law was designed. The crime for which Cook was arrested, failure to turn himself in when gazetted, was absolutely provable. There was proof that he was advertised in the *Gazette*, and he did not turn himself in after the (literal) deadline.

★★★

John Cook stood at the dock of the Old Bailey. This trial was important: it was one of the first Hawkhurst Gang trials under the new law. He stood accused of smuggling by two of the Folkestoners they had beaten up, Robert Worthington and Christopher Barret.* The prosecution's star witnesses had almost not made it to London to testify. As they were travelling, they were awakened from their beds by the gang, who marched Barret out into the street, to his likely death. When Barret reached the street, he turned his would-be assassin's pistol away. The gun went off, grazing Barret's lip, but giving him enough time to run for his life.** Worthington's would-be killer was no more successful; when Barret had gone down the stairs, the smuggler fired his pistol at Worthington, grazing his slipper and giving him enough time to also escape.[409]

Both the Attorney General and Solicitor General were personally prosecuting the case. Ryder gave the opening argument, outlining the smuggling law that had been published the year before and stressing the harms of smuggling and the necessity of doing something about it: 'for these are Crimes of too high a Nature, to be admitted of in any Country where Laws are made'.[410]

Ryder also stressed that Cook was no ordinary smuggler: 'The Prisoner was one of the Gang that went by the Name of the Hawkhurst Gang, where they have made themselves pretty famous, by the Terror they have spread in the Country.'[411] The gang weren't just smugglers, but a band of

---

*   It is reasonable to assume that Barret and Worthington were Folkestone gang smugglers, because Cook's ordinary account indicates that the reason he was arrested was on the evidence of the Folkestone men.

**   Firearms of the period were single shot and were slow to reload.

terrorist thugs. Cook was to be the first of many representatives of the Hawkhurst Gang to grace the dock at the Old Bailey.

The government chose to try Cook for the smuggling charge, rather than his failure to appear. He had broken that part of the smuggling law, but Ryder readily admitted the conditions for his gazetting had not been met. Cook's name had been published per the letter of the law, but the proclamations that needed to be made in the market towns were botched by the sheriff. The charge was unprosecutable.[412]

The gazetting system's complexity made it difficult to use in court. The method of ensuring that the suspect knew that they needed to appear had many moving parts. If one of those parts failed, or the prisoner could show that they genuinely didn't know what they were meant to do, the charge couldn't be prosecuted, but that was largely beside the point. The law was meant to give the government the means to break up the big smuggling gangs, not send a horde of part-timers to the gallows.

An East Anglian smuggler, John Harvey, was gazetted the same day as John Cook. An illiterate gamekeeper, he also failed to appear, but petitioned for a pardon soon after he landed in Newgate. Ryder was afraid of the precedent that it would set if 'I didn't know' was a legitimate defence for gazetting. Ryder recommended that the King not grant the pardon,[413] though it appears that Ryder was not without his sympathy for Harvey. Ryder tried him under the 1736 Act, even though the date of his offence took place six days after the 1746 Act took effect. Harvey was transported for seven years.[414]

Ryder shaped the case to be about whether Cook was present during the smuggling run in question, and relied on Barret and Worthington's testimony to establish this fact. It was particularly important for the government to establish that Cook had been armed, and was actually smuggling; that is, he was unloading goods from a cutter and not paying the appropriate taxes. The other key provision is that he was doing this with a group of people. It was illegal to go with firearms along the coast in a group of three or more, but not against the law to go with fewer than three.

Barret and Worthington, likely coached in what they needed to say by Ryder and Murray, delivered their testimony with brutal efficiency.* [415]

---

* The Old Bailey proceedings that are the source material for this were abridged trial transcripts, so it is possible that this case had more back and forth than is portrayed in the papers. However, Barret and Worthington seemed to know exactly what to say.

They said all the things that they needed to fulfil the charge that Cook had been smuggling at the time. Murray also included a line of questions around how the witnesses were attacked on their way to give this testimony. It wasn't just John Cook they were making a case against, but the whole Hawkhurst Gang.[416]

But as Cook's defence floundered, a surprise witness on his behalf made a case for Cook's character. One of the guards responsible for taking Cook to jail spoke up and said he had overheard Mr Bolton, the man the gang had tortured and almost sold into slavery two years before, say that Cook had saved the lives of the customs officers. As he was speaking, John Bolton himself entered the courtroom and began to testify.[417]

He told the court what the Hawkhurst Gang had done to him and his fellow officers two and a half years ago.[418] However bad his treatment had been at the hands of the gang, it would have been worse had Cook not intervened. Bolton told the court that he believed Cook was 'the chief Instrument of saving our Lives at that Time'.[419]

Incredulous, Ryder asked how Cook had the ability to prevent that much violence.* Bolton replied by describing how Cook had physically restrained his fellow gang members when they went to beat Bolton and his companions and how he had discovered the gang's plan to send them to France.[420]

Ryder brushed Bolton's testimony aside, trying to keep Bolton's altruism from ruining his test case. There were bigger considerations at stake. Ryder asked Bolton, 'Did not the Prisoner at that Time appear to be one of the Gang?'[421]

'Yes,' Bolton replied. That was all Ryder needed.

'This shews that the Prisoner had not arriv'd to that Pitch of Wickedness as some of his Companions; and this Declaration shews the Officers Gratitude,' he concluded.

---

* Throughout the sources around the Hawkhurst Gang, there seems to be some sort of restraining force whenever the gang was at its most violent. When Walsh was being assaulted by the gang after the ransack of Bailley's house, the customs report says that he'd have been killed had someone in the gang not stopped them. This is likely John Cook, or some sort of faction within the gang that Cook belonged to. Most of these smugglers were rough, violent men. There were few people willing to testify to their character like Bolton did for Cook.

The Idle Prentice Executed at Tyburn, William Hogarth, 1747.

Bolton's intervention came to nothing. The jury came back with a guilty verdict, Cook was to hang.[422]

Two weeks later, between seven and eight in the morning, John Cook and a fellow smuggler made their way to Tyburn, London's public gallows. All hope was lost. Cook had thought the gang would protect him, but he was left to face the rope alone. To the very day of his execution, he had hoped William Grey, his long-time master whom he had served faithfully for years, would come to his aid. Cook always believed that, should he get arrested and actually sentenced, Grey had the connections to make sure that he would never face the hangman. But Grey was already on the run from the law himself, having escaped out of Newgate a few months before, and was probably lying low.[423] Whether Grey was not able to help his faithful servant, or if he simply didn't care, will never be known. It didn't matter now. Cook and Ashcraft, the man he was to be executed with, travelled to their fates in a cart* flanked with soldiers, guards against any last-minute rescue.[424]

---

*   The sources do not indicate it was a cart, but it was standard practice.

They were also accompanied by the Ordinary* of Newgate. The men behaved well to their captors, attentively taking part in the final prayer. As the Ordinary was about to leave them, Cook asked that the Lord's prayer be repeated, the briefest extension of a life at its end. He regretted all the things he had done in his life and the people he had hurt. Grey had deserted him, but in that last prayer of his life, he forgave him in the same way that he hoped he would be forgiven. Both men wished they knew more prayers now, expressing their guilt. Gang life had led him here: praying that God had mercy on his soul in front of whatever spectators had come to watch a smuggler die.[425] Not even the man who he had saved, John Bolton, was able to save him.

The prayer finished and there was nothing left for Cook to do but die. The cart was withdrawn from under him.

Several months later, the dragoons that had arrested him shared the £500 reward for his capture.[426]

Cook's trial and conviction were published in *Proceedings of the Old Bailey* and his biography was published in *The Ordinary of Newgate's Account of the Behaviour, Confession and Dying Words of the Condemned Criminals Who Were Executed at Tyburn*. Both publications were read widely around London, a city with a voracious appetite for true crime stories. The 1746 Smuggling Act allowed smugglers to be tried in the London courts, rather than the jurisdiction where the actual offence took place. This was to mitigate the effects of the sympathetic or intimidated juries from acquitting smugglers, but it had an additional benefit for the government. All of the trials in the Old Bailey were publicised in the *Proceedings* and those executed were given a biography in the *Ordinary's Accounts*. The London trials were much more widely publicised than others held out in the counties. There was an additional microscope on the smuggling trials that had not been there before: the 'opinion out of doors', which was the common name for the swirling, pulsing mass of the London public sphere. Smuggling had been a second-rate issue when it wound its way through parliament in early 1746, but the trials brought into London would take it to the forefront of the rough-and-tumble politics of the capital.

---

*   Chaplain of the prison.

The *Ordinary's Accounts* were structured as a cautionary tale, and were meant to educate the public on what led criminals to the gallows. The Ordinary of Newgate would often intersperse the criminal biographies with lessons and moralising where the accused had gone wrong in life, and how to avoid the same fate.[427] In the case of John Cook, that was a very long explanation of the evils of smuggling. The Ordinary sets out to disabuse his readership of the perceived venality of the trade:*

> I found, by what passed between us, since their Conviction, especially Cook, that Men, who follow this unlawful Practice of Smuggling, have long been under a strong Prepossesion, that the Crime for which they were condemned was not so heinous in the Sight of God, as the Punishment was severe by the Laws of Men; and I am afraid, not only the unhappy Criminals themselves, but many well-meaning though unthinking Men labour under this fatal Mistake.[428]

The Ordinary laid out the social and economic harms of smuggling, interwoven with Cook's biography, citing the Hawkhurst Gang by name, saying that they are 'reckoned the most flagitious Crew of all that Set of People'.[429]

The Hawkhurst Gang were not the only smugglers who had been dragged into London. As the year wore on, the Suffolk gangs that had grown fat off the shift in the market would trickle in. But the Hawkhurst Gang were certainly the most famous, and were the particular target of Ryder and Murray. John Cook was the first member to stand trial, but he was by no means the last.

---

*   It is difficult to know exactly how much control of the press the government had in this period, and in particular the *Ordinary of Newgate's Accounts*. The government did have publications it controlled, but eighteenth-century press culture was more diverse and vibrant than a simple government megaphone. It is entirely possible that the Ordinary of Newgate was closely colluding with those trying to dismantle the big smuggling gangs in the government. However, it is equally likely that the Ordinary was more or less independent of government and competing for readership like the editor of any other for-profit publication. The tide of public opinion in other newspapers had already turned against smugglers, raising similar points to the Ordinary.

June 1747

Peter Tickner was likely asleep when the dragoons came for him around 4 a.m. There were those among the soldiers that knew him. He was Rough Tickner, a big man in the Hawkhurst Gang, and they were not taking any chances. Some of the dragoons swung around the back of the house to cut off any escape. Their instincts were correct, and they caught Tickner making a quick getaway out of the back, barely dressed. The dragoons told him to stop or they would fire, one exclaiming 'That's Rough Tickner.' The other replied, 'He was rough enough,' and told him he was under arrest. Allowing him to get dressed, they took him into custody. Tickner must have known this was the end for him, because he told the dragoons that he would kill himself.* They assured him that he did not need to go that far.[430]

Similar scenes were repeated across the summer of 1747 as the government arrested one Hawkhurst Gang member after another along with a variety of other smugglers. The government used the gazetting system to full effect and picked up gang members as soon as they could find enough evidence to prosecute. Jeremiah Curteis was arrested at the beginning of June for the same smuggling run that would send John Cook to the gallows. The dragoons found Curteis sleeping in an outhouse near Rye.[431] On the run and knowing that they were coming for him, he was probably sleeping in toilets to evade capture.

Curteis was examined before the Commissioner of Customs and taken to Newgate. Curteis had been taken before and rescued at least twice. His branch of the gang seemed exceptionally loyal and willing to rescue their leader whenever he managed to get thrown into jail. As he was taken to Newgate, the guards discovered and foiled yet another plot to break him out.[432] Curteis's gang would have to try again later.

Other Hawkhurst Gang members began to fill up the Old Bailey's docket. Cook was just the prelude, the main show would be in the autumn.

---

* The trial report from the Old Bailey says that he would 'case' himself, but the meaning is clear from the context.

In the early hours of 10 July, Curteis made his escape from Newgate.[*] He needed to get out, otherwise he would stand trial and almost certainly be convicted. He was imprisoned not with his fellow smugglers, but the Bibbie brothers, who had been in on the robbery of the Chester mail.[**] He was also imprisoned with William Cox, a forger who had been criss-crossing the UK, marrying wives wherever he went.[433] Cox was a hustler, and managed to organise and direct the smuggler and the two robbers in an escape attempt.[434]

Curteis had arranged with his men to wait for him on the outside when he made his way out. He wasn't just getting out of Newgate, he was getting out of the country. He arranged with Sam Hill and Abraham Walter, fresh from receiving his pardon for testifying before parliament, to assist in the escape. Hill would wait for Curteis when he escaped, and Walter could get him out of the country using his connections across the Channel.[435] Hill worked with Thomas Tennant, a lifeguard man, and the main contact with Walter. The stage was set.

However, the smugglers' preparations had been thrown into chaos. The escape was to take place a night earlier than planned. The posse that Hill and Tennant had arranged could not come. They were on their own.[436] Cox, who had more freedom around the prison than the others, walked to the others' cells at about 1 a.m. It was time. The Bibbies and Curteis broke the locks to their cells while Cox unbolted the external locks.[437] They went up the stairs towards the chapel, where the tools of their escape were waiting: some bed sheets tied into a rope, and a plank that stretched over to an adjacent roof. They walked or dragged themselves across this plank, where they would use the bed sheets to lower themselves into the press yard.[438]

Then the escapees began to part ways. Tying the sheets to a chimney, Curteis and Cox tried to climb down, falling in the process and making a noise that scared the Bibbies into trying another route through a badly constructed roof some distance away.[439] Curteis was hurt. Hill

---

[*]   This is another reconstruction of the events between several contradictory sources: Sam Hill's Ordinary Account, a pamphlet about the Bibbies that claims to be a direct account from the Bibbies' perspective, and newspaper accounts. Sam Hill was an outside observer to the proceedings and does contradict the Bibbies' account somewhat. Though there are some compelling similarities, such as how the Bibbies claim that Curteis fell and how Hill claims to have had to drag him out of the press yard.

[**]   It is not clear if it was the same robbery as Gabriel Tomkins.

Newgate prison, Thomas Malton, late eighteenth century.

was patiently waiting outside, occasionally entering the press yard to see what was happening. Hill heard irons clattering in the night and saw Tom Bibbie coming out of the press yard. Hill asked where Curteis was. Tom Bibbie's only reply was that he would shoot him if he didn't back off. William Bibbie followed shortly after and made the same threat. Whatever camaraderie the prisoners had evaporated the moment they reached the press yard. Curteis was on his own, saved only when Hill went in and found him bleeding on the ground. He carried him to Tennant, the trio disappearing into the night. Curteis was free.[440]

Within two weeks Curteis was seen back among the gang in Hawkhurst, planning to get to France.[441] The Bibbies stayed at large, Thomas Bibbie managed to stay hidden, but William Bibbie died a few weeks after escaping, in a stonecutter's yard.[442] Cox managed to slip away, to marry another day.[443]

***

At the end of July, the Treasury sent John Collier a letter to get his advice about the new militias around Hawkhurst.[444]

Goudhurst had been an active militia for months, but now there were more that had sprung up near the gang's headquarters. The Goudhurst militia had swelled to twenty-four members, Sturt seemed to have stepped down as the leader in favour of a pair of brothers named Standing. A Cranbrook blacksmith had formed a similar militia.[445] Calling themselves an association rather than a militia, they went so far as to forge official badges, replete with a royal crown and the motto of the Order of the Garter: *Honi Soit Qui Mal y Pense*, 'Shame be whoever thinks bad of it'.[446] A smaller militia had also formed in Ticehurst, another village nearby.[447]

In June, a few months after the battle of Goudhurst, the government had leaned into the growing militia movement. Following a legal opinion by Ryder earlier in the year, the government published an announcement in the *London Gazette* saying that any one of His Majesty's subjects, barring clergy, was allowed to assist in the apprehension of smugglers, permitting them to return force with force.[448] It was a problem that had vexed policing smuggling for years. Smugglers that shot, beat or killed customs officers were pursued for their crimes, but it was difficult to catch them, as well as prove that they had committed the offence. People working on behalf of the customs, on the other hand, were readily culpable in any acts of violence that they committed against suspected smugglers. If a smuggler was killed, like Thomas Peene a decade earlier, the incident was investigated as a murder to see if the response was appropriate. This worked reasonably well when it was just customs officers and soldiers having shootouts with smugglers, but now that civilians were getting into the anti-smuggling game, it opened a whole raft of legal questions. However, the militias were certainly useful and provided important backup for customs officers and the military. Ryder provided legal cover for these vigilantes by issuing the proclamation that whatever the military or the militias did in the course of apprehending smugglers was condoned by the government, and that they wouldn't be hauled into an assault or murder trial if things got violent.

It was a startling announcement, and an admission that law and order had broken down in Kent and Sussex. Smuggling may have been a problem in areas as diverse as Scotland, Suffolk and Wales, but only Kent and Sussex had spiralled so badly out of control that the government was largely powerless. It not only empowered civilians to respond in kind to smugglers' aggression, it also allowed them to use unprovoked force if it was in the service of apprehending a smuggler or disrupting a smuggling run. Justices of the peace could deputise anyone they needed in their anti-smuggling work, and the announcement warned those in an official position that neglecting their duty was a crime in itself.

The announcement, quoting Ryder and Murray, ended with the simple admission that this was all they could do to end the gangs in Kent and Sussex and restore order. The government was trying its best. 'And we don't know what further can be done, than by keeping a sufficient force in those parts, and giving strict orders to all officers, both civil and military, to use that force in support of the laws, and suppressing, subduing, and bringing to justice all such offenders, and by seeing such orders be obeyed.'[449]

The June announcement was Rodrigo Duterte* via George II. Kent and Sussex had slid into civil war and the government was providing a legal cover for what was already happening on the ground. In late May, before the announcement, the *Ipswich Journal* quoted a letter they had received from Goudhurst. Arthur Grey had beaten and robbed a lace seller travelling through Hawkhurst. Grey was unlikely to pay for the crime, because the government was too lenient with indemnity acts. Even if Grey were caught, some powerful man would make sure that he never saw trial. The letter concludes that government apathy and corruption had 'thrown this country into a state little better than civil war'.[450] They had had enough, and were taking matters into their own hands.

Declaring open season on smugglers, and distributing the state's monopoly on coercive force among the general population, is a dangerous genie to let out of the bottle. John Collier's bosses in the Board of Customs wrote to him, unsure whether the rise in vigilantism in the two counties was necessarily a good thing. The expanded Goudhurst militia had allied themselves with a group of thirty dragoons, and were frequently rummaging houses, searching for any hidden smugglers, generally doing what one would expect from a band of self-appointed law enforcement.[451] The militias may have

---

* A twenty-first-century Filipino president who famously encouraged extrajudicial murder against drug dealers.

been fighting back against the depredations of the Hawkhurst Gang, but there was also a significant monetary incentive to catch smugglers that was making the militias look like predators as well. By the summer, there were numerous smugglers that had passed their gazetting deadline, entitling whoever apprehended them to a handsome £500 reward, a substantial amount of money that could justify the expense of assembling a large crew and leaving existing occupations. But the militias were vigilantes, and were unlikely to respect anyone's civil liberties.

The Treasury notes that the militia were 'very diligent' in their pursuits and that all three militias would co-ordinate together if the need arose.[452] Dozens of men, allied with the local dragoons, was a substantial force, and a dangerous one if their energies were not used for the right reasons. They wanted Collier to figure out whether the militias were 'deserving of the protection and encouragement of the commissioners'.[453] Replacing one rapacious, heavily armed gang with another rapacious, heavily armed gang, this time with official badges, was not in anyone's interest.

Collier set to work finding out what little he could about the militias charging around the Kent–Sussex border. Sometime after receiving the Treasury's letter, he scrawled his investigation, some cursory notes, on a scrap of paper:

> [unreadable] Sturt called their captain, a bastard
> of Kirk Skinner a notorious smuggler
> two or three Standers, 1 or 2 of the
> [unreadable] the whole party at Goudhurst
> has heard of Cranbrook has heard of Ticehurst
> to beset all the houses at once
> this first exploit good.[454]

Collier replied in August with at least some tentative support for the militiamen. Their taking up arms was 'very laudable towards dispersing the infamous gang of smugglers in and about Hawkhurst'.[455] Having received his seal of approval, the militias had the green light to hunt the gang down. The Kent and Sussex civil war continued.

15

ON TRIAL

Autumn at the Old Bailey saw a bumper crop of smuggling trials, but some of the biggest names in the gang were missing: the Greys, Trip Stanford and Jeremiah Curteis.

First on the docket in early September was Thomas Purveryor. Christopher Barret and Robert Worthington reprised their roles as star witnesses. The counsel for the prosecution plainly laid out the government's goal:[456]

> This Prosecution is commenced in order, if possible, to break a desperate and wicked Gang of Men who have got together, and, for a long time, not only defrauded the publick Revenue, and fair Trader, but have likewise gone to that Height, that being armed and disciplined in Banditties, they have begun to be the Terror of the Publick; and, unless a timely Stop is put to these Proceedings, they will, in the end, strike at the Constitution itself.[457]

He was found guilty, and sentenced to death.

A month later Thomas Fuller went on trial, and once again it wasn't just an individual smuggler on trial, it was the whole gang. Ryder said in his opening remarks:

> The Prisoner liv'd at Hawkhurst in the County of Kent, a Place famous in the News-Papers for great Riots, great Disorders, committed by a Gang of Smugglers, and the Prisoner is one enlisted in that Gang, whose Business, together with the rest, is putting the Laws in defiance.[458]

However, unlike Cook, the gang members on trial in the autumn sessions came to court with a legal team ready to defend them. There were no public defenders in eighteenth-century London, and those caught in the court system without sufficient means were left to defend themselves.[459] Smugglers, particularly those that were in the upper echelons of the Hawkhurst Gang, did not have that problem. They could avail themselves of those who made their business defending well-off prisoners in Newgate, a seedy industry where it was believed that defence lawyers could make an argument for anything, conjuring false witnesses from a ready pool of willing fraudsters.[460] The gang relied on one of these lawyers, a man named Kelly. He was an Irish Catholic who made his living in the shady world of Newgate defence.

Henry Simon, the solicitor responsible for preparing prosecutions against the gang, wrote to Collier that Kelly 'received his assurances from his country, and his principals from his religion or from Hell itself'. Simon figured that he could summon forty or fifty fellow Irishmen or Catholics that would 'swear whatever he pleases to dictate'.[461]

Ryder and Murray stayed on their strategy; Fuller was guilty because he was armed with other people and carrying untaxed goods. They produced a witness, William Wills, who had known Fuller since childhood. He had seen them smuggling, armed with a carbine, carrying some oilskin bags underneath him.[462]

Fuller's defence counsel fought back. It is true that Fuller might have been armed and carrying something, but witnesses could not have known from mere sight that what Fuller was carrying were untaxed goods. There could have been anything in that oilskin bag. 'So all that amounts to what you saw was, you saw a parcel of People on Horseback with Oilskin Bags, and Tubs, but you can't tell whether it was Tea or Tobacco, or British Brandy.' Fuller's lawyer argued. Murray urged Wills to tell the court what he believed was in the bags, to which Wills replied tea. Fuller's counsel retorted back to Wills, 'Thou wouldst be very loathe to be hanged upon another man's Belief.' Wills sheepishly replied, 'Aye, so I should.' Murray tried to save the witness by shooting back, 'Or upon another Man's Evidence either.'[463] But the volley was lost, fifteen love to Fuller's team.

Ryder and Murray brought in another witness, William Wiseman, who testified in the very precise, targeted patter developed by the prosecution. Murray, anticipating a similar line of attack, asked him to tell the jury why he thought the bags contained tea. It was because smugglers never carry tea in anything else. Murray lined up an easy shot: why didn't Wiseman ask what was in the bags? 'They would have shot me dead if I had presumed to ask them,' Wiseman replied.

Fuller's lawyer responded with some courtroom theatrics. He asked Wiseman, 'Canst thou tell, Friend, what is in my hat?'

Wiseman, flustered, said that there was something in it, some sort of paper. Fuller's lawyer asked if there was anything else. Wiseman was at a loss. Fuller's lawyers had made their point, 'Thou canst just as well tell, what was in those casks, as what is in my hat.' He pressed further, regarding the casks Fuller was seen transporting, 'Or thou canst not tell, but there might be vinegar or verjuice* in the Casks.'

Murray jumped in, 'You must show it was verjuice.'

'I think otherwise,' Fuller's lawyer retorted. He was right. All he needed to do was introduce doubt that the goods were smuggled.[464]

Ryder and Murray needed to overcome the doubt that the items Fuller was carrying were in fact smuggled goods. They brought in the experts, customs officers, one of whom was John Bolton. The officers proceeded to hammer home the point that only smugglers used oilskin bags to transport tea, and that half anchor barrels were of no use to anyone who wasn't running goods.[465] The court did not know it, but one of the officers was actually a former smuggler.[466]

Fuller's defence tried to keep sowing doubt about the contents of the bags and casks, but it was ineffective in the face of three men who had, combined, seized thousands of bags of tea and many half anchors of brandy. Bolton said plainly in his testimony, 'Oil-skin Bags are the package for tea.'[467]

Fuller's defence team were on the ropes, they couldn't dispute the facts of the case and any doubt that the packages could have contained anything but tea and brandy had been resolved by the testimony of the officers.

Guilty. Death.[468]

Peter Tickner, who had been taken by the dragoons in the wee hours of the morning, was next up. His case rested on the testimony of a man named Gosling, a Hawkhurst attorney whom Tickner had hired to sue someone that owed him money. Gosling was a flawed witness from the

---

*   A type of sour grape juice used in cooking to sour food in a similar way to vinegar.

start, and Tickner's defence counsel did a thorough job of discrediting him. Tickner refused to pay Gosling for his legal services and Gosling was aggressively pursuing him to get the money. The feud got so heated that the defence questioned him about swords that he had bought that were allegedly to kill Tickner, though trying to go after a gangster like him was a dangerous proposition. Gosling had to leave Hawkhurst because he feared for his life. The story of lawsuits, swords and various farm animals changing hands as payments left the jury doubting Gosling's credibility. Tickner was acquitted on the smuggling charge.[469] The prosecution would have another try, though. He would return to court to answer another smuggling charge. This time under the 1736 law, which carried a smaller penalty.

Tickner's next trial was on 9 December. He was being tried along with his fellow gang member, James Hodges, alias Poison. The run they were being tried for was before 23 June 1746, so it fell under the old law, meaning they were at risk of transportation rather than death. However, this run was a much firmer case than Tickner's previous trial. The prosecution's star witness was someone who was most certainly at the run and had witnessed both men smuggling: John Bolton. Bolton told the whole story of his abduction and torture at the hands of the Hawkhurst Gang. It was hard to dispute Bolton's testimony. He had been captive on the beach that night at Lidlight, and he was certainly an expert on the methods and techniques of the gang. The defence's previous techniques of sowing doubt about the contents of barrels or assumptions about smugglers fell flat against Bolton's narrative. The defence counsel asked Bolton how he had come to Kent. Murray cut in, 'They carried him there and whipped him.'[470]

Guilty. Transportation.[471]

Tickner left the bar shaking his fists at Bolton and the other prosecution witnesses.[472] Bolton's explosive story of his treatment would be published in the *Proceedings*. It was one of the most detailed accounts of the smugglers' abuses yet published in the capital. 'Publishing this extraordinary account in this manner to the city of London had its immediate use, and I hope it will have its [use] even hereafter, the court was more thorough than ever I yet saw it,' Simon wrote to Collier after the trial.[473] Tickner's and Hodges's conviction was not just a legal victory, it was a powerful public relations victory for the government.

Samuel Austin's trial started the same day, after Tickner's and Hodges's, at about noon.[474] He was accused of participating in the same run that sent Fuller to the gallows. One witness to the prosecution, William Wyman, testified that he had actually received smuggled tea as payment for a horse. Austin's defence was that he didn't know anything about the run, and he had an alibi[475] courtesy of his defence solicitor, Mr Kelly. He had been at Park Fair in Cranbrook, then gone home and spent a quiet night in bed. His key witness was Thomas Cook, a tailor who was servant to one of the Austins' neighbours in Hawkhurst. He had gone to the fair with Austin and his wife, borrowing a horse and staying with the family that night. Cook woke up before Austin at 6 a.m., seeing him in bed with his wife.[476] He was a neatly dressed, presentable young man.[477] The perfect companion for a nice, family trip to the fair, and a great alibi.

Murray and Ryder took turns cross-examining Cook. Ryder fired questions at him for twenty minutes, trying to find a crack in his story. It was no use, he was unflappable. Cool under pressure, he weathered the questions from the top two lawyers in the United Kingdom with a grace beyond his years. While Ryder was doing his best to find a hole in Cook's story, someone whispered into Henry Simon's ear that Cook was actually the son of Austin's wife from a previous marriage. Simon let Ryder know this new, critical, titbit of information. Ryder had a new angle of attack.[478]

Ryder asked Cook if he was any relation to Austin. He replied no. The judge then asked Austin whether Cook was a relative of his. Austin also replied no. Ryder moved on to some other questions, before circling back with questions about Austin's wife's family.[479] Was Austin's wife married before? She was, to a man named Cook. Not immediately alarming, Cook is a common name, but he asked: how many children did she have from her previous husband? Three. What were their names? John, Mary and Thomas. How old were the children? Mary and John were small. How old was Thomas? About 18. Where does Thomas live? Cook cracked, he answered 'I am he.'[480]

That was enough. Cook knew it was over, he had been caught in a lie. Ryder went on the attack. Who had put him up to lying? Cook should speak up now to not repeat his perjury.[481] Ryder hoped that he could out Kelly, the smugglers' crooked defence solicitor,[482] but Cook would not give anybody up.[483] The Attorney General then motioned to the court that Cook be arrested for wilful and corrupt perjury in the face of the court. He was hauled off to Newgate.[484]

Kelly, perhaps feeling the pressure, rose to defend himself.* He made a long speech about his honour and was willing to show the court all the correspondence he had with Austin's other lawyers. The witnesses were just what were sent to him.[485] It wasn't his fault Cook lied.

The rest of the trial consisted of Ryder and Murray picking apart the remaining witnesses, now that Cook had been hauled off for perjury. Under intense scrutiny, the holes in the story began to widen. Murray capped off the questioning by concluding that Austin had delayed his trial because two witnesses needed to appear. When the trial date finally came, neither of them did. The missing witnesses were simply agents used to gather the current witnesses and construct the fictitious alibi.[486] The judge took an hour summing up the evidence. The jury did not even leave the bar. Conferring for only thirty minutes, they reached their verdict at about 5 p.m.[487]

Guilty. Death.[488]

The government had struck a major blow to the gang in autumn 1747. Several were sentenced to death, and two to transportation. But the big targets still remained: the Grey brothers, Curteis and Trip Stanford. The people that were swinging from the Tyburn gallows were dangerous smugglers, but were not the leadership, nor the gang's most notorious members. But as in many mafias, it is difficult to pin anything on the bosses. The government needed these men to hang, which meant that they needed to be arrested for smuggling after mid-1746, or murder. Smuggling charges needed credible witnesses, and there was also the small matter of catching them.

★★★

---

*   Simon's letters to Collier are not clear whether Kelly got up to speak before or after Cook was arrested.

William Grey was arrested by the Cranbrook Association in October 1747, but there was precious little to charge him with. Writing to Simon, Collier said that Grey was responsible for smuggling thousands of pounds of goods over the years and had beaten the customs service at every turn.[489] There must have been something to charge him with. The leaders of the gang still had tremendous personal wealth, so they must have been getting their money from somewhere. William Grey had recently built a house in Hawkhurst worth the princely sum of £1,500. Trip Stanford had built a more modest, but still extravagant, house worth £700. Simon replied that it would be wonderful if they could get at them, but left it at that.[490] They had no witnesses.

The task of getting witnesses was about to get harder because the military was starting to slowly withdraw from Kent in late 1747. George Walker, the smuggler turned customs man who testified at Thomas Fuller's trial, was afraid to go back into Kent because of the military pull-out.[491] He would surely have a target on his back, now that he had testified against the gang.

Arthur Grey was arrested in October 1747 on the evidence of John Bolton.[492] The charge was highway robbery;[493] beatings and torture were a harder case to prove than stealing Bolton's money and weapons when they captured him. Both the Grey brothers were now in prison as the court session hit its stride during the autumn. However, there was a problem. By late December, the Duke of Newcastle started asking why Arthur Grey had not yet been tried. The issue was simple: there were no witnesses willing to testify. 'I have not the least scrap of information against that fellow,' Simon wrote to Collier.[494]

They could try Arthur Grey with the charge for which he was arrested, robbing John Bolton on the highway, which carried a death sentence. But that offence could only be tried in Kent,[495] hiding the trial from public view and risking an acquittal from an intimidated or sympathetic jury. A trial in Kent would not be published in the *Proceedings* and Grey would not get a biography in the *Ordinary's Accounts* were he to hang. Quietly expiring on a small-time Kent gallows would not do for someone like Arthur Grey. 'The man has been very barbarous, assiduous, and obnoxious in smuggling with firearms,' Simon wrote, saying that Grey 'would very deservedly suffer at Tyburn'. Only the main stage would do for Grey. They needed to find evidence to convict him as a smuggler.[496] The Crown needed a witness that could testify to Grey participating in a run after 24 June 1746. The hunt was on.

Witnesses realised that testifying against the Hawkhurst Gang was not a recipe for an easy life. The government had made their point about the perils of smuggling, and perhaps thought the matter settled in Kent and Sussex. However, the gang was not going to go down that easily; there were enough members left at large willing to take revenge against witnesses. Walker realised he could not go home now that the dragoons were pulling out, and those that did return home could expect harassment and frequent death threats. Another witness, who the government hoped could be used in another trial, did not show up because he feared for his life, assuming he would be killed before he reached London. He had already been shot at on the road, which wounded his horse.[497] The next shot might find its target.

William Wyman's return home had been marked by a dedicated harassment campaign by the gang. One of the witnesses in Samuel Austin's trial, he had narrowly escaped an ambush by the gang, saved only by the fact that the gang couldn't successfully identify him. Wyman believed that his customs minder, riding officer John Polhill, had intentionally informed the gang of his identity. As a result, the gang would come to his house two or three times a week and threaten to kill him. Wyman went into hiding. He could not go back home, he couldn't work, and he thought the person responsible for keeping him safe had betrayed him. He begged the customs service for some sort of weekly payment so he could live while he was lying low.[498]

Despite the miserable state Wyman found himself in, William Skinner, one of the Cranbrook Association, knew Wyman had a job to do. Skinner was encouraging Wyman to act as a witness against another smuggler, which he and the Cranbrook Association had presumably captured the month before. The community needed to work together. The Cranbrook Association, much like the government, could only apprehend smugglers. They needed witnesses to prosecute them successfully. He wrote to him appealing to Wyman's better angels, and loftier considerations than mere survival. 'I hope your regard for your safety, and the love of your country will not suffer you to delay in a matter of so great importance but unto your utmost to bring him and all such villains to justice.'[499] The people fighting the smugglers were fighting for a higher purpose, and it was not just Wyman whose life was in danger. 'I and many of my neighbours are threatened with death, but we are resolved by the blessings of God upon our endeavours to rid the country of them.'[500] *

The search for a witness to try Arthur Grey finally bore fruit a few months later when John Polhill, perhaps to prove he was still a loyal customs man, found a willing volunteer, a Lydd blacksmith named John Pelham. ** He had evidence saying that he saw Grey, armed and unloading a boat near Lydd at a place called Jew's Gutt.[501] It ticked all the necessary boxes for a conviction under the 1746 Act, especially given the precedent set by the previous trials at the Old Bailey.

But he needed to testify in court, and given the countryside was crawling with smugglers out for revenge against informants and Polhill was potentially compromised, the 75 miles between Lydd and London might as well have been 7,500. Polhill protested his innocence, saying that Wyman was a liar and that he was always asking him for help getting out of trouble.[502] Even if Polhill wasn't corrupt, the path to London took them right through the heart of Hawkhurst Gang territory. There was also reason to believe that the gang had recently been reinvigorated: William Grey was no longer in custody.

At the end of March 1748, William Grey, along with another Hawkhurst Gang member, Thomas Kemp, managed to escape from Newgate. Their fellow gang members hatched a plot to spring them, pretending to be visitors, then knocking down the guard to get him out.[503] The plan, crude as it was, worked and the gang were soon fleeing deep into Kent. He was spotted in Tunbridge, then in Battle a little while later.[504]

Kent was still a war zone, William Grey was free, and the government needed to get Pelham to London so they could convict Arthur Grey.

---

*   It is very difficult if not impossible to determine what exactly Skinner and the other militiamen's motivations were. Skinner and his crew stood to gain £500 if Wyman testified. But even in modern conflicts like Afghanistan and Syria, determining whether an armed group are motivated by ideology, or by the prospect of financial or political reward, is difficult to do with any certainty. This is as true for the smugglers as it is for the militia. The reality is that it was likely a mixture of both. The prospect of financial reward does not invalidate genuine patriotic feelings or concern for the community. The eloquence of the letter suggests that Skinner may have been well off enough that he had something to lose. If that were the case, picking a fight with the most famous and fearsome smuggling gang in Britain was very risky and suggests that there may have been other motivations beyond the financial.

**   No relation to the Duke of Newcastle or his brother, Prime Minister Henry Pelham.

Collier hatched a clever plan: don't go by road at all. Pelham would go by sea, bypassing the inland gauntlet of lurking gangsters. Arthur Grey was charged with the smuggling offence, protesting that he should be tried for what he was originally arrested for, robbing John Bolton on the highway.[505] The prosecution commissioned a cutter, and Collier ordered Polhill to escort Pelham to London.[506] The plan worked and Pelham reached London safely. Grey's trial could proceed.

The trial itself was swift, efficient, and in some ways cathartic. Pelham was the main witness, laying out his evidence. There was no haggling over what was in the bags or the casks; that song and dance was already settled. There was no mistaking Arthur Grey, a minor celebrity that the King's counsel said was 'so very well known in that country'. Polhill also knew Grey, and testified that he had seen him and the gang heading to Lydd about the time of the run in question. Two material witnesses for Grey did not show up; either his legal team had collapsed, or by this time everyone on the smuggler side knew that the legal fight was a lost cause.[507] Ryder and Murray had set up a pattern for these prosecutions, and Murray followed the script to its deadly end.

Simon wrote to Collier, 'I hope that all apprehensions of Arthur's returning to Kent will be soon over, yesterday he was capitally convicted.' Simon thought that Grey's conviction might have been a turning point. 'The taking of so brutal a creature, I hope will be attended with good con-sequences.'[508] Grey hanged on the morning of 11 May 1748 with a Suffolk smuggler, William Rowland. When the deed was done, Rowland's body was handed over to his friends, who had hired a hearse to carry him back to Ipswich for burial. Grey's body, on the other hand, was hung in chains on Stamford Hill.[509]

William Grey's brother was dead, and by mid-May he was back in Newgate. He was swiftly put on trial, this time for an offence under the old 1736 law, either due to a clerical error, or because the wealthy William was able to bribe someone to change it. It is more likely that the Crown needed whatever conviction they could get. Transportation was better than nothing, and it was always difficult to pin anything on William Grey. He didn't fight the charge, pleading guilty and receiving seven years' trans-portation. The sentence was not appreciated back in Kent, where worries abounded that he would not actually serve his sentence and be back on the streets at the head of the gang. But it was not to be. Newgate and the county prisons the Greys frequented were rife with disease. William Grey likely succumbed to what was called 'gaol [jail] fever' shortly after his conviction. He died before he was ever transported.[510] The Greys were no more. Two down, two to go.

★★★

In April 1748, a body was recovered from a pond in Parham Park, Cecil Bishopp's estate. It was identified as Richard Hawkins, a labourer who had recently gone missing. The coroner's inquest returned that the man had been murdered.[511]

Hawkins was a labourer from a Sussex town near where Jeremiah Curteis had been operating; one of his stash houses was close to where Hawkins worked. After a run, Curteis had misplaced a small bag of tea, and had suspected Hawkins of taking it. Infuriated that someone should steal from him, even a relatively trivial amount of tea, Curteis and his crew abducted Hawkins, leading him at gunpoint to the Dog and Partridge alehouse. There they began to interrogate Hawkins, who continued to say he knew nothing of the missing tea.[512] They beat Hawkins and whipped him, pressing him for information. Curteis watched as his men kept beating the poor man. After the beating, the smugglers propped Hawkins in a chair by the fire. He sat slumped in the chair, bloody and bruised, then died. Curteis and the others took the body to the pond in Parham Park, weighed the arms and legs down with stones tied with ropes, then threw it into the water.[513]

16

POOLE

In September 1747, as the juries of the Old Bailey were sending many of the Hawkhurst Gang to the gallows, a smuggling cutter made its way to a run in Sussex.[514] The run was a new venture. Coming from the island of Guernsey in the western English Channel, the run was a risky bet for Sussex smugglers who usually bought their goods from France and Holland. The longer a cutter was at sea, the more chance it would fall to a revenue cutter or a privateer. But the deal was likely too good, so they took the risk.

The cutter carried a fortune of tea, 3,000lb, as well as brandy and some coffee. The laden cutter made its way to the rendezvous point, but as it passed near Poole, a town in West Sussex, it caught the attention of a customs vessel. Giving chase, the customs vessel bore down on the smugglers, who tried to shake it off, juking and using all their seamanship to try to escape. The chase lasted six hours, ending with the customs vessel firing several shots at the smugglers, forcing them to finally give up. It was a typical seizure: the customs men boarded their prey, finding the tea wrapped in oilskin bags and brandy in half ankers.[515]

The customs officers brought the cutter and its cargo back to Poole, stowing the brandy on the ground floor of the customs house, and the tea on the floor above.[516]

This was not something the smugglers could let go. Profits were down and they could not cope with losing that much cargo. A few years ago, a seizure like that could have just been written off as a loss, smuggling was so lucrative. But the times had been harder since the Jacobite Rebellion, and the subsequent crackdown on smuggling had disrupted their operation. The smuggling gang, which was based in Chichester, needed to get their goods back, but they hadn't the strength to break open a customs house unaided. Smuggling gangs all over the country were armed, but they were armed for defence. The Chichester gang didn't have the skills, experience or viciousness required to actually go on the offence with the customs service. There was only one gang in the area that was equipped to do that: the Hawkhurst Gang. Though the gang's leaders were either dead, imprisoned or on the run, there were still plenty of them left with the experience required to knock over an entire customs house. A crop of leaders had stepped up, and the gang was willing to help the Chichester gang rescue their goods, as long as they got their cut.

They met in a forest that was part of the Duke of Richmond's sprawling estate to plan the heist. Perhaps learning from their bad experiences working with other gangs, the Hawkhurst Gang made the partnership official; both gangs would all sign their names to the plan to break open the customs house and rescue the tea. The Hawkhurst Gang brought with them a little horse to store their weapons.[517]

The combined gang of around thirty smugglers rode into Poole at about 11 p.m., sending two scouts to see if the coast was clear. It was not. A sloop lay in the harbour, which made the Chichester smugglers grow fearful. If they tried to break up the customs house, the crew of the revenue cutter could simply train the sloop's guns on the door as they were breaking in, turning the gang into a bloody smear against the front of the building. The Chichester smugglers thought the job impossible, and began turning their horses away. The Hawkhurst Gang were unafraid, and told the shirking Chichester men that if they wouldn't do it, they would do it themselves. As the Chichester smugglers dithered, their second scout came back with better news. The tide was so low, the sloop wouldn't be able to train its guns at the door.[518]

Assured of their likely survival, the whole party started the job, picking their way through a little back alley to the seaside and the customs house. When they got close, they left their horses and snuck up to the customs house, taking a young fisherman they encountered prisoner. Reaching the front of the building, they broke open the heavy door. Two startled, terrified men had been sleeping just inside, who the gang also took prisoner.

Bashing their way through an interior door, they were finally at their target, the tea, which they quickly loaded onto their waiting horses.[519] Once out of Poole, they stopped at a nearby town to have breakfast, offering to sell the tea to passers-by.[520]

The heist was a huge success, but it was not a secret. Thirty heavily armed men and as many horses smashing a door down in the middle of the night is not even in the realm of subtlety. It was a smash and grab on a government facility right at a time when the authorities were trying to show that they were getting tough on smuggling gangs in general, and the Hawkhurst Gang in particular. Their post-raid breakfast was such an occasion that it was reported in the papers.[521] A crowd of hundreds came to watch the triumphant gang fresh from their heist. The smugglers had only come for the tea. The brandy was too bulky or not valuable enough to be worth the effort. The successful raid showed that, even without their normal leaders, the Hawkhurst Gang was still viable.

One of the assembled crowd was a man named Daniel Chater, a shoemaker who had worked with one of the Chichester smugglers at harvest time. Chater's acquaintance shook his hand and handed him a bag of tea, working the adoring crowd.[522]

The round-up for the heist was swift. A little over a week after the robbery, a group of dragoons arrested seven of the gang in a night raid.[523] Another Poole robber was arrested the same day as Arthur Grey's final arrest.[524] It wasn't difficult to find a gang of robbers that did nothing to hide the crime. The challenge, as always, was finding witnesses.

Daniel Chater told his neighbours that he knew one of the smugglers, putting him on the radar of the local customs officials as a potential witness. In February, the customs service sent William Galley, a local officer, to bring Chater in to give a statement. Galley and Chater set out to see Major Battine, Surveyor General for Sussex and a local justice of the peace, carrying a letter about their purpose.[525] They would never make it to their intended destination.

They had initially set out for Chichester but they were informed that Battine was in a nearby town. Continuing their meandering quest, they came to the White Hart pub, which unbeknownst to them was a smugglers' hangout. As they sat and drank, the pub landlord began to suspect that they might be informants or some other anti-smuggling agents.

She called her associates, including her two grown sons. They plied the two men with drink, trying to discern their purpose. Vacillating between conviviality and aggression, at one point one of the smugglers punched Galley in the face, only to soon make amends and continue drinking. Galley and Chater had drunk so much, they needed to lie down in another room of the pub. When they were asleep, the smugglers read the letter the two men were carrying. Their worst fears had been realised. They prevaricated about what to do with the men. They could send them to France, but they might come back, or they could confine them until the trial for the raid was over, and whatever sentence was passed on Chater's acquaintance, they would do the same to Chater and Galley.[526]

But some, undoubtedly drunk themselves, felt that they needed to teach the passed-out customs man and his informant a lesson. The smugglers beat them and abducted them from the pub, threatening to shoot anyone who told what they saw there.

The smugglers tortured Galley and Chater to death. They whipped, cut, tied them underneath horses and beat them. Galley might have been buried alive, the smugglers assuming he was dead. Chater lingered for days. They knew they had to kill him, but were unsure how to do it in a way where they were all culpable. They wanted everyone to be involved, so no one of them could inform on the others, initially floating the idea of shooting him by tying a long string to the trigger of a gun, allowing all of them to pull it at once. That method was too quick, though – they needed to make an example to other potential informants. Throwing him down a well after partially strangling him, they stoned him to death.[527]

The murders stayed undiscovered for a few months, though the suspicion of foul play was immediate. While they were whipping Galley on his horse, the smugglers took his coat off so their blows would be more painful. The bloody greatcoat was found on the side of the road, raising suspicion that something had happened to the two men. But no one knew whether they had been murdered, or kidnapped and sent to the galleys in France. The government posted a reward for information, but it wasn't until months later that an anonymous tipster let the authorities know where Galley's body was buried, and implicated a smuggler named William Steele, alias Hardware, in the murders. Steele was quickly taken into custody, where he described the murders and named his accomplices.[528] Details of the murders appeared in newspapers in late October.[529]

The most Noble PRINCE CHARLES DUKE of RICHMOND, LENOX, and AUBIGNY, &c &c.
Who Died Aug.t 8th 1750. Ætat. 49

From an Original Picture Presented by His Grace to the Corporation of the CITY of CHICHESTER.
Published by Geo. Smith, Painter at CHICHESTER.

Portrait of the Duke of Richmond (James MacArdell, 1750).

The crime turned what might have been an ultimately forgettable customs house raid into a national scandal. Not since John Bolton's capture had smugglers toyed with and so cruelly tortured a customs man and an informant. The murders were shocking and inexcusable, even for someone sympathetic to smugglers. Assaults, beatings and shootouts could be passed off as business. Cruel business, but business nevertheless. The Galley and Chater murders were excessive. They may have started off as the drunken mobbing of an informant, but they turned to excess in a way that commanded the public's and, perhaps more importantly, the political establishment of Sussex's attention.

Newcastle seems to have understood the gravity of the smuggling problem that he had helped unleash, and was already intensely interested in the trials of the Hawkhurst Gang.

The violence of the murders shocked his friend, the Duke of Richmond into action.[530] The Poole raid and the subsequent murders were planned and committed on or near Richmond's estate. It was literally too close to home for him. A military man, Richmond commanded troops on the Continent and recently fought the rebels in northern England. He knew death, but what had just happened was beyond the bounds of war, and was too big to ignore. He devoted himself to eradicating smuggling in Sussex. The murderers would pay, the Poole raiders would be brought to justice, and the remaining Hawkhurst Gang was going down.

17

THE HUNT

Steele's testimony about the murders made it to the highest levels of government, including the Prime Minister, Henry Pelham. 'I have read over Steele's examination and such a scene of villainy and barbarity I have never before heard or read of,' he wrote to Richmond in early November 1748.[531] Something needed to be done. High-profile murders tend to galvanise law enforcement into a narrow focus, putting a microscope on how they could let such a thing happen in the first place. By mid-1748, the trials of the Hawkhurst Gang and other smugglers had begun to wind down, with the focus shifting to the gangs in Suffolk, who had ballooned on the benefits of cheap Dutch tea.

The Hawkhurst Gang was broken as far as the government was concerned: the Greys were dead, Curteis was on the run and they couldn't build a case against Trip Stanford. The inheritors of the gang, the Kingsmill brothers, were not on the radar of the authorities. If the Hawkhurst Gang returned to being just another smuggling gang, instead of a violent cartel, that was a success. Before the murders came to light, violence in Sussex appeared to have returned to an acceptable level. The Cranbrook and Goudhurst militias seemed to have disbanded and returned to their lives.[532] Smuggling was always a violent enterprise, but it began to return to the type of violence that was common before the 1740s.

That assumption was dealt a blow by the Galley and Chater murders, bringing some of the focus back to Sussex. Pelham not only wanted the murderers caught, but also to get at the root of the problem, smuggling itself: 'the next best thing we can do is use our endeavours to suppress the practice of smuggling, for it is that profession that breeds up the young, idle fellows to these villainies'.[533] It became clear that it wasn't just enough to take out the leaders, they needed to root out as much of the gang as they could, because the leadership pool was deeper than they had imagined.

Richmond took to hunting smugglers with tremendous efficiency and attention to detail. Running the whole operation from his Goodwood estate, he and his staff kept detailed notes, meticulously gathered evidence, and leveraged a government prosecution machine that was already tuned for sending smugglers to the gallows. While the previous round of prosecutions against the Hawkhurst Gang focused on publicly trying members for smuggling in London, Richmond cast the net much wider, attempting to convict smugglers for whatever crimes he thought notorious enough. The Galley and Chater murders were first priority, followed closely by the Hawkhurst Gang's murder of Richard Hawkins. Richmond reopened years-old cold cases that remained persistently unsolvable, such as Thomas Carswell's 1740 murder.

Richmond was a general, used to commanding obedient troops to achieve a specific objective. Political nuance and legal precedent meant less to him than the men previously working to break up the smuggling gangs of the south-east, Dudley Ryder and William Murray. This wasn't a surgical strike on the gang's leadership with carefully crafted cases, curated witnesses and trial reports meant to maximise public opinion. Richmond's crusade was an almost indiscriminate dragnet, a mass round-up of the Sussex smuggling community. It may have started with the horror of the Galley and Chater murders, but it would grow into a scorched-earth war on smuggling. Richmond's hunt would stretch the eighteenth-century judicial system to its legal and political limit.

Agents delved deep into the seedy underbelly of Sussex, searching for their quarry. Their reports back to Richmond chronicle the colourful cast of Sussex's gangland: smugglers with names like Tall Boy, Slotch, Fatback, Apple Pye Tom and The Cackler. It quickly became clear that no smuggler in Sussex was safe, and they began to scatter, hiding from the law. Some tried to blend back in with the community and assume new identities. One even took the more theatrical approach of hiding in an ancient castle, haunting it like an angry ghost.[534]

Richmond's first investigation started close to home. Some of his game-keepers had shared company with the gang the night before the Poole raid. His gamekeepers were to prove innocent of any involvement, but Richmond's caution was understandable. The raid had been planned and staged on his property, so it stood to reason that the men who he paid to lurk about his forests might have been involved. He needed to make sure that there was no one on the inside of his household that could have been implicated.[535]

The government spent the autumn of 1748 rounding up anyone they thought might be associated with the murders, either charging them directly or getting them on smuggling charges. Anyone who was even tangentially related to the crime was questioned. The man who owned the turf house where they kept Chater, who had kicked the whole party out by saying, 'Don't murder him here, take him somewhere else and do it,' was brought in. Even a gardener who had unwittingly lent the group a ladder was taken in.[536]

The objective was to bring all these disparate crimes to trial as pub-licly as possible. That was going to be a challenge for the non-smuggling crimes that Richmond wanted to prosecute. The 1746 law allowed smug-gling charges to be tried anywhere, preferably the Old Bailey where the *Proceedings* would publish the trials to the chattering classes, hungry to read stories where criminals get their comeuppance. This was the reason the government waited for the perfect witness to try Arthur Grey at the Old Bailey, even though they could have hanged him for robbing John Bolton. County courts were not only more of a gamble, they didn't have the same spotlight as a trial at the Old Bailey. The press and the public had been howling for years about how the government was not serious about the rapacious smuggling gangs, or worse, suggesting that the authorities were holding back because they were getting something out of the gangs.

There was truth to both accusations. The government had, since 1740, been embroiled in an ever-escalating war with France, and seen off a rebellion that the French had supported, distracting the UK from the war. The gov-ernment, or at least Newcastle and his brother, was also getting something out of the current state of affairs. There is no doubt that Newcastle benefited electorally from the steady stream of smuggling prosecutions that he could help quash in exchange for political support. This was certainly true in the 1734 election and there is evidence to suggest that the practice continued at least until 1743.[537] However, Newcastle did seem to have had some change of heart after the Jacobite rebellion had cast the gangs in a different, more dangerous light. He had taken a personal interest in Arthur Grey's prosecution[538] and was behind Richmond's new push to exterminate the gangs.[539] But his reputation was not easily undone. The government didn't just need to get rid of the smuggling gangs in the south-east, they needed to do it publicly, and in a way that provided the best rebuff to accusations of shiftlessness or corruption.

The issue with focusing narrowly on the sort of smuggling cases that could be tried at the Old Bailey was that people arguably cared more about the other crimes that smugglers committed. The Galley, Chater and Hawkins murders were brutal, but the Hawkhurst Gang and others were also robbing people in their houses, sticking them up on the road, and generally terrorising the local population, especially since their smuggling operation had been disrupted. After the top leadership, bar Jeremiah Curteis and Trip Stanford, had died in jail or been executed, the gang had essentially become a group of armed paramilitaries, bandits that were open to providing muscle for other gangs.

Richmond needed to more broadly do what Ryder had done the year before: arrest and try the gangsters as publicly as possible. But Richmond, with the backing of the government, would need to do it in the counties outside the London political bubble. However, Kent and Sussex were still gang territory, and the balance of power was very different from that in London itself. Smuggling gangs could not muster the manpower in the capital, and while Newgate saw its share of daring escapes by the Hawkhurst Gang, it was probably more secure than the county jails. Judges and juries in Kent and Sussex were much more likely to either be sympathetic to or, more likely, intimidated by the threat of violence from the gang, a fear that also hindered actually apprehending suspects.[540] Richmond would have to take a different approach.

The first priority was the physical security of anybody involved in the investigation. Potential witnesses, whether they were suspects themselves or not, were kept under heavy guard in customs houses or in Chichester, a major town where a dedicated attack would be easier to spot. Upwards of fifty soldiers were used in the early days of the investigation to discourage any attempts to get at witnesses or suspects – a crude, early form of witness protection.[541] The smugglers had just tortured two men to death on the suspicion that they were snitches. They were clearly willing and able to do awful things to whoever crossed them.

The fear was that the smugglers would mount some sort of serious armed attack, tens or hundreds of smugglers, against any jails holding witnesses or prisoners (which in the case of Steele, were the same thing). The military resources used to protect anybody who could participate in the trial were substantial. Although the break-in at the Poole customs house was what started the whole affair, such buildings were still a harder sort of target that could be more easily defended in the event the gangs came out in force.[542] Customs houses were also separate from the jails that held the perpetrators of other crimes, which meant the flow of information was easier to control.

There was a palpable fear that there would be some sort of retaliation. Steele, the main witness to the murders, was afraid that his house would be burned down and his family killed if he were kept in the general prison population and was seen talking to the government.[543] The gangs apparently had eyes everywhere. They certainly had crooked lawyers floating around the London legal world* willing to tip the gang off to potential raids and prosecutions. It was very likely they kept an eye out for any informers in the prisons as well, saying nothing of the other prisoners in the jail.

Richmond spent large sums on the military power required to ensure that the witnesses he needed stayed alive long enough to testify at trial. It was an abundance of caution, but rooted in the knowledge that the government was operating on gang turf. Any rumours that came in were dutifully recorded, such as a sail merchant who reported a worrying exchange he had. A man approached him to buy some muskets – 500 to be exact. But not just any muskets, the good ones that the British tended to capture from the French. Having an inkling of what they might be used for, the merchant stalled, and reported the whole exchange to the government.[544] Purchasing that much firepower was suspicious and there was no way to know it was for a large-scale attack by the smugglers, but the point was that it could have been used in an armed attack. Richmond was not taking any chances.

---

*   The examples we know of were Heneage Norton, corrupt customs clerk, and Kelly, defence council for the Hawkhurst Gang.

Richmond had agents conducting the numerous simultaneous manhunts for the suspects, but he relied on Dudley Ryder, the Attorney General, to sort out the necessary legal details, ensuring they could actually try all the suspects who were filling jails and customs houses. Since these were murders, jurisdiction mattered to where the trials would take place. The worst-case scenario was that Galley was killed in one county and Chater in another, making a flashy, slam-dunk prosecution almost impossible. Ryder had to carefully determine just where the murders had taken place, and fortunately they were both in Sussex. All of the murderers could be tried together.[545]

The other issue was how to order the trials to achieve the best chance of convictions and maximum political impact. In the case of Galley's and Chater's murders, had the killers been involved in the Poole raid as well? What do they prosecute first, and how do those trade-offs play out? Trying the smuggling charge first would give them the advantage of the main stage, but would be harder to prove. The murder charges were easier to prove, Ryder was convinced the suspects were guilty, but the proceedings would take place in a relatively uncovered Sussex court. Ryder recommended to try the murders first, and any suspects that were acquitted would then be tried for smuggling.[546] It was better to get convictions than go for the political win.

As the autumn ground on into early winter, Richmond was frustrated at the lack of progress in apprehending the murderers, including Jeremiah Curteis and his accomplices for the murder of Hawkins. It wasn't just Steele who was quaking in his boots at the thought of what the gangs would do to informers, the whole county was intimidated out of co-operating. A beating or a load of blunderbuss shot to the face was never far away with Curteis and his ilk roaming around. And it wasn't just normal folks who were afraid to cross the gang: Richmond reported to Henry Pelham that he had heard several judges declare they would not participate in any legal action against smugglers.[547] Richmond wanted to loosen people's lips, especially those who had some involvement with the murders, and asked Henry Pelham to authorise pardons for those who would co-operate with the investigations.[548]

A pall of fear hung over the whole area, creating a paradox for Richmond: people would not feel safe until the smugglers were brought in, but people needed to feel safe enough from the smugglers' retaliation to help the government apprehend them.

The whole thing must have been infuriating for anyone working the case. The Poole robber had been greeted in the next town over with an adoring crowd and the raid was published in newspapers at the time. Yet, the government weren't able to get their hands on the men who had brutally killed one of that adoring crowd. Everyone in west Sussex was too scared to step up, lest they too wind up a broken heap at the bottom of a well.

The Hawkhurst Gang was also on the prowl, not only taking muscle-for-hire jobs, but branching into more terrifying forms of crime. The deaths of the Greys and other high-profile members meant that the gang was no longer potent enough to actually make any smuggling runs. Their networks must have been shattered, their capital dried up, and their community turned against them. Curteis, not one to let a bounty on his head deter him, led that gang in one of their new ventures: home invasions.

★★★

At around 8 p.m. one evening in August 1748, the Hawkhurst Gang approached a house owned by one Mr Wakeford, a wealthy Sussex man. Led by Curteis and John Mills, they dismounted their horses, leaving them with two of the gang that Wakeford and his servants would recognise. Only Curteis remained on his horse, riding up to the door and whistling for someone to answer. He asked for some beer from the probably bewildered servant that answered the door.

Curteis took the beer back to the rest of the gang, standing nearby, hesitant to start the job. He swore at them and told them to come on, whereby they rushed into the house behind him. Some paltry small beer was insufficient for the new, unexpected house guests, who wanted the good stuff. The servants must have known what was going on, and tried to stall as best they could. Mr Wakeford was in bed, you see, and he had the keys to where they kept the strong beer.

The smugglers kept up with the game, asking the servants to bring them to Wakeford, because they had information about some dangerous smugglers lurking around. At this point the gang either tired of their flimsy ruse, or everybody was truly on the same page. They rounded up the servants, forcing one maid to lead them by candlelight towards

Wakeford's bed chamber. Encountering a locked door at the top of the stairs, the gang began pounding it with the butts of their blunderbusses. But the door was tough, and Thomas Kingsmill had to wrench open the door with a metal spit he had taken from a nearby fireplace.

Mr Wakeford was unlikely to be getting much sleep at this point, an armed gang beating down the door near his bedroom. But he stayed in bed, either out of abject fear or because there was truly no place else for him to go. Finally smashing through the door, the smugglers ran into the bedroom to find his box bed,* a large wooden cabinet with a bed inside, reasonably common for the period. Wakeford must have lain terrified in the dark box, the noise coming closer and closer: muffled voices downstairs, loud bashing at the stairwell door, numerous footsteps running into his room, and finally the latch lifting on his bed's door.

Curteis shoved a carbine in Wakeford's face, demanding that he show them where he kept his money. He could only respond that he didn't have any money, a poor lie coming from a man sitting in such a large and well-furnished house. But the fact he managed a coherent response at all, staring down the barrel of a gun, sitting in a wooden box that may very well become his coffin, is impressive.

The Hawkhurst Gang didn't believe him, and threatened to cut him up while he lay in his bed, a more painful way to go since threatening to shoot him in the face was surprisingly ineffective. But Wakeford kept insisting that he had no money. If he wasn't going to tell them where his money was, he could at least tell them where he kept his silver plate. Wakeford pointed to a cabinet at the foot of his bed, which the gang emptied, then searched the house for anything of value. They managed to drag up some more silver, and about £14 along with some watches and other precious metal items. It wasn't nothing, but it was probably not what they were hoping for, being so fixated on the money that they thought Wakeford had.

Taking one last pass to see if Wakeford was lying to them, they threatened to kidnap him, possibly to France, if he wouldn't tell them where the money was. Still refusing to tell them, perhaps because he really didn't

---

*   The way the source describes what happened, I'm assuming it is a box bed. According to Thomas Winter's testimony, the smugglers ran into Wakeford's chamber, then lifted the latch to the chamber where he was lying. This must have meant that he had some sort of inner chamber that was most likely a box bed.

have any substantial money at home, the smugglers dragged him out of the house and towards their waiting horses. This was probably enough to convince them that Wakeford was telling the truth about his lack of funds. Leaving with a few threats about not going to the authorities, the gang rode off with their haul.[549]

★★★

For his part, Ryder advised against offering pardons for informants, and would take months to come around to the idea.[550] Richmond would have to continue the hunt with the legal powers he had available. Much like in the early 1740s, it was hard to catch these suspects, keep them in jail, and get them convicted in a county that was either crooked or scared to their wits' end.[551] This was going to take some special tools to get the job done. And there was only one man who could grease the political wheels enough to get them: Newcastle.

Richmond began hustling to have the non-smuggling trials taken out of the normal county assize courts* and into a special commission that he could control. These commissions were unusual, but had happened before, most notably to try Jacobite rebels after the 1715 and 1745 rebellions,[552] but they had to be granted ostensibly by the King, through the government. Richmond knew that Newcastle was key to getting his request granted. He wrote to Newcastle, asking him to pressure the chancellor to grant his request. Newcastle seemed hesitant, but Richmond was persistent.[553] Getting his special commission would allow him to more or less pick his judges, carefully avoiding the ones that were either too scared or corrupt to do their jobs.

The government eventually granted Richmond's request for a special court, and he set about planning the affair. It was his party, and no detail would be spared his attention for what was designed to be the trial of the century. He shopped around several towns in Sussex for the venue, but settled on Chichester, for a combination of convenience for the judges and securely delivering the prisoners to trial.[554]

But this party needed guests, and the government was rapidly filling up the list. In early November 1748, a newspaper ad ran putting a

---

*   Biannual court sessions that dealt with serious crimes such as murder, highway robbery and theft.

£500 bounty on the heads of eighty-five smugglers, a wide cross-section of the south-eastern smuggling fraternity.[555] It was a tasty incentive for the dragoons and agents who were already scouring the countryside for the murderers and anyone who broke open the customs house at Poole. The arrests piled up and the jails filled as the year drew to a close.

Rather than face the highly organised, large-scale resistance that the Hawkhurst Gang was known for, the manhunts for the gang were starting to appear like just that, hunts, of the sort where rich men use their resources to hunt an animal. Richmond sat at Goodwood, driving his red-coated hounds to flush out so many criminal foxes. Although unlike the foxes that men like Richmond hunted, many of the smugglers had it coming. One after the other, they were brought in by the dragoons, but some, like Curteis, evaded arrest. One suspected smuggler, pursued by government troops, decided to take fate into his own hands: throwing himself into the sea to drown, rather than face capture.[556]

Richmond thought that smuggling and, more importantly, the smuggling gangs in Sussex had been broken by December 1748.[557] The Hawkhurst Gang, or what was left of them, were certainly in survival mode. All that was left were the hardcore gang members who had seen and done too much to return to a normal life, even if they wanted to. Too few in number to do any meaningful smuggling, they survived using crude violence to commit whatever crime they could to eke out a living. The Wakeford robbery was likely a disappointment and a government investigation into the Poole raid revealed that the gang were paid in tea for providing the muscle needed to break open the customs house.[558] The smugglers whose bosses were dead simply gravitated to the remaining gang leaders, Curteis and Thomas Kingsmill, such as John 'Jockey' Brown, one of William Grey's servants, who was now working for Curteis.[559]

Henry Simon, the government lawyer who had been instrumental in the earlier prosecution against the Hawkhurst Gang, worked overtime during Christmas, organising the prosecution for the special trial sessions at Chichester, which were now scheduled for mid-January. Everyone was deeply concerned with making sure all the suspects actually stayed in jail before the trials and didn't get out on bail, in which case they would almost certainly flee. The smugglers, particularly the leaders of the Chichester gang, Jackson and Carter, had their own pack of lawyers trying to secure their release, including Heneage Norton, the smugglers' inside man in the customs service for the better part of two decades. However, the 1746 smuggling law came into good effect. Just charging them with a crime, even murder, made them eligible for bail, but the fact that all of them were also charged with failing to appear after being gazetted was key. That double charge, at least one being a felony, made bail almost impossible.[560] Simon would make sure that the murderers that had been apprehended would face trial.

The week before Christmas, Simon sent his clerk to deliver the news that the leaders of the murders, William Jackson and William Carter, would be tried at the special assizes. Though they had been in Newgate for a month, the news must have made their upcoming prosecutions real. No one was going to come and help them, and if they went to trial, it was unlikely that the government was going to go through all this trouble to not get a conviction. As the news sunk in, Carter was overcome with emotion, trembling with fear at the prospect they would likely see the wrong end of a rope before February. Jackson was already in poor health during his time in Newgate, and after the news of his indictment, Carter also turned for the worse. Carter or Jackson dying before their day in court would have been a disaster for the government, destroying any potential public relations value they might have. The government made sure they were well while they were confined, having a doctor keep healthy the men that Richmond desperately wanted to hang in a few weeks.[561]

As soon as the holidays were over, the final preparations for the trials at Chichester began. Richmond planned the trial like the high-profile, aristocratic event that it was. All of these well-to-do trial attendees needed places to stay befitting their social status. Richmond's agents took care of those details as well, assessing the suitability of the Bishop of Chichester's palace. They concluded that it would be suitable for the calibre of guests that Richmond was inviting, with the caveat that the palace had 'no knives nor forks fit for a gentleman'.[562] They did not forget about the suspects, though. An agent informed Richmond that the gibbets, cages used for displaying the bodies of hanged criminals, were ready and waiting for their expected occupants. Though they would not put them out before the trial.[563] They didn't want to be presumptuous, after all.

Richmond also made sure to invite the men who had worked so hard to fight smuggling over the last decade: John Collier and Henry Simon would accompany Richmond to the trials.[564]

Nothing was left to chance. The suspects were being held in London area jails, Newgate, New Gaol and Horsham; no doubt better guarded against escape attempts than when the Greys and Curteis were there. Under military guard, the prisoners were taken to Chichester in one large convoy and placed in heavy irons on their arrival; all except one, the still gravely ill Jackson. His jailers took the utmost care of him, he needed to be alive to stand trial. It was the gallows, not disease, that was supposed to kill him.[565]

The judges made their way to Chichester in somewhat more style. Setting out from London in a grand party of six coaches drawn by six horses, followed by sixty guards and attendants, they were entertained by Richmond at his hunting lodge on the way, reaching Chichester the Saturday before the trials were supposed to begin. On Sunday, the city aldermen (which included Richmond) attended a service at Chichester Cathedral, setting the stage for the trials to start the following day.[566]

The sermon described the murders in graphic detail, preparing the assembled aldermen for the main event tomorrow. Towards the end of the sermon, the preacher neatly summed up not only why these trials were taking place, but the point of the entire years-long campaign against the gangs. No doubt nodding at Richmond, he said how happy the kingdom was to have 'illustrious instances of persons' that 'they may be able, with the blessings of almighty God, if not correct all the abuses of these daring and outrageous people [smugglers], at least to give check to their insolence, and keep them within modest bounds'.[567] For all the talk of the damage that smuggling does, it was not about eradicating smuggling, or even the smugglers themselves. It was all about removing the smuggling gangs that overstepped previous social boundaries. It was their excesses that forced this reaction, their unravelling of the social contract in Kent and Sussex over the years. Smugglers were part of the social and political fabric of the area, but no one was willing to accept the violence that the gangs had unleashed.

On Monday, the trials for the murder of Galley and Chater began. The judges left their poorly-cutleried accommodation at the Bishop's Palace and went in a ceremonial procession to the Chichester guildhall, where Richmond and a selection of Sussex dignitaries, including Cecil Bishopp, waited to greet them.[568] The grand jury was summoned, and the trials began.

There was really no other way that the trials could have gone other than a guilty verdict. Richmond was not going to have his carefully planned event spoiled. The government's case was carefully laid out, summoning witnesses to establish the whereabouts of the suspects and victims to establish guilt, making the legal argument that even if all of them did not simultaneously strike the fatal blow, they were all guilty of murder. In the end, they didn't need any string tied to the trigger of a gun for them all to go down together. William Steele's testimony was the most damning, describing the torture Galley and Chater suffered in minute detail. There was little the smugglers' defence counsel could do except feebly challenge some of the witnesses' details.* The judge passed his inevitable sentence: guilty, death.[569]

The murderers were taken to a place called Broile in Sussex and hanged in front a large crowd of likely cheering spectators. The gibbets that had been stowed away ready were now used for their intended purpose, hanging the bodies as a warning to others. In the end, illness took Jackson before he could be hanged, dying four hours after his death sentence was passed down. The sheer stress was too much for his already fragile constitution.[570] Whatever justice Richmond wanted done had been done, Galley and Chater had been avenged.

The whole thing, with its pomp and finery, had the air of a kangaroo court that was not lost on those in attendance. After the trial, an anonymous pamphlet entitled 'A free Apology in Behalf of the Smugglers so far as their case affects the Constitution' was published, which criticised the 1746 law and the measures that the government had taken to break the gangs in the south-east, specifically the 'Butcheries at Chichester', decrying the 'cruel Ravages the law may sometimes give a sanction to'.[571] Richmond and the government had succeeded in showing that they were cracking down hard on smugglers with the full might and majesty of the Crown, perhaps too successfully. The law enforcement balance that democracies, even flawed ones like the eighteenth-century United Kingdom, must maintain is a delicate one. Crack down on organised crime too little, and be accused of not dealing with the problem. Enforce too much, and risk accusations of sliding into dictatorship.

---

*   It is difficult to know if, like the Old Bailey proceedings, the defence's role in the trial was truncated to create a clearer narrative. The account does seem to acknowledge most of the cross-examination, even the absence of it for certain witnesses.

However, Richmond was not going to take the blow in the press lightly; two could play the anonymous pamphlet game. Richmond published an account of the murders and the trials, under the pseudonym 'a Gentleman of Chichester'.* Richmond arguably won the messaging war over the trials. The Gentleman of Chichester's accounts of the trials enjoyed multiple editions, staying in print for almost a century.

The accounts of the trials focused on one central thesis: that smuggling was the root cause of all this barbarity. Smuggling was a crime, one that people thought was a minor crime, or at least a victimless crime. But everyone could now see what this minor crime led people to: murder, torture and near rebellion. Smuggling was bad, and led what otherwise might have been good men to do worse things.

There was a kernel of truth to the argument; probably none of it would have happened if it were not for smuggling. But it masked the culpability of the government, in both policy and individual actors, in creating a constellation of mafias that terrorised communities and murdered informants. It takes a village to raise a child, and it takes a nation to create entrenched, violent organised crime. The people prosecuting these murders had a hand in creating the system that wrought this violence, with electoral gamesmanship and draconian, reactionary laws. Few in the government would be willing to admit that, even if they realised it. It all got lost in the justifiable hand-wringing about revenue, the escalating violence and the paternalistic rhetoric of 'give unto Caesar what is Caesar's'.

With Galley's and Chater's murderers now hanging in chains, the investigations shifted to righting all the other wrongs committed by the Hawkhurst Gang: Curteis's murder of Richard Hawkins, Carswell's nearly decade-old murder, and the crime that started it all, the Poole raid.

The Chichester trials and their related investigations revealed how close men of substance were to the smuggling trade and the worst crimes associated with it. Henry Pelham wrote to Richmond after the trials, thanking him for his diligence in fighting smuggling and to deliver some titillating news. It appears that Jackson's wife had had a romantic connection with a mutual friend of theirs, an earl they called 'Tankey'. Pelham thought

---

* There is no proof that Richmond is the Gentleman of Chichester, but he is widely regarded as the author of the pamphlet in the literature and I see no evidence to suggest that he is not.

it all a big joke and promised to share a snigger with Richmond when they next saw Tankey, at the thought of him laying with a low-life's wife.[572]

But it shows that the rigid-seeming separation between the classes was permeable. Jackson was unlikely to be poor or working class (he had several lawyers trying to help him and Carter out), but he certainly was not the sort to be rubbing elbows with the earls and dukes of the country. Newcastle wasn't the only mover and shaker that had relationships with people actively involved in smuggling, nor was Tankey the only Sussex nobility connected to the smugglers caught in Richmond's dragnet.

The government had arrested a smuggler named Thomas 'Slotch' Lillywhite, one of the gang involved in the Poole raid. Lillywhite was young, 17 years old at the time of the crime, and was apparently a minor player in the incident. As the Hawkhurst Gang rode into town, Lillywhite was left to mind the horses. The fact that he had a smuggler-sounding alias suggests that this was not his first time in the smuggling game.[573] Like Gabriel Tomkins, he was starting young.

Lillywhite's arrest might have been unremarkable had it not been for one thing: he was married to Mary Owen, the daughter of Sarah Owen, who was housekeeper to Cecil Bishopp. But Mary was not just the daughter of Bishopp's housekeeper, she was Bishopp's illegitimate daughter. Bishopp was unusually fecund, producing a 'horde of beauty daughters'[574] that flitted around London society, hobnobbing at the very top of the social ladder. But it seems that he had produced one more daughter, who flitted around the sort of social scene that included young, presumably dashing smugglers named Slotch.*

Bishopp was in a bind. He had thrown whatever political weight he had supporting Richmond's purge of Sussex smugglers, and the Hawkhurst Gang in particular. Bishopp was one of the men standing with Richmond, greeting the judges at the Chichester trials. He wanted to be visibly anti-

---

*   There is no direct evidence that Cecil Bishopp is Mary Owen's father. However, his involvement with her and her family is unusual. Parham 1/3/4/5 in West Sussex Record Office show that Bishopp granted a cottage and garden to the very young (around 6-year-old) Mary Owen. In that manorial record, her father is listed as Walter Owen. Bishopp is certainly closely involved, and takes a lot of risks with his political career in order to assist his housekeeper's daughter, if she wasn't also his. Bishopp being Mary Owen's father is a widely held view, one that I share and present in this book.

smuggler, and now his illegitimate daughter's husband was sitting in jail waiting for one of Richmond's well-used gibbets. It seems like Bishopp was a good father, or at least a man that was loyal to the servant he had impregnated decades ago. He had to try and intervene, even if it meant crossing the man determined to string up every smuggler in the south-east.

A little over a week before the trials at Chichester started, Bishopp wrote to Richmond trying to get some leniency for Lillywhite. He appealed to Lillywhite's youth, claiming he was an innocent country boy caught up in the violent gang of thugs. Lillywhite didn't even see the customs house, being the gang's designated horse minder. Besides, there was no bloodshed during the raid and it was understandable that Lillywhite would go along with the gang; the whole raid was judged a 'gallant expedition' by the locals.[575] Unlike the Hawkhurst area, it seems as if the Chichester gang had not spent the last decade abusing the surrounding villages, and still enjoyed local support. The Hawkhurst Gang must have loved the adoration after the raid, since they had been hounded out of their own community by the militias.

Bishopp mentioned why he was intervening, but not directly. Lillywhite had recently been married to 'a young woman of good fortune and credible parents', failing to mention that he was one of those parents. Bishopp included, but lightly crossed out 'now big with child'.[576] It seemed that Bishopp had a grandchild on the way, who would soon be fatherless if he didn't save the foolish teenager from the gallows.

It must have been an awkward scene as they stood greeting the judges at Chichester, because Richmond was livid, not replying until the day of the trials. Fresh off of listening to graphic testimony of how Galley and Chater had been slowly tortured to death, Richmond penned a fiery reply. How could Bishopp vouch for a smuggler, having just listened to such a horror? Whatever Lillywhite's level of involvement, he was involved in the crime that precipitated these 'inhuman' murders.[577]

Richmond clearly laid out why Lillywhite needed to be punished, whatever mitigating circumstance Bishopp thought he had. Even if the common people in Sussex didn't think smuggling was a crime, there was no better way to disabuse them of that view than to actually punish the smugglers. But this paled in significance to a more pressing, political reason: the narrative that the Pelham government 'fanned' smuggling to keep electoral control over the countryside.[578]

That narrative had become an effective line of attack for opposition politicians in parliament. Richmond bitterly recalled how the administration's opponents had become so bold as to openly question the government's motivation for why they weren't doing more about the smuggling crisis. In the Commons, Admiral Vernon, who only a few years earlier had been guarding the Channel against the French, intimated that a plan to conscript smugglers into the navy had been abandoned because there were MPs that were actively helping the smugglers. Speaking in parliament, he said: 'it is the general opinion without doors,* that the smugglers have powerful protection somewhere; and nothing has yet been done, by which that opinion can be weakened'.[579]

The narrative was not new, it had been floating around in the press for years,[580] but the crisis precipitated by the Hawkhurst Gang had reached such a fever pitch that the accusation had more bite. Richmond seemed very sensitive to that line of attack as it crescendoed in London and spread to the Pelhams' political opponents in Sussex. Richmond was as angry at the politicians claiming that the Pelham government was protecting the smugglers as he was at the smugglers themselves, calling his political opponents 'bad men', Admiral Vernon being the chief bad man among them. Even the remaining Jacobites, or at least the people Richmond thought were Jacobites, were piling on the 'the Pelhams were protecting the smugglers' argument.[581]

Unfortunately for Richmond, the Pelhams' political enemies weren't entirely wrong in their accusations. Newcastle had been using smuggling prosecutions as a source of political leverage for years, at least up until the mid-1740s and likely after. Even in Richmond's papers, there is an account of a smuggler that seems to have been released in part on the suggestion that Newcastle thought he should be freed.[582] Richmond must have understood what Newcastle was doing, but was a good soldier, standing by his boss and friend even in the face of accusations that had some merit to them. However, there doesn't seem to be any indication that this cosy relationship with the smugglers had any impact on government policy towards smuggling. The 1746 Smuggling Act was about as harsh as anti-smuggling policy could get, and the government had taken extreme measures in Kent and Sussex, like condoning violence towards smugglers.

---

* The 'opinion without doors' was an early way of referring to general public opinion. 'Without doors' was an archaic way of saying 'out doors'.

Richmond concluded his blistering letter to Bishopp by saying there would be no leniency for Lillywhite; he would be tried at the Old Bailey with the rest of the Poole raiders.[583] Bishopp would need to figure out another way of saving his son-in-law.

★★★

About a month after the Chichester trials, another crop of smugglers faced trial at the normal assizes at East Grinstead, a town in Sussex. The Chichester trials were a big, flashy set piece meant to show the power and majesty of the government in dealing with the worst kind of smugglers, while the East Grinstead trials were business as usual, albeit with some of the Galley and Chater murderers, one of Hawkins's murderers, and whichever Wakeford robbers could be rounded up.

Richmond had been able to take significant chunks out of the remaining Hawkhurst Gang that was still at large. Thomas Kingsmill, the leader of the Poole raid and long-term member, had been taken, along with William Grey's former servant, Jockey Brown, among a host of others hauled in for whatever charge they could get to stick, from smuggling to highway robbery. But the ever-slippery Curteis was still on the run. Curteis had always been different. He had been a leader in the Hawkhurst Gang since the Hastings Outlaws disintegrated in 1744, but he had always been a man who existed somewhere in the English Channel, effortlessly sliding back and forth between France and England. This likely made him a hard man to capture, probably spending only part of his time riding around as the terror of Kent and Sussex. The Treasury even sent two agents to Collier specifically to find Curteis in June 1748,[584] but their efforts seem to have come to nothing. He had apparently joined the French army in the Irish Brigade,[585] a unit for disaffected people from the British Isles and a precursor to the French Foreign Legion.

The remaining Galley and Chater murderer was swiftly and thoroughly sent to the gallows with a similar set of witnesses to those at Chichester.[586] Jockey Brown, who had been riding around with Curteis since William Grey died, was hanged for a highway robbery.[587] John Mills, the only Hawkhurst Gang member to have the dubious distinction of being involved in the Hawkins and Chater murder, saw his day in court. Twenty days after beating Hawkins to death in the back of the Dog and Partridge pub, he was among the group deciding whether to murder Galley and Chater.[588] Mills went to the gallows, the only one of the gang involved in the Hawkins murder to hang.

With the gang being in such a ragged state and the heat on them so intense, there were several members willing to turn King's evidence in exchange for clemency. The most damning was Thomas Winter, one of Curteis's men who had been involved in the Wakeford robbery and the Hawkins murder.

There was also Thomas Border, who had been involved in the Carswell murder in 1740. A few years before, it is unlikely that any of these men would have even considered snitching, lest they suffer the same fate as Club James. But times were different, the gang was fragmented, and it was clear that smugglers were actually staying in jail to face trial. It was better to be the informant than to be the one in the dock facing execution.

In one instance, an informant had been actively involved in apprehending his follow gang members. William Pring, looking for a pardon, made a deal with the government to deliver some of his associates in the gang. Pring knew that Mills was wanted for the murders, and that he was with the Kemp brothers, who used to be high up in the Hawkhurst Gang, one of which had already managed to escape the noose in early 1748.[589] Pring went out to Bath and Bristol, where the gangsters had been hiding out,* trying to sell some of the few smuggled goods that they had managed to run. Their normal buyers in London must have dried up, given that Bristol is significantly further to travel.

Meeting them in Bristol, Pring convinced them that they should come with him to his house in Kent, telling them he had a job robbing a local farmer that they could help with. Lured with the prospect of another score, they went with him to Kent, where they were quickly arrested.[590] There is apparently no honour among thieves.

The Kemps, who had survived in the gang life for as long as any, finally went to the gallows, unrepentant to the end. They refused to admit to the clergyman who attended their executions that smuggling was wrong, though they would admit that the robberies they had

---

* The source does not explicitly say that they were hiding out, but it is reasonable to assume it factored into their motivation. Bristol is a long way away to sell goods that could be sold in London.

committed were. However, they would not have had to do them if they hadn't been driven out of their homes out of fear of being arrested as smugglers.[591] The gang had been scattered out of Hawkhurst, and had to resort to desperate measures. What made the Hawkhurst Gang different from other smuggling gangs was that they could not just return to a normal life after their smuggling operation had dried up, they had done too much and made too many enemies. Had they tried to do that, it is possible that more of them would have survived. But they were professional gangsters to the end, and died like gangsters.

The assizes at Rochester in Kent had another crop of Hawkhurst Gang members go to the gallows for various crimes, another harvest of fruit from Richmond's fatal tree.[592]

On 5 April 1749, the trial for the Poole raid began at the Old Bailey. Richmond had managed to round up five of the gang involved in the raid that had so far escaped prosecution: Thomas Kingsmill, William Fairall, Richard Perin, Thomas Lillywhite and Richard Glover. This was the final blow that Richmond would strike on the last remnants of the Hawkhurst Gang, who had terrorised Kent and Sussex for the better part of a decade, who were going down not for all the smuggling, violence and murder they had done over the years, but for robbing a customs house.

Some of the defendants were lawyered up and ready to fight it out, literally to the death. The trial laid out the events of that night, and William Steele reprised his well-practised testimony. The Chichester smugglers had hired the Hawkhurst Gang, whom they called the 'East Country People', to break open the customs house, and share the recovered tea out with them. Kingsmill was the ring leader of the expedition, insisting that the gang get their haul, despite the timidity of the Chichester smugglers. Lillywhite and Perin were left to mind the horses as the gang made the break-in. Lillywhite was young and had never been with the gang before, and Perin, whose nickname was Pain, ironically had arthritis that disqualified him from the heavy lifting.[593]

There was little that the government had not revealed in previous trials, but they made a convincing case, producing multiple witnesses that placed the defendants at the raid, even if two of the defendants had the uninspiring job of holding the horses.[594]

The two Hawkhurst Gang leaders, Kingsmill and Fairall, had nothing to say in their defence, other than to deny their involvement. The days of the gang being able to afford a lawyer to defend them in court were long gone. The others, either from their own means, or through the support of a wealthy patron, had lawyers that tried to mitigate their charges with character witnesses, or by showing that they were not armed.[595]

Glover claimed that he had been forced to go along in the raid by his brother-in-law, who had threatened to shoot him in the head if he did not. He backed up this assertion with a bevy of character witnesses that swore he had never been a smuggler before. Perin's character witness was less inspiring, saying that he was a good carpenter, and he had never seen him skip work to go smuggling, but had to admit that he did hear rumours that Perin was a smuggler.

Lillywhite had the biggest ace in the hole; his secret father-in-law, Cecil Bishopp, had likely paid for his defence council. Throughout the trial, his lawyer hammered at every government witness about one key fact: whether Lillywhite was armed during the raid. Lillywhite advanced the story of the foolish boy who had been invited on a ride, and ended up working with the most notorious gang in the south-east.

Bishopp had not only likely paid for the defence, he personally appeared in court to testify to Lillywhite's character. It was the ultimate act of sticking his neck out. Bishopp knew that Richmond, and by extension the government, was ardent that Lillywhite pay for his involvement in the raid. Bishopp was still a political hustler, and must have known that he was probably throwing his political career away. But Lillywhite was family, even if he had married his illegitimate daughter.[596]

Bishopp testified in court that Lillywhite had married his housekeeper's daughter, glossing over the fact that she was his daughter as well, and that he would never have consented to the match if he did not think that Lillywhite was of good character. He also pointed out that Lillywhite's wife had left him a fortune, a subtle nod that Lillywhite was more to him than just his housekeeper's daughter's husband.[597]

As the trial ended, the judge summed up the evidence against the defendants, noting that if the jury thought there was not enough evidence against Lillywhite, they could acquit him. The jury only deliberated for fifteen minutes before reaching their verdict.[598]

Kingsmill, Perin and Fairall were found guilty, sentenced to death. Glover managed to convince the jury that he had been coerced, being found guilty but recommended for a pardon. Lillywhite was acquitted and immediately released by the court; reunited with his young bride, baby boy, and no doubt relieved father-in-law.[599]

Kingsmill and Fairall were defiant to the end, partying it up in prison before the trial and refusing to admit that they had done anything wrong, even as their execution approached. Like many leaders of the Hawkhurst Gang, they had what would now be considered an extreme libertarian view of taxes. In regard to the Poole raid, Kingsmill and Fairall didn't think they had stolen anything from the King in his warehouse because that tea was never the King's to begin with. It was the property of the smugglers who bought it.[600]

The Hawkhurst men were taken from Newgate to Tyburn on 26 April 1749, under heavy guard. Transported in a cart, they received one last prayer, the Ordinary recommending God have mercy on their souls just before 'the Cart was withdrawn from under them, whilst they called on the Lord to receive their Souls'. The tightening rope silenced the praying men. Kingsmill's and Fairall's bodies were taken away and hung in chains near where they had grown up, an ignominious return of their villages' sons. Kingsmill was from Goudhurst, hanging close to where his brother was shot dead by the militia almost exactly two years before.[601]

18

AFTERMATH

After the Poole raid trials, Richmond's crusade ended in a bloody denouement. A few Hawkhurst Gang members who had previously escaped capture went to the gallows. But the government had moved on to the new smuggling hotspot, Suffolk, efficiently using the 1746 law to put the Suffolk gangs on a legal conveyor belt that terminated at a noose. The smuggling trials in the Old Bailey almost became routine, some only containing a scant few lines to record a guilty verdict.

Richmond was intent on making sure that the Hawkhurst Gang hanged, and needed to make sure every possible route they had to escape the rope was closed off to them. He had caught wind of people petitioning on behalf of Richard Mapesden, who had been convicted in July, and that meant that there was still a chance of his pardon. Richmond, likely aware that Newcastle might use the pardon for a deal, appealed directly to his friend. 'I really hope no such application, whoever it comes from, will be listened to.'[602]

Almost a decade after he was killed, Carswell's murder was solved, or at least avenged. Three of the murderers were convicted in summer 1749,[603] but there were still a lot of his murderers that still needed to be caught; thirty smugglers bore down on him that winter's night. The main instigator of the incident, Trip Stanford, was arrested along with Jockey Tom, two of the gang that had seen little of a jail until now.

Thomas Border, who had been one of the gang, had turned King's evidence, so there was now a credible case against the two leaders, but the law would save Stanford from the gallows. Wealthy before he got into the smuggling game, he had hired a lawyer who was able to concoct a tortuous defence: that night, Stanford had first raised the alarm, gathering the gang together to recover the goods, which meant that he had hired the Hawkhurst Gang to save the tea that Carswell had seized. It wasn't his fault that the gang went on to kill Carswell, he had not told them to do that. Hard as it was to accept, he was technically correct.[604] The jury acquitted him. Jockey Tom, however, was not so lucky. He hanged for Carswell's murder.[605]

But one man would outlive most of the Hawkhurst Gang, if only for a short time. Gabriel Tomkins, the incorrigible criminal, the old man of smuggling, finally met his end. A life of crime was ended by his robbing the Chester mail in 1746. He was arrested almost three years later, in early 1749.[606] The next year, he was tried and sentenced to death for the robbery, hanging in chains near Bedford.[607] He was around 60 years old when he went to the gallows, a ripe old age for anyone in the period, much less a man who spent his entire life as a violent criminal. Tomkins had been a smuggler, customs officer and highway robber. He had escaped numerous gunfights, being shot through the arm, transportation, and an attempted kidnapping. He had led a very full, albeit criminal, life. This was his inevitable end.

By mid-1749, the Hawkhurst Gang was no more, a collection of hanged bodies and men deep in hiding. The pace of smuggling trials at the Old Bailey began to taper off over the next few years, targeting the Suffolk gangs that had taken over the major smuggling routes. They were likely as large and successful as the Hawkhurst Gang, but never caused a political crisis like the gang created during the 1740s.

What made the Hawkhurst Gang different is that they unmoored themselves from any of the wider communities of eighteenth-century Kent and Sussex. They ceased to be part of the agricultural community that relied on smuggling to sell their wool, they broke the unspoken rules of the conflict between revenue man and smuggler, their excesses alienated them from any political relationships that they had, and they subjugated the surrounding villages. They followed the typical arc of organised crime, that starts in a tight-knit community, and ends in excesses that brings a wider crackdown from authorities who can no longer ignore the problem. The gang became detached from anything that could have restrained their behaviour, and the violence spiralled out of control.

A revenue-hungry government had an interest in combatting smuggling, but was constrained by Whigish politics that sought a limited state, preserving personal liberties, values we cherish in western democracies to this day. The crisis centred on the Hawkhurst Gang was one of the first instances in British history where law enforcement had to walk the fine line between fighting crime and respecting what we would call civil liberties today. The gang was able to flourish for a time in the shadows of the legal system, benefiting from a symbiotic relationship with political elites who used smuggling as a way to steer electoral outcomes. In the end, lofty political ideals gave way to the brutal practicality of laws passed to crush smuggling.

The demise of the Hawkhurst Gang was not the end of smuggling in the region, which would continue until the early nineteenth century, when a dedicated preventative service and a shift towards income taxes made it unviable. The gangs in the late 18th century were just as large as the Hawkhurst Gang at its height, but did not provoke a similar rolling political crisis. In fact, the government seemed more intent on punishing the local population for supporting the smugglers than they were fighting the gangs. In 1784, Prime Minister William Pitt the younger, in a show of strength, marched troops down to Deal and burned every boat on the beach for their support of smugglers, ruining the livelihoods of an entire town for years.[608]

Historians have often argued that the popular and government reaction to the gang was driven by fears of Jacobitism. However, this ignores concerns in the press and private government documents about the gang well before the Jacobite rebellion had started. There was little direct concern about smugglers' support for the Stuart dynasty. Rather, the concern was more around the gang's potential allegiance with the French, and their violent excesses. The crackdown on the gang wasn't because they were Jacobites, it was because they had become dangerous rebels in their own right.[609] They had broken down law and order in Kent and Sussex, so much so that the citizenry felt they needed to take matters into their own hands.

Richmond died in August 1750, and with him any lingering desire to aggressively pursue smugglers. He had sent most of his targets to the gallows, but one stubbornly avoided his grasp – Jeremiah Curteis. Whether through his service to the French military, or his seemingly effortless Channel crossings, he remained a free man. A year before he died,

Richmond sent an agent with a ship to Dunkirk to try and trick Curteis and any accomplices back to the UK to face justice. The agent returned, but only just. After some initial successes and near misses, Curteis realised who Richmond's agent was, and tried to make sure that he never returned. The agent narrowly escaped Dunkirk with his life.[610]

Nature did what Richmond could not. In 1753, the *Gentleman's Magazine* noted in its list of notable deaths for the month 'Jeremiah Curteis, the noted smuggler, at Dunkirk'.[611] Curteis was around 36 years old at the time of his death from smallpox.[612] He died a smuggler in one of the spiritual homes of smuggling in the English Channel. A life cut short, but not by the noose.

Henry Pelham died in 1754, leaving Newcastle to step in as Prime Minister. He would spend two separate terms in office, presiding over the start of the French and Indian War. He was one of the most influential politicians of his time, and had in part built his political empire on a cosy relationship with criminals.

Before his trial for the murder of Carswell, possibly about to meet his maker, Trip Stanford wrote a will leaving his ill-gotten gains to his family: wife Mary, son James, and daughters Mary, Sarah and Elizabeth. Stanford left his 70-acre farm in Hawkhurst, called Fulling Mill, to his brothers. While he awaited trial, the farm was occupied by one Walter Tickner, probably a relation of Peter Tickner, a Hawkhurst Gang member hanged a few years before. It all sounded like a very normal will for a nice family, if the writer of the will wasn't about to be tried for murder. But Stanford's will was premature. He would live another decade, dying around 1760.[613] Stanford, unlike most of his fellows, lived long enough to enjoy the fruits of his time leading the gang.

Smuggling gangs came and went, but it was the Hawkhurst Gang that people remembered a century later. The accounts of the trials published by Richmond, under the name Gentleman of Chichester, stayed in print until at least the 1830s, capturing people's imagination for generations. Its moralising, anti-smuggling rhetoric had a life long after the gang had gone, and the smuggling trade had ceased to be a major force in Kent and Sussex. The Hawkhurst Gang meant something not only to the people at the time, but also to people decades later. They were a reminder of a very dangerous period in British history when, for a brief time, a criminal gang had *de facto* control over large swathes of two counties. A time when men like the Greys, Trip Stanford and Jeremiah Curteis were the law, doing what they wanted, taking what they wanted, and bringing terrible violence down upon whoever tried to stop them.

The Hawkhurst Gang is an integral, violent part of the history of tea, the British national drink. Tea made them, and it was so many bags of tea stolen from a customs house that eventually ended them. The teabags that we nonchalantly put in our mugs every morning have a deep, criminal history.

EPILOGUE

In June 1750, Horace Walpole wrote a letter to his friend and fellow MP George Montagu, who had just moved to Hawkhurst, a quieter place than it had been in the past few years.

Smuggling had not disappeared in the region. Walpole would later describe a journey he had through the 'wretched village' of Robertsbridge, near the site where Carswell died. There was no room at the inn, because it was full of smugglers, licking their wounds after a recent shootout with the customs men. Perhaps some of the men had ridden with the Hawkhurst Gang a few years before. The sides were more evenly matched. Walpole and his party were allowed to pass by, unmolested.[614] The smugglers had returned to just being smugglers rather than rebellious *mafiosi*, and the ancient contest between revenue man and smuggler continued as it had always done. A modicum of sanity had returned to the Kent and Sussex border.

Walpole's letter to Montagu was much more upbeat, gently ribbing him about his new home. 'You are agent from the Board of Trade to the smugglers.' He had found an old newspaper with some wanted smugglers' names: 'John Price alias Miss Marjoram, Bob Plunder, Bricklayer Tom, and Robin Cursemother', his friend's new neighbours. Walpole jokes that his sister, when she returned from a spa, would go from drinking the therapeutic water 'to sip nothing but run [smuggled] brandy'.[615]

Smuggling, and Hawkhurst, had become a bit of a joke. The sort of place that had a rough past, but was now a better place to live. Almost like a friend moving to Chicago and telling them to say hello to Al Capone.

The smugglers might still be there and the illicit industry still humming along, but the bad old days of terrible violence, murderous gangsters and roving militias were gone. There was still crime and the gangs were still a problem for the government, but people could move on with their lives, and respectable people could live there. The gang left an indelible mark on the area. They would be remembered for decades and centuries to come.

Walpole ended the letter to his friend, 'Adieu, I expect that in return for this long tale, that you tell me of your frolics with Robin Cursemother, and some of Miss Marjoram's bon mots.'[616]

NOTES

1 'Kent', *Kentish Gazette* (May 1847).
2 Douglas Hay et al., *Albion's Fatal Tree: Crime and Society in Eighteenth-Century England*, Pantheon Books, 1975, p.119.
3 Ibid., p.120.
4 'Obituary', *Sun* (Aug. 1829), BL_0002194_18290807_005_0001.pdf; 'To Be Sold', *South Eastern Gazette* (Oct. 1847).
5 Hay et al., *Albion's Fatal Tree*, p.120.
6 Paul Muskett, 'What was the Ordinary of Newgate?', Open History 139.36. Microsoft Word document supplied by author.
7 Mary Waugh, *Smuggling in Kent and Sussex 1700–1840*, Countryside Books, 1985.
8 Henry Jones, 'The Enigma of "General" Sturt and the Battle of Goudhurst – 1747 (Part 1)', *Bygone Kent 20* (2000), pp.358–365; Henry Jones, 'The Enigma of "General" Sturt and the Battle of Goudhurst – 1747 (Part 2)', *Bygone Kent 20* (2000), pp.392–400; Henry Jones, 'The Battle of Wingham: The Beginning of the End for the Hawkhurst Gang', *Bygone Kent 22* (2002), pp.161–167; Henry Jones, 'The Hawkhurst Gang: James (Alias Trip Stanford)', *Bygone Kent 24* (2004), pp.230–237; Henry Jones, 'The Hawkhurst Gang: A Winter's Tale', *Bygone Kent 21* (2001), pp.659–666; Henry Jones, 'The Hawkhurst Gang: The Gray Brothers', *Bygone Kent 20* (2000), pp.667–673; Henry Jones, 'The Hawkhurst Gang: The Trial and Tribulations of John Cook', *Bygone Kent 20* (2000), pp.711–718; Henry Jones, 'The Hawkhurst Gang: Thomas Fuller', *Bygone Kent 21* (2001), pp.304–309; Henry Jones, 'A Lucky Escape', *Bygone Kent 20* (2000), pp.560–565.
9 Paul Muskett, 'Military operations against smuggling in Kent and Sussex, 1698–1750', *Journal of the Society for Army Historical Research* 52.210 (1974), pp.89–110; P. Muskett, 'Aspects of English Smuggling in the Eighteenth Century', PhD thesis, Open University, 1996; Paul Muskett, 'Soliciting for Profit', *Criminal Law and Justice Weekly* 179 (June 2015). Supplied by author.

10 Old Bailey Proceedings Online (www.oldbaileyonline.org, version 8.0, 24 September 2022), July 1740, trial of James Watmore (t17400709-39). (Accessed 24/9/2022).

11 Ibid.

12 Old Bailey Proceedings Online (www.oldbaileyonline.org, version 8.0, 24 September 2022), January 1740, trial of Elizabeth Taverner , alias Howard Hannah Sargeway, alias French Hannah (t17400116-36). (Accessed 24/9/2020).

13 Ibid.

14 Ibid.

15 Ibid.

16 T. Short, *Discourses on Tea, Sugar, Milk, Made-wines, Spirits, Punch, Tobacco, &c: With Plain and Useful Rules for Gouty People*, Zentralantiquariat der Deutschen Demokratischen Republik, 1750, p.11.

17 Ibid., p.13.

18 Ibid., p.13.

19 Ibid., p.12.

20 Ibid., p.12–13.

21 Ibid., p.12.

22 Ibid., p.13.

23 P.D. Huet, *Memoirs of the Dutch Trade in All the States, Empires, and Kingdoms in the World: Shewing Its First Rise and Amazing Progress: After what Manner the Dutch Manage and Carry on Their Commerce; Their Vast Dominions and Government in the Indies, and by what Means They Have Made Themselves Masters of All the Trade of Europe … A Treatise Very Neccessary for Every Englishman, Tr. from the French, Now Printed at Amsterdam*, Eighteenth-century collections online, C. Rivington, 1719, p.116.

24 Short, *Discourses on Tea, etc.*, p.14.

25 *An Universal History, from the Earliest Account of Time* v. 29. T. Osborne, 1759, p.556; Leonard Blussé. 'Chinese Trade to Batavia during the days of the V.O.C.', (1979), ISSN. 0044-8613, p.209.

26 Blussé, 'Chinese Trade to Batavia during the days of the V.O.C.', p.203.

27 *An Universal History, from the Earliest Account of Time*, p.556.

28 *An Universal History, from the Earliest Account of Time*, p.556; *The Political State of Great Britain*. v. 49. J. Baker and T. Warner, 1735, p.69.

29 *The Political State of Great Britain*, p.69.

30 Old Bailey Proceedings Online (www.oldbaileyonline.org, version 8.0, 10 March 2021), October 1747, trial of Thomas Fuller (t17471014-4). (Accessed 3/10/2021), p.2.

31 Ibid., p.2.

32 Jones, 'The Hawkhurst Gang: James (Alias Trip Stanford)', p.231; Waugh, *Smuggling in Kent and Sussex*, p.73; Weather in History 1700 to 1749 AD. premium.weatherweb.net/weather-in-history-1700-to-1749-ad (Accessed 6/10/2021).

33 Jones, 'The Hawkhurst Gang: The Gray Brothers', p.667.

NOTES

34   Jones, 'The Hawkhurst Gang: James (Alias Trip Stanford)', p.231.

35   Jones, 'The Hawkhurst Gang: James (Alias Trip Stanford)', pp.231–32, *Stamford Mercury* (1741). British Newspaper Archive (Accessed 1/10/2021).

36   Jones, 'The Hawkhurst Gang: James (Alias Trip Stanford)', p.232.

37   WSRO, Goodwood Ms. 156.

38   Ibid.

39   Roy Frank Hunnisett, *East Sussex Coroners' Records 1688–1838*, Vol. 89, Steve Parish, 2005, p.199.

40   WSRO, Goodwood Ms. 156.

41   Ibid.

42   Great Britain. Parliament. House of Commons. Journals of the House of Commons. British history online v. 25. order of the House of Commons, 1745, p.104.

43   SAY/286 ESRO.

44   *Stamford Mercury* (1741). British Newspaper Archive (Accessed 1/10/2021).

45   Short, *Discourses on Tea, etc.*, p.19.

46   Parker, H., *Of the use of tobacco, tea, coffee, chocolate and drams*, 1722, p.12.

47   P.A. Motteux, *A Poem Upon Tea* v. 17. J. Tonson, 1712, p.1.

48   Short, *Discourses on Tea, etc.*, p.24.

49   Parker, H., Of the use of tobacco …, p.14.

50   E.F. Haywood, *The Female Spectator*, v. 2. T. Gardner, 1748, p.84.

51   Parker, H., *Of the use of tobacco* …, p.12.

52   Short, *Discourses on Tea, etc.*, p.28.

53   Short, *Discourses on Tea, etc.*, p.25; J. Hanway, *A Journal of Eight Days Journey from Portsmouth to Kingston Upon Thames, with Miscellaneous Thoughts, Moral and Religious, in a Series of Letters: To which is Added, and Essay on Tea*, 1756, p.216.

54   *The Universal Magazine*, v. 1. Pub. for J. Hinton, 1747, p.161.

55   Hanway, *A Journal of Eight Days* …, p.216.

56   Short, *Discourses on Tea, etc.*, p.30.

57   Ibid., p.25.

58   Hanway, *A Journal of Eight Days* …, p.215.

59   Ibid., p.216.

60   Commons, Journals of the House of Commons, p.103.

61   W. Coxe, *Memoirs of the Life and Administration of Sir Robert Walpole, Earl Of Orford: With Original Correspondence and Authentic Papers, Never Before Published. In Three Volumes. Containing The Correspondence From 1730 To 1745*, 3, Cadell and Davies, 1798, p.129.

62   K. Dovey, *Framing Places: Mediating Power in Built Form*, Architext, Taylor & Francis, 2002, ISBN 9781134688975, Chapter 7.

63   Women in St Stephen's Chapel 1548–1834, UK Parliament (Accessed 9/7/2021).

64   Paul Langford et al., *The Excise Crisis: Society and Politics in the Age of Walpole*, Oxford [Eng.]: Clarendon Press, 1975, p.44.

65   Coxe, *Memoirs of the Life and Administration of Sir Robert Walpole* …, p.129.

66 Ibid., p.130.

67 'First Parliament of George II: Sixth session (part 3 of 5, from 27/2/1733)', in *The History and Proceedings of the House of Commons, Vol. 7, 1727–1733* (London, 1742), pp.304–353. British History Online, www.british-history. ac.uk/commons-hist-proceedings/vol7/pp304-353 (Accessed 13/6/21).

68 Coxe, *Memoirs of the Life and Administration of Sir Robert Walpole*, p.129.

69 'First Parliament of George II: Sixth session (part 3 of 5, from 27/2/1733)', in *The History and Proceedings of the House of Commons, Vol. 7, 1727–1733* (London, 1742), pp.304–353. British History Online, www.british-history. ac.uk/commons-hist-proceedings/vol7/pp304-353 (Accessed 13/6/2021).

70 Langford et al., *The Excise Crisis* ..., pp.27–28.

71 Ibid., pp.5–8.

72 José Jurado Sánchez. 'Military expenditure, spending capacity and budget constraint in eighteenth-century Spain and Britain', *Revista de Historia Económica, Journal of Iberian and Latin American Economic History 27.1* (2009), pp.141–174.

73 Langford et al., *The Excise Crisis* ..., p.32.

74 Ibid., p.39.

75 Ibid., p.46.

76 *Caledonian Mercury* (Apr. 1733), British Newspaper Archive (Accessed 20/6/2021).

77 Langford et al., *The Excise Crisis* ..., p.46.

78 Oxford, Bodleian Library HFL: B 762 Engl Gallery: digital.bodleian.ox.ac. uk/objects/c3ff6124-a7b7-4023-ab18-7c12497c3ddd/, p.154.

79 Ibid., p.155.

80 Ibid., p.173.

81 Ibid., p.173.

82 Ibid., p.173.

83 Ibid., p.174.

84 *London Gazette*, 'Page 1', Iss. 6748, 28 January 1728, www.thegazette.co.uk/ London/issue/6748/page/1 (Accessed 18/9/2021).

85 D. Defoe, *Mercurius Politicus*, University Microfilms, 1716, p.60; 'Treasury Books and Papers: January 1729', *Calendar of Treasury Books and Papers, Vol. 1, 1729–1730*, ed. William A. Shaw (London, 1897), pp.1–13, British History Online www.british-history.ac.uk/cal-treasury-books-papers/vol1/pp1-13 (Accessed 9/9/2021).

86 *Caledonian Mercury* (Apr. 1732), British Newspaper Archive (Accessed 9/9/2021).

87 Oxford, Bodleian Library HFL: B 762 Engl Gallery: digital.bodleian.ox.ac. uk/objects/c3ff6124-a7b7-4023-ab18-7c12497c3ddd, p.174.

88 *The Gentleman's Magazine*, No. XXV, 1733, p.267.

89 Renaud Morieux, *The Channel: England, France and the construction of a maritime border in the eighteenth century*, vol. 23. Cambridge University Press, 2016, p.252.

90 Ibid., p.259.

NOTES

91 D. Defoe, *A Tour Thro' the Whole Island of Great Britain: Divided into Circuits or Journies. Giving a Particular and Diverting Account of Whatever is Curious and Worth Observation*, v. 1. G. Strahan. W. Mears. R. Francklin. S. Chapman. R. Stagg, and J. Graves, 1724, p.46.

92 Ibid., p.49.

93 H. Hicks, *The Poll for Knights of the Shire to Represent the County of Kent; in which is Inserted, Not Only the Names of the Electors and Candidates, But Also Every Person's Freehold and Place of Abode*, 1734, p.248.

94 1911 Encyclopædia Britannica/Newcastle, Dukes of, Wikisource, the free online library (Accessed 11/9/2021).

95 Langford et al., *The Excise Crisis …*, p.11.

96 Bishopp, Sir Cecil, 6th Bt. (d.1778), of Parham, Suss., History of Parliament Online. www.histparl.ac.uk/volume/1715-1754/member/bishopp-sir-cecil-1778 (Accessed 17/1/2022); Penryn – History of Parliament Online. www.historyofparliamentonline.org/volume/1715-1754/constituencies/penryn (Accessed 11/7/2021).

97 *Ipswich Journal* (Sept. 1733), British Newspaper Archive (Accessed 11/7/2021).

98 *Ipswich Journal* (Dec. 1733), British Newspaper Archive (Accessed 30/5/2021).

99 Ibid.

100 Timothy J. McCann et al., *The Correspondence of the Dukes of Richmond and Newcastle, 1724–1750*. Vol. 73, Sussex Record Society, 1984, p.9.

101 *Newcastle Courant* (Dec. 1733), British Newspaper Archive (Accessed 12/7/2021).

102 Sussex, History of Parliament Online (Accessed 12/7/2021).

103 McCann et al., *The Correspondence of the Dukes of Richmond and Newcastle*, p.70.

104 Richard Saville, *The Letters of John Collier of Hastings, 1731–1746*, 2016, p.xxxiii.

105 Ibid., p.xxxiii–xxxiv.

106 'Warrants for Minor Appointments: 1733', *Calendar of Treasury Books and Papers, Vol. 2, 1731–1734*, ed. William A. Shaw (London, 1898), pp.516–525, British History Online www.british-history.ac.uk/cal-treasury-books-papers/vol2/pp516-525 (Accessed 12/7/2021).

107 Saville, *The Letters of John Collier*, p.xxxiv.

108 Sussex, History of Parliament Online.

109 R. Platt, *Smuggling in the British Isles: A History*, Tempus Series, Tempus, 2007, ISBN 9780752442495, p.84.

110 James Alexander Williamson, *The English Channel: A History*, World Publishing Company, 1959, p.202.

111 *The Gentleman's Magazine*, No. XXV, 1733, p.492.

112 Defoe, *A Tour Thro' the Whole Island of Great Britain*, p.54.

113 W. Symonds, *A New-years-gift to the Parliament, Or, England's Golden Fleece Preserv'd, in Proposals Humbly Laid Before this Present Parliament. Printed in the year*, 1702, p.13.

114 Platt, *Smuggling in the British Isles: A History*, p.84.

115 Symonds, *England's Golden Fleece Preserv'd*, p.13.

116 Ibid., pp.14–15.

117 Defoe, *A Tour Thro' the Whole Island of Great Britain*, p.53; Symonds, *England's Golden Fleece Preserv'd*, p.13.

118 Symonds, England's Golden Fleece Preserv'd, p.13.

119 Defoe, *A Tour Thro' the Whole Island of Great Britain*, p.54.

120 John Beattie, 'The Royal pardon and criminal procedure in early modern England', *Historical Papers/Communications historiques 22.1* (1987), pp.9–22.

121 WSRO, Goodwood Ms. 155.

122 Basil Williams. 'The Duke of Newcastle and the Election of 1734', *English Historical Review* (1897), pp.448–488.

123 Ibid., pp.470–472.

124 Ibid., p.471.

125 Saville, *The Letters of John Collier*, p.xxxiv.

126 *Caledonian Mercury* (May 1734), British Newspaper Archive (Accessed 30/5/2021).

127 Langford et al., *The Excise Crisis …*, p.120.

128 *Stamford Mercury* (1741). British Newspaper Archive (Accessed 1/10/2021).

129 'Warrants, Letters, etc.: 1734, January–June', *Calendar of Treasury Books and Papers, Vol. 2, 1731–1734*, ed. William A. Shaw (London, 1898), pp.590–615, British History Online www.british-history.ac.uk/cal-treasury-books-papers/vol2/pp590-615 (Accessed 14/7/2021).

130 Langford et al., *The Excise Crisis …*, p.134.

131 Ibid., p.150.

132 Horace Walpole. *The Yale Edition of Horace Walpole's Correspondence*, Yale University Press, 1937, v. 9, p.141.

133 Ibid., v. 35, pp.140–141.

134 SAY/275 ESRO.

135 'Warrants for Minor Appointments: 1745', *Calendar of Treasury Books and Papers, Vol. 5, 1742–1745*, ed. William A. Shaw (London, 1903), pp.837–848, British History Online www.british-history.ac.uk/cal-treasury-books-papers/vol5/pp837-848 (Accessed 17/7/2021).

136 'Warrants for Minor Appointments: 1732', *Calendar of Treasury Books and Papers, Vol. 2, 1731–1734*, ed. William A. Shaw (London, 1898), pp.353–361, British History Online www.british-history.ac.uk/cal-treasury-books-papers/vol2/pp353-361 (Accessed 21/7/2021).

137 SAY/287 ESRO.

138 Ibid.

139 SAY/284 ESRO; SAY/287 ESRO.

140 SAY/287 ESRO.

141 Hunnisett, *East Sussex Coroners' Records 1688–1838*, p.199.

142 Record Transcription: Thomas Peen, England Marriages 1538–1973, findmypast.co.uk, www.findmypast.co.uk/transcript?idR⁻_855967541 (Accessed 14/7/2021).

143 SAY/287 ESRO.

144 SAY/286 ESRO.

145 SAY/287 ESRO.

146 Ibid.

147 Ibid.

148 Hunnisett, *East Sussex Coroners' Records 1688–1838*, p.199.

149 SAY/287 ESRO.

150 Hunnisett, *East Sussex Coroners' Records 1688–1838*, p.199.

151 Oxford, Bodleian Library HFL: B 762 Engl Gallery: digital.bodleian.ox.ac. uk/objects/c3ff6124-a7b7-4023-ab18-7c12497c3ddd, p.1225.

152 Great Britain. *An Act for Indemnifying Persons who Have Been Guilty of Offences Against the Laws Made for Securing the Revenues of Customs and Excise: And for Enforcing Those Laws for the Future*, eighteenth-century collections online, John Baskett, 1736, pp.73–75.

153 Ibid., pp.60–61.

154 Ibid., pp.69–71.

155 Ibid., pp.88–90.

156 Ibid., p.106.

157 Muskett, 'Aspects of English Smuggling in the Eighteenth Century', pp.340–342.

158 Britain, *An Act for Indemnifying Persons* ..., p.123.

159 Ibid., p.124.

160 Oxford, Bodleian Library HFL: B 762 Engl Gallery: digital.bodleian.ox.ac. uk/objects/c3ff6124-a7b7-4023-ab18-7c12497c3ddd, pp.1226–1229.

161 Ibid., pp.1230–1232.

162 Ibid., pp.1231–1232.

163 Ibid., p.1234.

164 Ibid., p.1238.

165 Ibid., p.1240.

166 Paul Muskett, 'Gabriel Tomkins Smuggler, Customs Officer, Sheriff's Bailif and Highwayman, Part 2', *Sussex History* 1, 2 (1981–82). Typewritten copy supplied by author, p.22.

167 Ibid., p.20.

168 *Derby Mercury* (Feb. 1736), British Newspaper Archive (Accessed 17/8/2021); *Newcastle Courant* (Feb. 1737), British Newspaper Archive (Accessed 8/17/2021); *Stamford Mercury* (June 1738), British Newspaper Archive (Accessed 17/8/2021).

169 Saville, *The Letters of John Collier*, p.90.

170 Muskett, 'Gabriel Tomkins Smuggler ...', p.20.

171 Ibid., p.20.

172 Ibid., p.21.

173 Ibid., p.21.

174 Saville, *The Letters of John Collier*, p.90.

175 Ibid., p.90.

176 *London Gazette*, 'Page 1', Iss. 5954, 9 May 1721, www.thegazette.co.uk/ London/issue/5954/page/1 (Accessed 28/9/2021).

177 Charles G. Harper, *The Smugglers* (Accessed 6/1/2021), pp.31–33; Muskett, 'Gabriel Tomkins Smuggler ...', p.21.
178 Muskett, 'Gabriel Tomkins Smuggler ...', p.21.
179 Saville, *The Letters of John Collier*, pp.151–152.
180 Muskett, 'Gabriel Tomkins Smuggler ...', p.22.
181 Record Transcription: Gabriel Tomkins England Births & Baptisms 1538–1975 — findmypast.co.uk. www.findmypast.co.uk/transcript?idR‾_22085371821 (Accessed 25/9/2021).
182 *London Gazette*, 'Page 1', Iss. 6748, 28 January 1728, www.thegazette.co.uk/London/issue/6748/page/1.
183 Muskett, 'Gabriel Tomkins Smuggler ...', p.22.
184 *Derby Mercury* (May 1740), British Newspaper Archive (Accessed 22/8/2021).
185 CUST/148/12/639 TNA.
186 Williamson, *The English Channel*, pp.107–108.
187 CUST/148/12/709-719 TNA.
188 CUST/148/12/579-586 TNA.
189 Jones, 'The Hawkhurst Gang: James (Alias Trip Stanford)', p.231.
190 Old Bailey Proceedings Online (www.oldbaileyonline.org, version 8.0, 27 Jan. 2022), Ordinary of Newgate's Account, May 1748 (OA17480511). (Accessed 27/1/2022).
191 Old Bailey Proceedings Online (www.oldbaileyonline.org, version 8.0, 21 January 2022), Ordinary of Newgate's Account, August 1749 (OA17490804). (Accessed 21/1/2022).
192 Old Bailey Proceedings Online (www.oldbaileyonline.org, version 8.0, 24 September 2022), Ordinary of Newgate's Account, December 1747 (OA17471221). (Accessed 24/9/2022).
193 Muskett, 'Gabriel Tomkins Smuggler ...', p.20; Waugh, *Smuggling in Kent and Sussex*, p.73.
194 *London Gazette*, 'Page 3', Iss. 8660, 21 July 1747 (undefined), British Newspaper Archive (Accessed 25/1/2022).
195 CUST/148/12/629 TNA.
196 Yann Gobert-Sergent, 'Pêche, course et contrebandiers: le port de Boulogne de Louis XIV à Napoléon Ier (1680–1815)', PhD thesis, ACRB Éd., 2004, p.66.
197 Ibid., pp.52, 63.
198 Old Bailey Proceedings Online (www.oldbaileyonline.org, version 8.0, 21 December 2020), Ordinary of Newgate's Account, March 1752 (OA17520323). (Accessed 21/12/2020).
199 James S. Cockburn. 'Patterns of violence in English society: homicide in Kent 1560–1985', *Past & Present* 130 (1991), pp.70–106.
200 Waugh, *Smuggling in Kent and Sussex*, p.74.
201 André Zysberg. 'La société des galériens au milieu du XVIIIe siècle'. fre. (1975). issn. 0395-2649, p.45; Jean-Baptiste Xambo, 'Servitude et droits de transmission. La condition des galériens de Louis XIV', *Revue dhistoire moderne contemporaine* 2 (2017), pp.157–183.

202 Zysberg, 'La société des galériens au milieu du XVIIIe siècle', p.49.

203 CUST/148/12/629 TNA.

204 CUST/148/12/613 TNA.

205 Record Transcription: Abraham Walter England Births & Baptisms 1538–1975, findmypast.co.uk. www.findmypast.co.uk/transcript?idR⁻_882978291. (Accessed 6/11/2021).

206 SP/36/63/3/0061-0068 TNA.

207 McCann et al., *The Correspondence of the Dukes of Richmond and Newcastle*, p.xxxi.

208 Ibid., pp.108, 122.

209 Gobert-Sergent, *Pêche, course et contrebandiers*, pp.52, 63.

210 Robert Tombs and Isabelle Tombs, *That Sweet Enemy: The French and the British from the Sun King to the Present*, Random House, 2007, p.39.

211 SP/36/63/3/0061-0068 TNA.

212 Ibid.

213 Ibid.

214 Ibid.

215 Ibid.

216 Ibid.

217 Ibid.

218 Hay et al., *Albion's Fatal Tree*, p.147. Though Walter is never mentioned by Winslow, the timing is the same and it is almost certainly him.

219 SP/36/63/3/0061-0068 TNA.

220 SP/36/77/2/0060-0061 TNA.

221 Hunnisett, *East Sussex Coroners' Records 1688–1838*, p.200; CUST/148/12/681 TNA.

222 Hunnisett, *East Sussex Coroners' Records 1688–1838*, p.200.

223 CUST/148/12/639 TNA.

224 CUST/148/12/605 TNA.

225 *Kentish Weekly Post* or *Canterbury Journal* (Feb. 1741), British Newspaper Archive (Accessed 16/11/2021).

226 Waugh, *Smuggling in Kent and Sussex*, p.74.

227. *Kentish Weekly Post* or *Canterbury Journal* (Feb. 1741), British Newspaper Archive (Accessed 16/11/2021).

228 Waugh, *Smuggling in Kent and Sussex*, p.74.

229 CUST/148/12/561 TNA.

230 Jones, 'The Hawkhurst Gang: James (Alias Trip Stanford)', p.233.

231 CUST/148/12/667 TNA; Waugh, Smuggling in Kent and Sussex, p.75.

232 *Derby Mercury* (Oct. 1743), British Newspaper Archive (Accessed 22/11/2021).

233 'Warrants for Minor Appointments: 1735,' *Calendar of Treasury Books and Papers, Vol. 3, 1735–1738*, ed. William A. Shaw (London, 1900), pp.145–155, British History Online (Accessed 24/4/2021), www.british-history.ac.uk/cal-treasury-books-papers/vol3/pp145-155 (Accessed 25/4/2021); 'Warrants for Minor Appointments: 1736', *Calendar of Treasury Books and Papers, Vol. 3,*

1735–1738, ed. William A. Shaw (London: Her Majesty's Stationery Office, 1900), pp.282–291, British History Online (Accessed 24/4/2021), www.british-history.ac.uk/cal-treasury-books-papers/vol3/pp282-291 (Accessed 25/4/2021).

234 C. King and J. Stagg, *The True State of England*, 1734, p.118.

235 Old Bailey Proceedings Online (www.oldbaileyonline.org, version 8.0, 24 October 2021), April 1742, trial of John Bolton, alias Bolter (t17420428-46) (Accessed 28/10/2021).

236 'Warrants for the Payment of Money: 1742, January–March,' *Calendar of Treasury Books and Papers, Vol. 5, 1742–1745*, ed. William A. Shaw (London, 1903), pp.158–171, British History Online (Accessed 25/4/2021), www.british-history.ac.uk/cal-treasury-books-papers/vol5/pp158-171 (Accessed 4/25/2021).

237 'Warrants for Minor Appointments: 1740,' *Calendar of Treasury Books and Papers, Vol. 4, 1739–1741*, ed. William A Shaw (London: Her Majesty's Stationery Office, 1901), pp.419–433, British History Online (Accessed 25/4/2021), www.british-history.ac.uk/cal-treasury-books-papers/vol4/pp419-433 (Accessed 25/4/2021).

238 Record Transcription: Kent Baptisms, Thomas Quaif, findmypast.co.uk (Accessed 6/8/2022).

239 Old Bailey Proceedings Online (www.oldbaileyonline.org, version 8.0, 24 October 2021), April 1742, trial of John Bolton, alias Bolter (t17420428-46).

240 Commons, *Journals of the House of Commons*, p.104; CUA Ch(H), Political Papers, 41, 19.

241 CUST/148/12/647-648 TNA; Saville, *The Letters of John Collier*, p.xxxix.

242 CUST/148/12/647-648 TNA.

243 Saville, *The Letters of John Collier*, p.xxxix.

244 Ibid., pp.xxxiv, 272, 391.

245 Sussex – History of Parliament Online.

246 CUST/148/12/647-648 TNA.

247 Ibid.

248 Saville, *The Letters of John Collier*, pp.xxxix–xl; CUST/148/12/647-648 TNA.

249 CUST/148/12/647-648 TNA.

250 Saville, *The Letters of John Collier*, pp.xxxix, 274.

251 *Derby Mercury* (July 1744), British Newspaper Archive (Accessed 11/12/2021).

252 Ibid.

253 Winslow, Cal, *Sussex Smugglers*, p.141 In: Hay et al., *Albion's Fatal Tree*, p.141. Winslow citation indicates that Collier pleaded with Newcastle in 1747, but the matter was resolved by then. Given that Collier said that Grayling was in Newgate, Winslow must have been mistaken about the date, citing it as 1747 instead of 1744.

254 Saville, *The Letters of John Collier*, p.xl.

255 Gobert-Sergent, 'Pêche, course et contrebandiers', p.52.

256 *Stamford Mercury* (Nov. 1744), British Newspaper Archive (Accessed 11/12/2021).

257 CUST/148/12/673-675 TNA.

258 Ibid.

259 OBPO Ordinary of Newgate's Account, March 1752 (OA17520323).

260 CUST/148/12/673-675 TNA; OBPO Ordinary of Newgate's Account, March 1752 (OA17520323); *Stamford Mercury* (Nov. 1744), British Newspaper Archive (Accessed 20/12/2021).

261 CUST/148/12/673-675 TNA.

262 Ibid.

263 Ibid.

264 Ibid.

265 Ibid.

266 *Derby Mercury* (Nov. 1744), British Newspaper Archive (Accessed 23/12/2021); *Newcastle Courant* (Nov. 1744), British Newspaper Archive (Accessed 12/23/2021).

267 *Stamford Mercury* (Nov. 1744), British Newspaper Archive (Accessed 23/12/2021).

268 *Stamford Mercury* (Nov. 1744), British Newspaper Archive (Accessed 23/12/2021).

269 Old Bailey Proceedings Online (www.oldbaileyonline.org, version 8.0, 21 November 2020), December 1747, trial of Peter Tickner James Hodges, commonly called and known by the name of Poison (t17471209-52). (Accessed 26/11/2020).

270 T29/30/107 TNA.

271 OBPO trial of Peter Tickner, James Hodges (t17471209-52).

272 OBPO trial of Peter Tickner, James Hodges (t17471209-52); Old Bailey Proceedings Online (www.oldbaileyonline.org, version 8.0, 15 January 2022), Ordinary of Newgate's Account, July 1747 (OA17470729). (Accessed 15/1/2022).

273 OBPO trial of Peter Tickner, James Hodges (t17471209-52).

274 Ibid.

275 *Newcastle Courant* (Dec. 1744), British Newspaper Archive (Accessed 15/1/2022).

276 OBPO trial of Peter Tickner, James Hodges (t17471209-52).

277 Ibid.

278 Jones, 'The Hawkhurst Gang: The Trial and Tribulations of John Cook', p.715; OBPO Ordinary of Newgate's Account, July 1747 (OA17470729).

279 OBPO Ordinary of Newgate's Account, July 1747 (OA17470729).

280 Ibid.

281 OBPO trial of Peter Tickner, James Hodges (t17471209-52).

282 *Newcastle Courant* (Dec. 1744), British Newspaper Archive (Accessed 15/1/2022).283 OBPO Ordinary of Newgate's Account, March 1752 (OA17520323).

284 Ibid.

285 Ibid.

286 OBPO trial of Peter Tickner, James Hodges (t17471209-52).
287 Ibid.
288 Ibid.
289 Ibid.
290 OBPO trial of Peter Tickner, James Hodges (t17471209-52); OBPO Ordinary of Newgate's Account, March 1752 (OA17520323).
291 OBPO Ordinary of Newgate's Account, March 1752 (OA17520323).
292 Jones, 'A Lucky Escape', pp.563–564.
293 Ibid., p.564.
294 *Derby Mercury* (Jan. 1745), British Newspaper Archive (Accessed 15/1/2022).
295 *Newcastle Courant* (Dec. 1744), British Newspaper Archive (Accessed 15/1/2022).
296 *Ipswich Journal* (Dec. 1744), British Newspaper Archive (Accessed 15/1/2022).
297 G. Murray, *A Particular Account of the Battle of Culloden … In a letter from an officer of the Highland army* [i.e. Lord George Murray], *to his friend at London*, T. Warner, 1749, pp.16–18.
298 *Derby Mercury* (Jan. 1745), British Newspaper Archive (Accessed 15/1/2022).
299 Muskett, 'Aspects of English Smuggling in the Eighteenth Century', pp.340–342.
300 T29/30/101 TNA.
301 T29/30/106 TNA; T27/26/158 TNA.
302 *Derby Mercury* (Feb. 1745), British Newspaper Archive (Accessed 17/1/2022).
303 *Newcastle Courant* (Feb. 1745), British Newspaper Archive (Accessed 17/1/2022).
304 *Derby Mercury* (June 1745), British Newspaper Archive (Accessed 17/1/2022).
305 *Stamford Mercury* (Feb. 1745), British Newspaper Archive (Accessed 15/1/2022).
306 *Stamford Mercury* (Apr. 1745), British Newspaper Archive (Accessed 19/1/2022).
307 *Derby Mercury* (Apr. 1745), British Newspaper Archive (Accessed 17/1/2022).
308 *The Gentleman's Magazine* (London, England). v. 15, F. Jefferies, 1745, p.205.
309 *Newcastle Courant* (Feb. 1745), British Newspaper Archive (Accessed 17/1/2022).
310 *Derby Mercury* (Feb. 1745), British Newspaper Archive (Accessed 17/1/2022).
311 Dan Bogart, 'Political party representation and electoral politics in England and Wales, 1690–1747', *Social Science History* 40.2 (2016), pp.271–303.
312 Ibid., p.271.
313 F.J. McLynn, 'Issues and Motives in the Jacobite Rising of 1745', *The Eighteenth Century* 23.2 (1982), pp.97–133.
314 Ibid., p.99.
315 Tombs and Tombs, *That Sweet Enemy*, p.38.
316 SAY/87 ESRO.
317 Tombs and Tombs, *That Sweet Enemy*, pp.39–40.
318 Saville, *The Letters of John Collier*, p.320.
319 McCann et al., *The Correspondence of the Dukes of Richmond and Newcastle*, p.197.

320 Ibid.
321 *Caledonian Mercury* (Dec. 1745), British Newspaper Archive (Accessed 19/1/2022).
322 Saville, *The Letters of John Collier*, p.320.
323 Ibid., p.320.
324 SP/36/77/2/151 TNA.
325 SP/36/77/2/159-160 TNA.
326 Saville, *The Letters of John Collier*, p.327.
327 SAY/87 ESRO. This document is hard to read, but it seems that Jockey Tom was involved in calling the constable, at least according to Collier's investigation.
328 Saville, *The Letters of John Collier*, pp.32 –329.
329 Ibid., p.329.
330 Ibid., p.332.
331 Bishopp, Sir Cecil, 6th Bt. (d.1778), of Parham, Suss., History of Parliament Online.
332 SAY/85 ESRO; SAY/87 ESRO.
333 Saville, *The Letters of John Collier*, p.329.
334 McCann et al., *The Correspondence of the Dukes of Richmond and Newcastle*, p.206.
335 Ibid., pp.xxxi–xxxii.
336 Ibid., p.202.
337 Hay et al., *Albion's Fatal Tree*, p.157.
338 *Newcastle Courant* (Mar. 1746), British Newspaper Archive (Accessed 20/11/2022).
339 *Caledonian Mercury* (1746), British Newspaper Archive (Accessed 26/5/2022).
340 *Newcastle Courant* (Feb. 1746), British Newspaper Archive (Accessed 21/1/2022).
341 Commons, *Journals of the House of Commons*, p.101.
342 Ibid., p.102.
343 Ibid., p.102.
344 Ibid., p.103.
345 Ibid., pp.103–104.
346 Ibid., p.104.
347 Ibid., p.105.
348 Ibid., p.102.
349 Ibid., p.103.
350 Ibid., p.104.
351 Ibid., p.105.
352 Ibid., p.105.
353 *Caledonian Mercury* (Feb. 1746), British Newspaper Archive (Accessed 20/1/2022).
354 *Kentish Weekly Post or Canterbury Journal* (Jan. 1746), British Newspaper Archive (Accessed 20/1/2022).
355 Commons, *Journals of the House of Commons*, p.106.
356 Ibid., p.105.

357 Ibid., p.106.

358 Ibid., p.106.

359 Ibid., p.109.

360 Ibid., p.110.

361 Walpole, *The Yale Edition of Horace Walpole's Correspondence*, p.272.

362 Commons, *Journals of the House of Commons*, pp.116, 130, 133, 164, 176, 177.

363 *Derby Mercury* (1746), British Newspaper Archive (Accessed 26/5/2022).

364 *Derby Mercury* (Mar. 1746), British Newspaper Archive (Accessed 20/1/2022).

365 Hay et al., *Albion's Fatal Tree*, p.155.

366 'Memorandum of Lieutenant William Higginson, General Evans Regiment of Dragoons to the Lords Commissioners of HM's Treasury', *Catalogue of the manuscripts in the Library of the Inner Temple*, ed. Conway Davies. Typed transcript provided by Paul Muskett, pp.394–413.

367 *Derby Mercury* (Apr. 1746), British Newspaper Archive (Accessed 20/1/2022); *Kentish Weekly Post* or *Canterbury Journal* (May 1746), British Newspaper Archive (Accessed 20/1/2022).

368 *Kentish Weekly Post* or *Canterbury Journal* (Apr. 1746), British Newspaper Archive (Accessed 20/1/2022).

369 OBPO Ordinary of Newgate's Account, March 1752 (OA17520323).

370 Ibid.

371 *Anno Regni Georgii II, Regis Magnae Britanniae, Franciae, & Hiberniae, Decimo Nono: At the Parliament Begun and Holden at Westminster, the First Day of December, Anno Dom. 1741, in the Fifteenth Year of the Reign of Our Sovereign Lord, George the Second ... And from Thence Continued by Several Prorogations to the Seventeenth Day of October, 1745, Being the Fifth Session of this Present Parliament. Thomas Baskett, printer to the King, and by the assigns of Robert Baskett*, 1745, p.530.

372 Hay et al., *Albion's Fatal Tree*, p.134.

373 *Anno Regni Georgii II*, p.531.

374 Ibid., pp.535–536.

375 Ibid., pp.537–538.

376 Ibid., p.540.

377 *Stamford Mercury* (Sept. 1746), British Newspaper Archive (Accessed 23/1/2022).

378 Muskett, 'Gabriel Tomkins Smuggler ...', p.22.

379 *Stamford Mercury* (Sept. 1746), British Newspaper Archive (Accessed 23/1/2022).

380 Ryder, Dudley (1691–1756), of Tooting, Surr., History of Parliament Online (Accessed 1/1/2021).

381 Ibid.

382 Murray, Hon. William (1705–93), of Ken Wood, Mdx, History of Parliament Online (Accessed 6/1/2021).

383 Ibid.

384 Jones, 'General Sturt, Part 1', p.364.

385 *Derby Mercury* (Apr. 1747), British Newspaper Archive (Accessed 21/1/2022).

386 Ibid.
387 Jones, 'General Sturt, Part 1', p.360.
388 Derby Mercury (Apr. 1747), British Newspaper Archive (Accessed 21/1/2022).
389 Ibid.
390 Jones, 'General Sturt, Part 1', p.362.
391 Ibid., p.361.
392 *Ipswich Journal* (1746), British Newspaper Archive (Accessed 27/9/2022).
393 *Derby Mercury* (Apr. 1747), British Newspaper Archive (Accessed 21/1/2022).
394 *Stamford Mercury* (Nov. 1746), British Newspaper Archive (Accessed 21/1/2022).
395 *Derby Mercury* (Mar. 1747), British Newspaper Archive (Accessed 21/1/2022).
396 *Derby Mercury* (Jan. 1747), British Newspaper Archive (Accessed 21/1/2022); *Derby Mercury* (Feb. 1747), British Newspaper Archive (Accessed 21/1/2022).
397 Jones, 'The Battle of Wingham: The Beginning of the End for the Hawkhurst Gang', pp.161–163.
398 Muskett, 'Gabriel Tomkins Smuggler …', p.23.
399 Jones, 'The Battle of Wingham: The Beginning of the End for the Hawkhurst Gang', p.165.
400 *Kentish Weekly Post* or *Canterbury Journal* (Apr. 1747), British Newspaper Archive (Accessed 21/1/2022); OBPO Ordinary of Newgate's Account, August 1749 (OA17490804).
401 Jones, 'The Battle of Wingham: The Beginning of the End for the Hawkhurst Gang', p.165.
402 OBPO Ordinary of Newgate's Account, August 1749 (OA17490804).
403 OBPO Ordinary of Newgate's Account, July 1747 (OA17470729).
404 *Derby Mercury* (Apr. 1747), British Newspaper Archive (Accessed 21/1/2022).
405 OBPO Ordinary of Newgate's Account, August 1749 (OA17490804).
406 OBPO Ordinary of Newgate's Account, July 1747 (OA17470729).
407 *London Gazette*, 'Page 2', Iss. 8632, 14 April 1747, www.thegazette.co.uk/London/issue/8632/page/2 (Accessed 24/1/2022).
408 *Kentish Weekly Post* or *Canterbury Journal* (July 1747), British Newspaper Archive (Accessed 24/1/2022); *Derby Mercury* (Nov. 1747), British Newspaper Archive (Accessed 24/1/2022).
409 Old Bailey Proceedings Online (www.oldbaileyonline.org, version 8.0, 3 November 2020), July 1747, trial of John Cook (t17470715-1). (Accessed 8/11/2020).
410 Ibid.
411 Ibid.
412 Ibid.
413 SP/36/97/0142-0152 [Check Folios] TNA.
414 Old Bailey Proceedings Online (www.oldbaileyonline.org, version 8.0, 24 January 2022), October 1747, trial of John Harvey (t17471014-6). (Accessed 8/11/2020).

415 OBPO trial of John Cook (t17470715-1); Muskett, 'Soliciting for Profit', p.430.
416 OBPO trial of John Cook (t17470715-1).
417 Ibid.
418 Ibid.
419 Ibid.
420 Ibid.
421 Ibid.
422 Ibid.
423 Jones, 'The Hawkhurst Gang: The Gray Brothers', p.668.
424 OBPO Ordinary of Newgate's Account, July 1747 (OA17470729).
425 Ibid.
426 *Derby Mercury* (Nov. 1747), British Newspaper Archive (Accessed 24/1/2022).
427 Ordinary of Newgate's Accounts (Accessed 29/9/2022).
428 OBPO trial of John Cook (t17470715-1).
429 Ibid.
430 Old Bailey Proceedings Online (www.oldbaileyonline.org, version 8.0, 25 January 2022), October 1747, trial of Peter Lickner (t17471014-2). (Accessed 26/11/2020).
431 *Ipswich Journal* (May 1747), British Newspaper Archive (Accessed 21/1/2022); *Kentish Weekly Post* or *Canterbury Journal* (June 1747), British Newspaper Archive (Accessed 21/1/2022).
432 *Ipswich Journal* (May 1747), British Newspaper Archive (Accessed 21/1/2022).
433 W. Tutty, *The Want of a Religious Education and Keeping Bad Company, Destructive to Virtuous Principles. A Sermon Preach'd the 20th of March, the Sunday Before the Conviction of Two Convicts, Viz. Thomas Bibby, for Robbing the Chester Mail, and Thomas Flack, for Robbery Upon the Highway, to which is Added, Their Life and Confession, with a particular Account of their Behaviour from the Time of their Condemnation, to that of their Execution*, H. Kent, 1747, p.42; *Derby Mercury* (July 1747), British Newspaper Archive (Accessed 25/1/2022); *London Gazette*, 'Page 2', Iss. 8660, 21 July 1747 (undefined), British Newspaper Archive (Accessed 25/1/2022).
434 Tutty, *A Sermon Preached*, p.42.
435 OBPO Ordinary of Newgate's Account, March 1752 (OA17520323).
436 Ibid.
437 Tutty, *A Sermon Preached*, p.43.
438 Ibid.
439 Ibid.
440 OBPO Ordinary of Newgate's Account, March 1752 (OA17520323).
441 *Derby Mercury* (July 1747), British Newspaper Archive (Accessed 25/1/2022).
442 *London Gazette*, 'Page 2', Iss. 8660, 21 July 1747, www.thegazette.co.uk/London/issue/8660/page/1. (Accessed 21/1/2022).
443 *London Gazette*, 'Page 3', Iss. 8660, 21 July 1747, www.thegazette.co.uk/London/issue/8660/page/1. (Accessed 21/1/2022).
444 SAY/298 ESRO.

445 Ibid.
446 Tim Browning, *The Militiamen*. From materials provided by the Cranbrook Museum.
447 SAY/298 ESRO.
448 SAY/296 ESRO; SAY/297 ESRO.
449 SAY/296 ESRO.
450 *Ipswich Journal* (May 1747), British Newspaper Archive (Accessed 21/1/2022).
451 SAY/298 ESRO.
452 Ibid.
453 Ibid.
454 SAY/299 ESRO.
455 SAY/300 ESRO.
456 Old Bailey Proceedings Online (www.oldbaileyonline.org, version 8.0, 26 January 2022), September 1747, trial of Thomas Puryour, otherwise called and known by the Name of Blacktooth (t17470909-36) (Accessed 26/1/2022).
457 Ibid.
458 OBPO trial of Thomas Fuller (t17471014-4).
459 Muskett, 'Soliciting for Profit', p.429.
460 Ibid., p.430.
461 SAY/307 ESRO.
462 OBPO trial of Thomas Fuller (t17471014-4).
463 Ibid.
464 Ibid.
465 Ibid.
466 Jones, 'The Hawkhurst Gang: Thomas Fuller', pp.308–309.
467 OBPO trial of Thomas Fuller (t17471014-4).
468 Ibid.
469 OBPO trial of Peter Tickner (t17471014-2).
470 OBPO trial of Peter Tickner, James Hodges (t17471209-52).
471 Ibid.
472 SAY/304 ESRO.
473 Ibid.
474 Ibid.
475 Old Bailey Proceedings Online (www.oldbaileyonline.org, version 8.0, 26 January 2022), December 1747, trial of Samuel Austin (t17471209-55) (Accessed 26/1/2022).
476 Ibid.
477 SAY/304 ESRO.
478 Ibid.
479 Ibid.
480 OBPO trial of Samuel Austin (t17471209-55).
481 Ibid.
482 SAY/307 ESRO.
483 OBPO trial of Samuel Austin (t17471209-55).

484 SAY/304 ESRO.
485 SAY/307 ESRO.
486 OBPO trial of Samuel Austin (t17471209-55).
487 SAY/304 ESRO.
488 OBPO trial of Samuel Austin (t17471209-55).
489 SAY/301 ESRO.
490 SAY/302 ESRO.
491 Ibid.
492 *Derby Mercury* (Oct. 1747), British Newspaper Archive (Accessed 26/1/2022).
493 Ibid.
494 SAY/308 ESRO.
495 Ibid.
496 Ibid.
497 SAY/305 ESRO.
498 SAY/313 ESRO.
499 SAY/314 ESRO.
500 Ibid.
501 SAY/317 ESRO.
502 SAY/318 ESRO.
503 OBPO Ordinary of Newgate's Account, March 1752 (OA17520323); SAY/320 ESRO.
504 Jones, 'The Hawkhurst Gang: The Gray Brothers', p.669; SAY/320 ESRO.
505 SAY/319 ESRO.
506 SAY/321 ESRO.
507 Old Bailey Proceedings Online (www.oldbaileyonline.org, version 8.0, 27 January 2022), April 1748, trial of Arthur Gray (t17480420-23) (Accessed 27/1/2020).
508 SAY/325 ESRO.
509 OBPO Ordinary of Newgate's Account, May 1748 (OA17480511).
510 Jones, 'The Hawkhurst Gang: The Gray Brothers', pp.671–673.
511 *Kentish Weekly Post* or *Canterbury Journal* (Dec. 1748), British Newspaper Archive (Accessed 28/1/2022).
512 A Gentleman of Chichester, *A Full and Genuine History of the Inhuman and Unparrallell'd Murders of Mr William Galley, A Customs House Officer at the Port of Southampton: and Mr Daniel Chater, a Shoemaker at Fordingbridge in Hampshire.* 1779, pp.42–43; Jones, 'The Hawkhurst Gang: A Winter's Tale', p.662.
513 Jones, 'The Hawkhurst Gang: A Winter's Tale', p.663.
514 Chichester, *A Full and Genuine History*, p.1.
515 Old Bailey Proceedings Online (www.oldbaileyonline.org, version 8.0, 27 January 2022), April 1749, trial of Thomas Kingsmill, alias Staymaker William Fairall, alias Shepherd Richard Perin, alias Pain, alias Carpenter Thomas Lillewhite Richard Glover (t17490405-36). (Accessed 27/1/2020).
516 Ibid.
517 Ibid.
518 Ibid.

519 Ibid.
520 *Derby Mercury* (Oct. 1747), British Newspaper Archive (Accessed 27/1/2022).
521 Ibid.
522 Chichester, *A Full and Genuine History*, p.2.
523 *Derby Mercury* (Oct. 1747), British Newspaper Archive (Accessed 28/1/2022).
524 *Derby Mercury* (Oct. 1747), British Newspaper Archive (Accessed 26/1/2022).
525 Chichester, *A Full and Genuine History*, p.3.
526 Ibid., pp.3–8.
527 Ibid., pp.9–30.
528 Ibid., pp.9–30.
529 *Derby Mercury* (Oct. 1748), British Newspaper Archive (Accessed 28/1/2022).
530 McCann et al., *The Correspondence of the Dukes of Richmond and Newcastle*, p.xxxi.
531 Ibid., p.276.
532 Browning, *The Militiamen*.
533 McCann et al., *The Correspondence of the Dukes of Richmond and Newcastle*, p.277.
534 WSRO, Goodwood Ms. 155.
535 Ibid.
536 Chichester, *A Full and Genuine History*, pp.37–41.
537 WSRO, Goodwood Ms. 155.
538 SAY/308 ESRO.
539 WSRO, Goodwood Ms. 155.
540 Ibid.
541 Ibid.
542 Ibid.
543 Ibid.
544 Ibid.
545 Ibid.
546 Ibid.
547 McCann et al., *The Correspondence of the Dukes of Richmond and Newcastle*, pp.277–278; WSRO, Goodwood Ms. 155.
548 McCann et al., *The Correspondence of the Dukes of Richmond and Newcastle*, pp.277–278.
549 WSRO, Goodwood Ms. 155.
550 WSRO, Goodwood Ms. 155; Hay et al., *Albion's Fatal Tree*, p.146.
551 WSRO, Goodwood Ms. 155.
552 *Ipswich Journal* (1746), British Newspaper Archive (Accessed 22/8/2022); M. Foster, *A Report of Some Proceedings on the Commission of Oyer and Terminer and Goal Delivery for the Trial of the Rebels in the Year 1746 in the County of Surry*, Sarah Cotter, 1767, pp.2, 249.
553 McCann et al., *The Correspondence of the Dukes of Richmond and Newcastle*, pp.278–279.
554 Ibid., p.281.

555 WSRO, Goodwood Ms. 154.
556 Ibid.
557 WSRO, Goodwood Ms. 155.
558 Ibid.
559 Ibid.
560 Ibid.
561 Ibid.
562 Ibid.
563 Ibid.
564 Ibid.
565 Chichester, *A Full and Genuine History*, pp.46–47.
566 Ibid., pp.47–49.
567 Ibid., p.315. This is a document of the sermon that is included in the scanned copy in Google Books. The actual pamphlet page is 25.
568 Ibid., p.49.
569 Ibid., pp.49–150.
570 Ibid., p.151.
571 *A Free Apology in Behalf of the Smugglers, So Far as Their Case Affects the Constitution*. anonymous pamphlet, 1749, p.18.
572 McCann et al., *The Correspondence of the Dukes of Richmond and Newcastle*, p.281.
573 John Bishop, 'The Strange Case of Thomas Lillywhite – Was He a Smuggler?', *The Sussex Family Historian* 4.9 (1981), p.283.
574 Walpole, *The Yale Edition of Horace Walpole's Correspondence*, v. 35, p.300.
575 WSRO, Goodwood Ms. 155.
576 Ibid.
577 Ibid.
578 Ibid.
579 Great Britain, Parliament, House of Commons and J. Almon, *The Debates and Proceedings of the British House of Commons 1743–74,* vol. 1746–1749; *The Debates and Proceedings of the British House of Commons 1743–74* J. Almon and S. Bladon, 1770, p.263.
580 *The Scots Magazine* (1745), British Newspaper Archive (Accessed 6/8/2022), This is a larger version of the same article excerpted from the 1745 *Gentleman's Magazine*, with additional commentary. I have not been able to find a copy of the original, p.179.
581 WSRO, Goodwood Ms. 155.
582 WSRO, Goodwood Ms. 154.
583 WSRO, Goodwood Ms. 155.
584 SAY/326 ESRO.
585 Chichester, *A Full and Genuine History*, p.205.
586 Ibid., pp.172–180.
587 Ibid., pp.208–210.
588 Ibid., p.205.

589 Old Bailey Proceedings Online (www.oldbaileyonline.org, version 8.0, 29 September 2022), January 1748, trial of Thomas Kemp (t17480115-29). (Accessed 29/9/2020).

590 Chichester, *A Full and Genuine History*, pp.201–203.

591 Ibid., p.223.

592 Ibid., pp.224–230.

593 Ibid., p.242.

594 OBPO trial of Thomas Kingsmill, William Fairall, Richard Perin, Thomas Lillewhite, Richard Glover (t17490405-36); Chichester, *A Full and Genuine History*, pp.236–254.

595 OBPO trial of Thomas Kingsmill, William Fairall, Richard Perin, Thomas Lillewhite, Richard Glover (t17490405-36); Chichester, *A Full and Genuine History*, pp.254–260.

596 OBPO trial of Thomas Kingsmill, William Fairall, Richard Perin, Thomas Lillewhite, Richard Glover (t17490405-36); Chichester, *A Full and Genuine History*, pp.258–259.

597 OBPO trial of Thomas Kingsmill, William Fairall, Richard Perin, Thomas Lillewhite, Richard Glover (t17490405-36); Chichester, *A Full and Genuine History*, pp.258–259.

598 Chichester, *A Full and Genuine History*, p.259.

599 OBPO trial of Thomas Kingsmill, William Fairall, Richard Perin, Thomas Lillewhite, Richard Glover (t17490405-36); Chichester, *A Full and Genuine History*, p.259.

600 Chichester, *A Full and Genuine History*, pp.260–261.

601 Old Bailey Proceedings Online (www.oldbaileyonline.org, version 8.0, 10 July 2022), Ordinary of Newgate's Account, April 1749 (OA17490426), www.oldbaileyonline.org/browse.jsp?div=OA17490426 (Accessed 10/7/2022).

602 McCann et al., *The Correspondence of the Dukes of Richmond and Newcastle*, p.286. McCann identifies the subject of this letter in a footnote as William Fairall. However, due to the date of the letter, it is Richard Mapesden who was tried twice at the Old Bailey in 1749, once in April for failing to appear, and once in July for the Reculver run.

603 Hay et al., *Albion's Fatal Tree*, p.164.

604 SP/36/112/2/50-51 TNA.

605 Hay et al., *Albion's Fatal Tree*, p.165.

606 *Derby Mercury* (1749), British Newspaper Archive (Accessed 10/7/2022).

607 *Derby Mercury* (1750), British Newspaper Archive (Accessed 10/7/2022).

608 Platt, *Smuggling in the British Isles: A History*, p.131.

609 Hay et al., *Albion's Fatal Tree*, p.157.

610 WSRO, Goodwood Ms. 155.

611 E. Cave, *The Gentleman's Magazine*, Early English newspapers v. 23, E. Cave, jun. at St John's Gate, 1753, p.99.

612 *Derby Mercury* (1753), British Newspaper Archive (Accessed 10/8/2022).

613 Notes on TNA PRO 11/865/147 provided courtesy of the Cranbrook Museum; *Sussex Advertiser* (1760), British Newspaper Archive (Accessed 13/7/2022).
614 Walpole, *The Yale Edition of Horace Walpole's Correspondence*, v. 35, p.137.
615 Ibid., vol. 9, pp.105–106.
616 Ibid., vol. 9, p.110.

BIBLIOGRAPHY

1911 Encyclopædia Britannica/Newcastle, Dukes of, Wikisource, *the free online library,* en.wikisource.org/wiki/1911_Encyclop\ per centC3\ per centA6dia_ Britannica/Newcastle,_Dukes_of (Accessed 11/9/2021).

An Universal History, from the Earliest Account of Time, v. 29, T. Osborne, 1759, books.google.co.uk/books?id=k35w37N4Gg8C.

Anno Regni Georgii II, Regis Magnae Britanniae, Franciae, & Hiberniae, Decimo Nono: At the Parliament Begun and Holden at Westminster, the First Day of December, Anno Dom. 1741, in the Fifteenth Year of the Reign of Our Sovereign Lord, George the Second … And from Thence Continued by Several Prorogations to the Seventeenth Day of October, 1745, Being the Fifth Session of this Present Parliament. Thomas Baskett, printer to the King, and by the assigns of Robert Baskett, 1745, books.google. co.uk/books?id=Xxc2AQAAMAAJ.

Bogart, Dan, 'Political party representation and electoral politics in England and Wales, 1690–1747', *Social Science History* 40.2 (2016), pp.271–303.

Browning, Tim, *The Militiamen.* From materials provided by the Cranbrook Museum.

Cockburn, James S., 'Patterns of violence in English society: homicide in Kent 1560–1985', *Past & Present* 130 (1991), pp.70–106.

'Memorandum of Lieutenant William Higginson, General Evans Regiment of Dragoons to the Lords Commissioners of HM's Treasury', *Catalogue of the manuscripts in the Library of the Inner Temple.* ed. Conway Davies. Typed transcript provided by Paul Muskett, pp.394–413.

Gobert-Sergent, Yann, 'Pêche, course et contrebandiers: le port de Boulogne de Louis XIV à Napoléon Ier (1680–1815)', PhD thesis, ACRB Éd., 2004.

Hay, Douglas et al., *Albion's Fatal Tree: Crime and Society in Eighteenth-Century England,* Pantheon Books, 1975.

Hunnisett, Roy Frank, *East Sussex Coroners' Records 1688–1838,* Vol. 89, Steve Parish, 2005.

Jones, Henry, 'A Lucky Escape', *Bygone Kent* 20 (2000), pp.560–565.
— 'The Battle of Wingham: The Beginning of the End for the Hawkhurst Gang', *Bygone Kent* 22 (2002), pp.161–167.
— 'The Enigma of "General" Sturt and the Battle of Goudhurst – 1747 (Part 1)', *Bygone Kent* 20 (2000), pp.358–365.
— 'The Enigma of "General" Sturt and the Battle of Goudhurst – 1747 (Part 2)', *Bygone Kent* 20 (2000), pp.392–400.
— 'The Hawkhurst Gang: A Winter's Tale', *Bygone Kent* 21 (2001), pp.659–666.
— 'The Hawkhurst Gang: James (Alias Trip Stanford)', *Bygone Kent* 24 (2004), pp.230–237.
— 'The Hawkhurst Gang: The Gray Brothers', *Bygone Kent* 20 (2000), pp.667–673.
— 'The Hawkhurst Gang: The Trial and Tribulations of John Cook', *Bygone Kent* 20 (2000), pp.711–718.
— 'The Hawkhurst Gang: Thomas Fuller', *Bygone Kent* 21 (2001), pp.304–309.
Jurado Sánchez, José, 'Military expenditure, spending capacity and budget constraint in eighteenth-century Spain and Britain', *Revista de Historia Económica, Journal of Iberian and Latin American Economic History* 27.1 (2009), pp.141–174.
Langford, Paul et al., *The Excise Crisis: Society and Politics in the Age of Walpole*, Oxford, Clarendon Press, 1975.
McCann, Timothy J. et al., *The Correspondence of the Dukes of Richmond and Newcastle, 1724–1750*, Vol. 73, Sussex Record Society, 1984.
McLynn, F.J., 'Issues and Motives in the Jacobite Rising of 1745', *The Eighteenth Century* 23.2 (1982), pp.97–133.
Morieux, Renaud, *The Channel: England, France and the construction of a maritime border in the eighteenth century*, Vol. 23, Cambridge University Press, 2016.
Muskett, Paul, 'Gabriel Tomkins Smuggler, Customs Officer, Sheriff's Bailif and Highwayman, Part 2', *Sussex History* 1, 2 (1981–82). Typewritten copy supplied by author.
— 'Military operations against smuggling in Kent and Sussex, 1698–1750', *Journal of the Society for Army Historical Research* 52.210 (1974), pp.89–110.
— 'Soliciting for Profit', *Criminal Law and Justice Weekly* 179 (June 2015). Supplied by author.
— 'What was the Ordinary of Newgate?', *Open History* 139.36. Microsoft Word document supplied by author.
Notes on TNA PRO 11/865/147 provided courtesy of the Cranbrook Museum.
Saville, Richard, *The Letters of John Collier of Hastings, 1731–1746*, 2016.
Tombs, Robert and Isabelle Tombs, *That Sweet Enemy: The French and the British from the Sun King to the present*, Random House, 2007.
Walpole, Horace, *The Yale Edition of Horace Walpole's Correspondence*, Yale University Press, 1937.
Waugh, Mary, *Smuggling in Kent and Sussex 1700–1840*, Countryside Books, 1985.
Williams, Basil, 'The Duke of Newcastle and the Election of 1734', *English Historical Review* (1897), pp.448–488.

BIBLIOGRAPHY

Williamson, James Alexander, *The English Channel: A History*, World Publishing Company, 1959.

Xambo, Jean-Baptiste, 'Servitude et droits de transmission. La condition des galériens de Louis XIV', *Revue dhistoire moderne contemporaine* 2 (2017), pp.157–183.

Newspaper Archives

Caledonian Mercury (Apr. 1732), British Newspaper Archive (Accessed 9/9/2021), www.britishnewspaperarchive.co.uk/viewer/bl/0000045/17320406/004/0003.

Caledonian Mercury (Apr. 1733), British Newspaper Archive (Accessed 20/6/2021), www.britishnewspaperarchive.co.uk/viewer/bl/0000045/17330402/006/0003.

Ipswich Journal (Sept. 1733), British Newspaper Archive (Accessed 11/7/2021), www.britishnewspaperarchive.co.uk/viewer/BL/0000191/17330908/005/0003

Ipswich Journal (Dec. 1733), British Newspaper Archive (Accessed 30/5/2021), www.britishnewspaperarchive.co.uk/viewer/bl/0000191/17331215/004/0002.

Newcastle Courant (Dec. 1733), British Newspaper Archive (Accessed 21/7/2021), www.britishnewspaperarchive.co.uk/viewer/bl/0000085/17331208/007/0002.

Caledonian Mercury (May 1734), British Newspaper Archive (Accessed 30/5/2021), www.britishnewspaperarchive.co.uk/viewer/bl/0000045/17340523/002/0001.

Derby Mercury (Feb. 1736), British Newspaper Archive (Accessed 17/8/2021), www.britishnewspaperarchive.co.uk/viewer/BL/0000189/17360203/004/0001

Newcastle Courant (Feb. 1737), British Newspaper Archive (Accessed 17/8/2021), www.britishnewspaperarchive.co.uk/viewer/bl/0000085/17370205/006/0001.

Stamford Mercury (June 1738), British Newspaper Archive (Accessed 17/8/2021), www.britishnewspaperarchive.co.uk/viewer/bl/0000254/17380608/002/0002.

Derby Mercury (May 1740), British Newspaper Archive (Accessed 22/8/2021), www.britishnewspaperarchive.co.uk/viewer/bl/0000189/17400529/015/0004.

Stamford Mercury (1741), British Newspaper Archive (Accessed 10/1//2021), www.britishnewspaperarchive.co.uk/viewer/bl/0000254/17410122/008/0004.

Kentish Weekly Post or *Canterbury Journal* (Feb. 1741), British Newspaper Archive (Accessed 16/11/2021), www.britishnewspaperarchive.co.uk/viewer/BL/0003200/17410221/007/0004.

Derby Mercury (Oct. 1743), British Newspaper Archive (Accessed 22/11/2021), www.britishnewspaperarchive.co.uk/viewer/bl/0000189/17431013/004/0001.

Derby Mercury (July 1744), British Newspaper Archive (Accessed 11/12/2021), www.britishnewspaperarchive.co.uk/viewer/BL/0000189/17440727/007/0001

Stamford Mercury (Nov. 1744), British Newspaper Archive (Accessed 11/12/2021), www.britishnewspaperarchive.co.uk/viewer/BL/0000254/17441115/003/0002

Stamford Mercury (Nov. 1744), British Newspaper Archive (Accessed 20/12/2021), www.britishnewspaperarchive.co.uk/viewer/bl/0000254/17441122/005/0002.

Derby Mercury (Nov. 1744), British Newspaper Archive (Accessed 23/12/2021), www.britishnewspaperarchive.co.uk/viewer/bl/0000189/17441116/004/0001.

Newcastle Courant (Nov. 1744), British Newspaper Archive (Accessed 23/12/2021), www.britishnewspaperarchive.co.uk/viewer/bl/0000085/17441117/010/0002.

Stamford Mercury (Nov. 1744), British Newspaper Archive (Accessed 23/12/2021), www.britishnewspaperarchive.co.uk/viewer/bl/0000254/17441115/005/0003.

Stamford Mercury (Nov. 1744), British Newspaper Archive (Accessed 23/12/2021), www.britishnewspaperarchive.co.uk/viewer/bl/0000254/17441129/004/0002.

Newcastle Courant (Dec. 1744), British Newspaper Archive (Accessed 15/1/2022), www.britishnewspaperarchive.co.uk/viewer/BL/0000085/17441222/004/0001

Ipswich Journal (Dec. 1744), British Newspaper Archive (Accessed 15/1/2022), www.britishnewspaperarchive.co.uk/viewer/BL/0000191/17441229/004/0001

Derby Mercury (Jan. 1745), British Newspaper Archive (Accessed 15/1/2022), www.britishnewspaperarchive.co.uk/viewer/BL/0000189/17450104/010/0003

Derby Mercury (Feb. 1745), British Newspaper Archive (Accessed 17/1/2022), www.britishnewspaperarchive.co.uk/viewer/bl/0000189/17450208/016/0004.

Newcastle Courant (Feb. 1745), British Newspaper Archive (Accessed 17/1/2022), www.britishnewspaperarchive.co.uk/viewer/bl/0000085/17450223/010/0002.

Derby Mercury (June 1745), British Newspaper Archive (Accessed 17/1/2022), www.britishnewspaperarchive.co.uk/viewer/bl/0000189/17450607/006/0002.

Stamford Mercury (Feb. 1745), British Newspaper Archive (Accessed 15/1/2022), www.britishnewspaperarchive.co.uk/viewer/BL/0000254/17450214/005/0002

Stamford Mercury (Apr. 1745), British Newspaper Archive (Accessed 19/1/2022), www.britishnewspaperarchive.co.uk/viewer/bl/0000254/17450411/005/0003.

Derby Mercury (Apr. 1745). British Newspaper Archive (Accessed 17/1/2022), www.britishnewspaperarchive.co.uk/viewer/bl/0000189/17450419/011/0003.

Caledonian Mercury (Dec. 1745), British Newspaper Archive (Accessed 19/1/2022), www.britishnewspaperarchive.co.uk/viewer/bl/0000045/17451224/006/0003.

The Scots Magazine (1745). British Newspaper Archive (Accessed 6/8/2022), This is a larger version of the same article excerpted in the 1745 *Gentleman's Magazine*, with additional commentary. I have not been able to find a copy of the original, www.britishnewspaperarchive.co.uk/viewer/BL/0000545/17450405/003/0027

Newcastle Courant (Mar. 1746), British Newspaper Archive (Accessed 20/1//2022), www.britishnewspaperarchive.co.uk/viewer/bl/0000085/17460301/007/0001.

Caledonian Mercury (1746), British Newspaper Archive (Accessed 26/5/2022), www.britishnewspaperarchive.co.uk/viewer/BL/0000045/17460207/008/0003

Newcastle Courant (Feb. 1746), British Newspaper Archive (Accessed 21/1/2022), www.britishnewspaperarchive.co.uk/viewer/bl/0000085/17460201/005/0001.

Caledonian Mercury (Feb. 1746), British Newspaper Archive (Accessed 20/1/2022), www.britishnewspaperarchive.co.uk/viewer/bl/0000045/17460204/003/0001.

Kentish Weekly Post or Canterbury Journal (Jan. 1746), British Newspaper Archive (Accessed 20/1/2022), www.britishnewspaperarchive.co.uk/viewer/ bl/0003200/17460129/018/0004.

Derby Mercury (1746), British Newspaper Archive (Accessed 26/5/2022), www.britishnewspaperarchive.co.uk/viewer/bl/0000189/17460627/013/0002.

Derby Mercury (1746), British Newspaper Archive (Accessed 26/5/2022), \
www.britishnewspaperarchive.co.uk/viewer/bl/0000189/17460620/016/0004.

Derby Mercury (Mar. 1746), British Newspaper Archive (Accessed 1/20/2022),
www.britishnewspaperarchive.co.uk/viewer/bl/0000189/17460328/021/0004.

Derby Mercury (Apr. 1746), British Newspaper Archive (Accessed 20/1/2022),
www.britishnewspaperarchive.co.uk/viewer/bl/0000189/17460418/013/0003.

Kentish Weekly Post or Canterbury Journal (May 1746), British Newspaper Archive
(Accessed 20/1/2022), www.britishnewspaperarchive.co.uk/viewer/
BL/0003200/17460531/006/0003.

Kentish Weekly Post or Canterbury Journal (Apr. 1746), British Newspaper
Archive (Accessed 20/1/2022), www.britishnewspaperarchive.co.uk/viewer/
bl/0003200/17460402/004/0002.

Stamford Mercury (Sept. 1746), British Newspaper Archive (Accessed 23/1/2022),
www.britishnewspaperarchive.co.uk/viewer/bl/0000254/17460904/004/0002.

Ipswich Journal (1746), British Newspaper Archive (Accessed 27/9/2022), www.
britishnewspaperarchive.co.uk/viewer/bl/0000191/17460712/002/0001.

Stamford Mercury (Nov. 1746), British Newspaper Archive (Accessed 21/1/2022),
www.britishnewspaperarchive.co.uk/viewer/bl/0000254/17461127/003/0002.

Ipswich Journal (1746), British Newspaper Archive (Accessed 22/8/2022),
www.britishnewspaperarchive.co.uk/viewer/bl/0000191/17460712/008/0002.

Derby Mercury (Apr. 1747), British Newspaper Archive (Accessed 21/1/2022),
www.britishnewspaperarchive.co.uk/viewer/bl/0000189/17470424/010/0003.

Derby Mercury (Apr. 1747), British Newspaper Archive (Accessed 21/1/2022),
www.britishnewspaperarchive.co.uk/viewer/bl/0000189/17470410/005/0001.

Derby Mercury (Mar. 1747), British Newspaper Archive (Accessed 21/1/2022),
www.britishnewspaperarchive.co.uk/viewer/bl/0000189/17470304/005/0001.

Derby Mercury (Jan. 1747), British Newspaper Archive (Accessed 21/1/2022),
www.britishnewspaperarchive.co.uk/viewer/bl/0000189/17470101/007/0003.

Derby Mercury (Jan. 1747), British Newspaper Archive (Accessed 21/1/2022),
www.britishnewspaperarchive.co.uk/viewer/bl/0000189/17470129/015/0004.

Derby Mercury (Feb. 1747), British Newspaper Archive (Accessed 21/1/2022),
www.britishnewspaperarchive.co.uk/viewer/bl/0000189/17470226/010/0003.

Kentish Weekly Post or Canterbury Journal (Apr. 1747), British Newspaper
Archive (Accessed 21/1/2022), www.britishnewspaperarchive.co.uk/viewer/
bl/0003200/17470401/005/0004.

Kentish Weekly Post or Canterbury Journal (July 1747), British Newspaper Archive
(Accessed 24/1/2022), www.britishnewspaperarchive.co.uk/viewer/
BL/0003200/17470701/005/0002.

Derby Mercury (Nov. 1747), British Newspaper Archive (Accessed 24/1/2022),
www.britishnewspaperarchive.co.uk/viewer/bl/0000189/17471127/008/0001.

Ipswich Journal (May 1747), British Newspaper Archive (Accessed 21/1/2022),
www.britishnewspaperarchive.co.uk/viewer/bl/0000191/17470530/011/0002.

Kentish Weekly Post or Canterbury Journal (June 1747), British Newspaper
Archive (Accessed 21/1/2022), www.britishnewspaperarchive.co.uk/viewer/
bl/0003200/17470617/004/0003.

Derby Mercury (July 1747), British Newspaper Archive (Accessed 25/1/2022), www.britishnewspaperarchive.co.uk/viewer/bl/0000189/17470710/007/0002.

Derby Mercury (July 1747), British Newspaper Archive (Accessed 25/1/2022), www.britishnewspaperarchive.co.uk/viewer/bl/0000189/17470724/004/0002.

Ipswich Journal (May 1747), British Newspaper Archive (Accessed 21/1/2022), www.britishnewspaperarchive.co.uk/viewer/bl/0000191/17470530/004/0001.

Derby Mercury (Oct. 1747), British Newspaper Archive (Accessed 26/1/2022), www.britishnewspaperarchive.co.uk/viewer/bl/0000189/17471023/009/0003.

Derby Mercury (Oct. 1747), British Newspaper Archive (Accessed 27/1/2022), www.britishnewspaperarchive.co.uk/viewer/bl/0000189/17471009/015/0004.

Derby Mercury (Oct. 1747), British Newspaper Archive (Accessed 28/1/2022), www.britishnewspaperarchive.co.uk/viewer/bl/0000189/17471016/017/0004.

Kentish Weekly Post or *Canterbury Journal* (Dec. 1748), British Newspaper Archive (Accessed 28/1/2022), www.britishnewspaperarchive.co.uk/viewer/bl/0003200/17481231/004/0002#.

Derby Mercury (Oct. 1748), British Newspaper Archive (Accessed 28/1/2022), www.britishnewspaperarchive.co.uk/viewer/bl/0000189/17481014/002/0001.

Derby Mercury (1749), British Newspaper Archive (Accessed 10/7/2022), www.britishnewspaperarchive.co.uk/viewer/bl/0000189/17490112/008/0003.

Derby Mercury (1750), British Newspaper Archive (Accessed 10/7/2022), www.britishnewspaperarchive.co.uk/viewer/bl/0000189/17500323/006/0002.

Derby Mercury (1753), British Newspaper Archive (Accessed 10/8/2022), www.britishnewspaperarchive.co.uk/viewer/bl/0000189/17531019/009/0003.

Sussex Advertiser (1760), British Newspaper Archive (Accessed 13/7/2022), www.britishnewspaperarchive.co.uk/viewer/bl/0000260/17600721/009/0004.

Other Archives

CUA Ch(H), Political Papers, 41, 19.

CUST/148/12/561 TNA.

CUST/148/12/579-586 TNA.

CUST/148/12/605 TNA.

CUST/148/12/613 TNA.

CUST/148/12/629 TNA.

CUST/148/12/639 TNA.

CUST/148/12/647-648 TNA.

CUST/148/12/647-648 TNA.

CUST/148/12/667 TNA.

CUST/148/12/673-675 TNA.

CUST/148/12/681 TNA.

BIBLIOGRAPHY

CUST/148/12/709-719 TNA.
SAY/275 ESRO.
SAY/284 ESRO.
SAY/286 ESRO.
SAY/287 ESRO.
SAY/296 ESRO.
SAY/297 ESRO.
SAY/298 ESRO.
SAY/299 ESRO.
SAY/300 ESRO.
SAY/301 ESRO.
SAY/302 ESRO.
SAY/304 ESRO.
SAY/305 ESRO.
SAY/307 ESRO.
SAY/308 ESRO.
SAY/313 ESRO.
SAY/314 ESRO.
SAY/317 ESRO.
SAY/318 ESRO.
SAY/319 ESRO.
SAY/320 ESRO.
SAY/321 ESRO.
SAY/325 ESRO.
SAY/326 ESRO.
SAY/85 ESRO.
SAY/87 ESRO.
SP/36/112/2/50-51 TNA.
SP/36/63/3/0061-0068 TNA.
SP/36/77/2/0060-0061 TNA.
SP/36/77/2/151 TNA.
SP/36/77/2/159-160 TNA.
SP/36/97/0142-0152 TNA.
T27/26/158 TNA.
T29/30/101 TNA.
T29/30/106 TNA.
T29/30/107 TNA.
WSRO, Goodwood Ms. 154.
WSRO, Goodwood Ms. 155.
WSRO, Goodwood Ms. 156.

Online

Beattie, John, 'The Royal pardon and criminal procedure in early modern England', *Historical Papers/Communications historiques* 22.1 (1987), pp.9–22.

Bishop, John, 'The Strange Case of Thomas Lillywhite – Was He a Smuggler?', *The Sussex Family Historian* 4.9 (1981).

Bishopp, Sir Cecil, 6th Bt. (d.1778), of Parham, Suss., History of Parliament Online, www.histparl.ac.uk/volume/1715-1754/member/bishopp-sir-cecil-1778. (Accessed 17/1/2022).

Blussé, Leonard, 'Chinese Trade to Batavia during the days of the V.O.C'. (1979). ISSN: 0044-8613. DOI: 10.3406/arch.1979.1509, www.persee.fr/doc/arch_0044-8613_1979_num_18_1_1509.

Britain, Great, *An Act for Indemnifying Persons who Have Been Guilty of Offences Against the Laws Made for Securing the Revenues of Customs and Excise: And for Enforcing Those Laws for the Future.* Eighteenth-century collections online. John Baskett, 1736, books.google.co.uk/books?id=-Dc7AQAAMAAJ.

Cave, E., *The Gentleman's Magazine.* Early English newspapers v. 23, E. Cave, jun. at St John's Gate, 1753, books.google.co.uk/books?id=HUQDAAAAMAAJ.

Chichester, A Gentleman of, *A Full and Genuine History of the Inhuman and Unparrallell'd Murders of Mr William Galley, A Customs House Officer at the Port of Southampton: and Mr Daniel Chater, a Shoemaker at Fordingbridge in Hampshire.* 1779, books.google.co.uk/books?id=56FnVQr2hlsC.

Commons, Great Britain, Parliament, House of, *Journals of the House of Commons,* British history online v. 25. Order of the House of Commons, 1745, books. google.co.uk/books?id=X0JIAQAAMAAJ.

Commons, Great Britain, Parliament, House of and J. Almon, *The Debates and Proceedings of the British House of Commons 1743–74 volume: 1746–1749.* The Debates and Proceedings of the British House of Commons 1743–74, J. Almon and S. Bladon, 1770, books.google.co.uk/books?id=C_Z28GR-NlcC.

Coxe, W., *Memoirs of the Life and Administration of Sir Robert Walpole, Earl Of Orford: With Original Correspondence and Authentic Papers, Never Before Published. In Three Volumes. Containing The Correspondence From 1730 To 1745,* 3, Cadell and Davies, 1798, books.google.co.uk/books?id=rDNPAAAAcAAJ.

Defoe, D., *A Tour Thro' the Whole Island of Great Britain Divided Into Circuits Or Journies. Giving a Particular and Diverting Account of Whatever is Curious and Worth Observation.* v. 1, G. Strahan, W. Mears, R. Francklin, S. Chapman, R. Stagg, and J. Graves, 1724, books.google.co.uk/books?id=ZG9bAAAAQAAJ.

— *Mercurius Politicus,* University Microfilms, 1716, books.google.co.uk/books?id=6PA5AQAAMAAJ.

Dovey, K., *Framing Places: Mediating Power in Built Form,* Architext, Taylor & Francis, 2002. ISBN 9781134688975, books.google.co.uk/books?id=6OyFAgAAQBAJ.

BIBLIOGRAPHY

'First Parliament of George II: Sixth session (part 3 of 5, from 27/2/1733)', in
*The History and Proceedings of the House of Commons: Vol. 7, 1727–1733 (London,
1742)*, pp.304–353. British History Online, www.british-history.ac.uk/
commons-hist-proceedings/vol7/pp304-353 (Accessed 13 June 2021).

Foster, M., *A Report of Some Proceedings on the Commission of Oyer and Terminer
and Goal Delivery for the Trial of the Rebels in the Year 1746 in the County of Surry.*
Sarah Cotter, 1767, books.google.co.uk/books?id=uYY0AAAAIAAJ.

Hanway, J., *A Journal of Eight Days Journey from Portsmouth to Kingston Upon
Thames, with Miscellaneous Thoughts, Moral and Religious, in a Series of
Letters: To which is Added, and Essay on Tea*, 1756, books.google.co.uk/
books?id=S5kaAAAAYAAJ.

Harper, Charles G., *The Smugglers*, www.gutenberg.org/files/45856/45856-
h/45856-h.htm. (Accessed 6/1/2021).

Haywood, E.F., *The Female Spectator*. v. 2. T. Gardner, 1748, books.google.co.uk/
books?id=fHFbAAAAcAAJ.

Hicks, H., *The Poll for Knights of the Shire to Represent the County of Kent;
in which is Inserted, Not Only the Names of the Electors and Candidates, But
Also Every Person's Freehold and Place of Abode*, 1734, books.google.co.uk/
books?id=zz1cAAAAcAAJ.

Huet, P.D., *Memoirs of the Dutch Trade in All the States, Empires, and Kingdoms in the
World: Shewing Its First Rise and Amazing Progress: After what Manner the Dutch
Manage and Carry on Their Commerce; Their Vast Dominions and Government
in the Indies, and by what Means They Have Made Themselves Masters of All the
Trade of Europe ... A Treatise Very Neccessary for Every Englishman. Tr. from the
French, Now Printed at Amsterdam.* Eighteenth-century collections online. C.
Rivington, 1719, books.google.co.uk/books?id=8bVJAAAAMAAJ.

'Kent', *Kentish Gazette* (May 1847). BL_0000235_18470504_039_0004.pdf, www.
britishnewspaperarchive.co.uk/viewer/bl/0000235/18470504/039/0004.

Motteux, P.A., *A Poem Upon Tea*. v. 17, J. Tonson, 1712, books.google.co.uk/
books?id=7PNbAAAAQAAJ.

Murray, G., *A Particular Account of the Battle of Culloden ... In a letter from an officer
of the Highland army [i.e. Lord George Murray], to his friend at London*, T. Warner,
1749, books.google.co.uk/books?id=y0ZfAAAAcAAJ.

Murray, Hon. William (1705–93), of Ken Wood, Mdx, History of Parliament Online,
www.historyofparliamentonline.org/volume/1715-1754/member/murray-
hon-william-1705-93 (Accessed 6/1/2021).

Muskett, P., 'Aspects of English Smuggling in the Eighteenth
Century', PhD thesis, Open University, 1996, books.google.co.uk/
books?id=Oy9tuAAACAAJ.

'Obituary', *Sun* (Aug. 1829), BL_0002194_18290807_005_0001.pdf, www.
britishnewspaperarchive.co.uk/viewer/bl/0002194/18290807/005/0001.

Parker, H., *Of the use of tobacco, tea, coffee, chocolate and drams*, 1722, books.google.
co.uk/books?id=a5hkAAAAcAAJ.

Old Bailey Proceedings Online (www.oldbaileyonline.org, version 8.0, 03

November 2020), July 1747, trial of John Cook (t17470715-1). (Accessed 8/11/2020), www.oldbaileyonline.org/browse.jsp?id=t17470715-1-defend30\&div=t17470715-1.

Old Bailey Proceedings Online (www.oldbaileyonline.org, version 8.0, 10 July 2022), Ordinary of Newgate's Account, April 1749 (OA17490426), www.oldbaileyonline.org/browse.jsp?div=OA17490426. (Accessed 10/7/2022).

Old Bailey Proceedings Online (www.oldbaileyonline.org, version 8.0, 10 March 2021), October 1747, trial of Thomas Fuller (t17471014-4). (Accessed 10/3/2021), www.oldbaileyonline.org/browse.jsp?id=t17471014-4\&div=t17471014-4.

Old Bailey Proceedings Online (www.oldbaileyonline.org, version 8.0, 15 January 2022), Ordinary of Newgate's Account, July 1747 (OA17470729). (Accessed 15/1/2022), www.oldbaileyonline.org/browse.jsp?id=OA17470729&div=OA17470729.

Old Bailey Proceedings Online (www.oldbaileyonline.org, version 8.0, 21 December 2020), Ordinary of Newgate's Account, March 1752 (OA17520323). (Accessed 21/12/2020), www.oldbaileyonline.org/browse.jsp?id=OA17520323\&div=OA17520323.

Old Bailey Proceedings Online (www.oldbaileyonline.org, version 8.0, 21 January 2022), Ordinary of Newgate's Account, August 1749 (OA17490804). (Accessed 21/1/2022), www.oldbaileyonline.org/browse.jsp?id=OA17490804\&div=OA17490804.

Old Bailey Proceedings Online (www.oldbaileyonline.org, version 8.0, 21 November 2020), December 1747, trial of Peter Tickner James Hodges, commonly called and known by the name of Poison (t17471209-52). (Accessed 26/11/2020), www.oldbaileyonline.org/browse.jsp?id=t17471209-52\&div=t17471209-52.

Old Bailey Proceedings Online (www.oldbaileyonline.org, version 8.0, 24 January 2022), October 1747, trial of John Harvey (t17471014-6). (Accessed 8/11/2020), www.oldbaileyonline.org/browse.jsp?id=t17471014-6-off26\&div=t17471014-6.

Old Bailey Proceedings Online (www.oldbaileyonline.org, version 8.0, 24 October 2021), April 1742, trial of John Bolton, alias Bolter (t17420428-46), www.oldbaileyonline.org/browse.jsp?id=t17420428-46&div=t17420428-46. (Accessed 28/10/2021).

Old Bailey Proceedings Online (www.oldbaileyonline.org, version 8.0, 24 September 2022), January 1740, trial of Elizabeth Taverner, alias Howard Hannah Sargeway, alias French Hannah (t17400116-36). (Accessed 24/9/2020), www.oldbaileyonline.org/browse.jsp?id=t17400116-36-off171&div=t17400116-36.

Old Bailey Proceedings Online (www.oldbaileyonline.org, version 8.0, 24 September 2022), July 1740, trial of James Watmore (t17400709-39). (Accessed 24/9/2022), www.oldbaileyonline.org/browse.jsp?id=t17400709-39-off200&div=t17400709-39.

BIBLIOGRAPHY

Old Bailey Proceedings Online (www.oldbaileyonline.org, version 8.0, 24 September 2022), Ordinary of Newgate's Account, December 1747 (OA17471221). (Accessed 24/9/2022), www.oldbaileyonline.org/browse.jsp?id=OA17490804\&div=OA17490804.

Old Bailey Proceedings Online (www.oldbaileyonline.org, version 8.0, 25 January 2022), October 1747, trial of Peter Lickner (t17471014-2). (Accessed 26/11/2020), www.oldbaileyonline.org/browse.jsp?id=t17471014-2-off7\&div=t17471014-2.

Old Bailey Proceedings Online (www.oldbaileyonline.org, version 8.0, 26 January 2022), December 1747, trial of Samuel Austin (t17471209-55), www.oldbaileyonline.org/browse.jsp?id=t17471209-55-off244\&div=t17471209-55. (Accessed 26/1/2022).

Old Bailey Proceedings Online (www.oldbaileyonline.org, version 8.0, 26 January 2022), September 1747, trial of Thomas Puryour, otherwise called and known by the Name of Blacktooth (t17470909-36). www.oldbaileyonline.org/browse.jsp?id=t17470909-36-off152\&div=t17470909-36. (Accessed 26/1/2022).

Old Bailey Proceedings Online (www.oldbaileyonline.org, version 8.0, 27 January 2022), April 1748, trial of Arthur Gray (t17480420-23). (Accessed 27/1/2020), www.oldbaileyonline.org/browse.jsp?id=t17480420-23-off146\&div=t17480420-23.

Old Bailey Proceedings Online (www.oldbaileyonline.org, version 8.0, 27 January 2022), April 1749, trial of Thomas Kingsmill, alias Staymaker William Fairall , alias Shepherd Richard Perin, alias Pain, alias Carpenter Thomas Lillewhite Richard Glover (t17490405-36). (Accessed 27/1/2020), www.oldbaileyonline.org/browse.jsp?id=t17490405-36\&div=t17490405-36.

Old Bailey Proceedings Online (www.oldbaileyonline.org, version 8.0, 27 January 2022), Ordinary of Newgate's Account, May 1748 (OA17480511). (Accessed 27/1/2022), www.oldbaileyonline.org/browse.jsp?div=OA17480511.

Old Bailey Proceedings Online (www.oldbaileyonline.org, version 8.0, 29 September 2022), January 1748, trial of Thomas Kemp (t17480115-29). (Accessed 29/9/2020), www.oldbaileyonline.org/browse.jsp?id=t17480115-29&div=t17480115-29.

Oppression whether by Tyranny, or Law An Enemy to all, A Free Apology in Behalf of the Smugglers, So Far as Their Case Affects the Constitution. By an Enemy to All Oppression, Whether by Tyranny, Or Law, W. Owen, 1749, books.google.co.uk/books?id=CO6wvGM5o2gC.

Ordinary of Newgate's Accounts, www.oldbaileyonline.org/static/Ordinarys-accounts.jsp. (Accessed 29/9/2022).

Oxford, Bodleian Library HFL: B 762 Engl Gallery: digital.bodleian.ox.ac.uk/objects/c3ff6124-a7b7-4023-ab18-7c12497c3ddd

London Gazette, 'Page 1', Iss. 5954, 9 May 1721, www.thegazette.co.uk/London/issue/5954/page/1. (Accessed 28/9/2021).

London Gazette, 'Page 1', Iss. 6748, 28 January 1728, www.thegazette.co.uk/London/issue/6748/page/1. (Accessed 18/9/2021).

London Gazette, 'Page 2', Iss. 8660, 21 July 1747 (undefined), British Newspaper Archive (Accessed 25/1/2022), www.thegazette.co.uk/London/issue/8660/page/2.

London Gazette, 'Page 2', Iss. 8632, 14 April 1747, www.thegazette.co.uk/London/issue/8632/page/2. (Accessed 24/1/2022).

London Gazette, 'Page 3', Iss. 8660, 21 July 1747 (undefined), British Newspaper Archive (Accessed 25/1/2022), www.thegazette.co.uk/London/issue/8660/page/3.

Penryn – History of Parliament Online, www.historyofparliamentonline.org/volume/1715-1754/constituencies/penryn. (Accessed 11/7/2021).

Platt, R., *Smuggling in the British Isles: A History*, Tempus Series, Tempus, 2007. ISBN: 9780752442495, books.google.co.uk/books?id=RdToAgAACAAJ.

Record Transcription: Abraham Walter England Births & Baptisms 1538–1975, findmypast.co.uk. www.findmypast.co.uk/transcript?idR_882978291. (Accessed 6/11/2021).

Record Transcription: Gabriel Tomkins England Births & Baptisms 1538–1975, findmypast.co.uk, www.findmypast.co.uk/transcript?idR_22085371821. (Accessed 25/9/2021).

Record Transcription: Kent Baptisms, Thomas Quaif, findmypast.co.uk, www.findmypast.co.uk/transcript?id=GBPRS/B/82193578/1. (Accessed 6/8/2022).

Record Transcription: Thomas Peen – England Marriages 1538–1973, findmypast.co.uk. www.findmypast.co.uk/transcript?idR_855967541. (Accessed 14/7/2021).

Ryder, Dudley (1691–1756), of Tooting, Surr., History of Parliament Online, www.historyofparliamentonline.org/volume/1715-1754/member/ryder-dudley-1691-1756. (Accessed 6/1/2021).

Short, T., *Discourses on Tea, Sugar, Milk, Made-wines, Spirits, Punch, Tobacco, &c: With Plain and Useful Rules for Gouty People*, Zentralantiquariat der Deutschen Demokratischen Republik, 1750, books.google.co.uk/books?id=51NQAQAAIAAJ.

Sussex, History of Parliament Online, www.historyofparliamentonline.org/volume/1715-1754/constituencies/sussex. (Accessed 12/7/2021).

Symonds, W., *A New-years-gift to the Parliament, Or, England's Golden Fleece Preserv'd, in Proposals Humbly Laid Before this Present Parliament, Printed in the year, 1702*, books.google.co.uk/books?id=epNEAQAAMAAJ.

The Gentleman's Magazine (London, England) v. 15, F. Jefferies, 1745, books.google.co.uk/books?id=f2YdAQAAMAAJ.

The Gentleman's Magazine, No. XXV for the year 1733, 1733, books.google.co.uk/books?id=WPVdAAAAcAAJ.

The Political State of Great Britain v. 49, J. Baker and T. Warner, 1735, books.google.co.uk/books?id=oqRCAQAAMAAJ.

The True State of England, C. King and J. Stagg, 1734, books.google.co.uk/books?id=qqM_AAAAYAAJ.

The Universal Magazine v. 1, Pub. for J. Hinton, 1747, books.google.co.uk/books?id=PTc2AAAAMAAJ.

BIBLIOGRAPHY

'To Be Sold', *South Eastern Gazette* (Oct. 1847), www.britishnewspaperarchive. co.uk/viewer/bl/0001097/18471012/056/0008.

'Treasury Books and Papers: January 1729', *Calendar of Treasury Books and Papers, Vol. 1, 1729–1730*, ed. William A. Shaw (London, 1897), pp.1–13, British History Online, www.british-history.ac.uk/cal-treasury-books-papers/vol1/ pp1-13 (Accessed 9 September 2021).

Tutty, W., *The Want of a Religious Education and Keeping Bad Company, Destructive to Virtuous Principles. A Sermon Preach'd the 20th of March, the Sunday Before the Conviction of Two Convicts, Viz. Thomas Bibby, for Robbing the Chester Mail, and Thomas Flack, for Robbery Upon the Highway, to which is Added, Their Life and Confession, with a particular Account of their Behiviour from the Time of thier Condemnation, to that of their Execution*, H. Kent, 1747, books.google.co.uk/ books?id=h0FfAAAAcAAJ.

'Warrants for Minor Appointments: 1732', *Calendar of Treasury Books and Papers, Vol. 2, 1731–1734*, ed. William A. Shaw (London, 1898), pp.353–361, British History Online www.british-history.ac.uk/cal-treasury-books-papers/vol2/ pp353-361 (Accessed 21 July 2021).

'Warrants for Minor Appointments: 1733', *Calendar of Treasury Books and Papers, Vol. 2, 1731–1734*, ed. William A. Shaw (London, 1898), pp.516–525, British History Online www.british-history.ac.uk/cal-treasury-books-papers/vol2/ pp516-525 (Accessed 12 July 2021).

'Warrants for Minor Appointments: 1735', *Calendar of Treasury Books and Papers, Vol. 3, 1735–1738*, ed. William A. Shaw (London: Her Majesty's Stationery Office, 1900), pp.145–155, British History Online, www.british-history. ac.uk/cal-treasury-books-papers/vol3/pp145-155. (Accessed 25/4/2021).

'Warrants for Minor Appointments: 1736', *Calendar of Treasury Books and Papers, Vol. 3, 1735–1738*, ed. William A. Shaw (London: Her Majesty's Stationery Office, 1900), pp.282–291, British History Online, www.british-history. ac.uk/cal-treasury-books-papers/vol3/pp282-291. (Accessed 25/4/2021).

'Warrants for Minor Appointments: 1740,' *Calendar of Treasury Books and Papers, Vol. 4, 1739-1741*, ed. William A. Shaw (London: Her Majesty's Stationery Office, 1901), pp.419–433, British History Online, www.british-history.ac.uk/ cal-treasury-books-papers/vol4/pp419-433. (Accessed 25/4/2021).

'Warrants for Minor Appointments: 1745', *Calendar of Treasury Books and Papers, Vol. 5, 1742–1745*, ed. William A. Shaw (London, 1903), pp.837–848, British History Online www.british-history.ac.uk/cal-treasury-books-papers/vol5/ pp837-848 (Accessed 17/7/2021).

'Warrants for the Payment of Money: 1742, January-March', *Calendar of Treasury Books and Papers, Volume 5, 1742–1745*, ed. William A. Shaw (London: His Majesty's Stationery Office, 1903), pp.158–171, British History Online, accessed April 25, 2021, www.british-history.ac.uk/cal-treasury-books-papers/vol5/pp158-171. (Accessed 25/4/2021).

'Warrants, Letters, etc.: 1734, January–June', *Calendar of Treasury Books and Papers, Volume 2, 1731–1734*, ed. William A Shaw (London, 1898), pp.590-615, British History Online www.british-history.ac.uk/cal-treasury-books-papers/

vol2/pp590-615 (Accessed 14/7/2021).

Weather in History 1700 to 1749 AD, premium.weatherweb.net/weather-in-history-1700-to-1749-ad. (Accessed 10/6/2021).

Women in St Stephen's Chapel 1548–1834, UK Parliament, www.parliament.uk/about/living-heritage/building/palace/ststephenschapel/ststephensthehouseof-comonns/women-st-stephens-chapel/. (Accessed 7/9/2021).

Zysberg, André. 'La société des galériens au milieu du XVIIIe siècle', fre. (1975). ISSN: 0395-2649. DOI: 10.3406/ahess.1975.293587, www.persee.fr/doc/ahess_0395-2649_1975_num_30_1_293587.

INDEX

INDEX